Caring for
PERENNIALS

Caring for PERENNIALS

What to do AND when to do it

Janet Macunovich

Photographs by Steven Nikkila

A Storey Publishing Book

STOREY

Storey Communications, Inc.
Schoolhouse Road
Pownal, Vermont 05261

The mission of Storey Communications is to serve our customers
by publishing practical information that encourages personal independence
in harmony with the environment.

Edited by Deborah Burns

Cover design by Meredith Maker

Text design and production by Cynthia McFarland

Production assistance by Mark Tomasi, Erin Lincourt and Allyson Hayes

Line drawings by Brigita Fuhrmann, except for the following: Judy Eliason, pages 98, 103 and 123;
    Allison Kolesar, page 147; Elayne Sears, page 47; Ray Wood, page 155.

Indexed by Northwind Editorial Services

Copyright © 1996 Janet Macunovich
Photographs © 1996 Steven Nikkila / Perennial Favorites

The information in this book is true and complete to the best of our knowledge. All recommendations are made without guarantee on the part of the author or Storey Communications, Inc. The author and publisher disclaim any liability in connection with the use of this information. For additional information please contact Storey Communications, Inc., Schoolhouse Road, Pownal, Vermont 05261.

Storey Publishing books are available for special premium and promotional uses and for customized editions. For further information, please call the Custom Publishing Department at 1-800-793-9396.

Printed in the United States by Vicks Lithograph and Printing Company

10 9 8 7 6 5 4 3 2

Library of Congress Cataloging-in-Publication Data

Macunovich, Janet, 1955–
    Caring for perennials : what to do and when to do it / Janet Macunovich
        p.   cm.
    "A Storey Publishing book."
    Includes bibliographical references and index.
    ISBN 0-88266-957-5 (pbk. : alk. paper)
      1. Perennials.   I. Title.
SB434.M32
    635.9'32—dc20   96-27505
                                                                              CIP

Contents

Dedication

To Robert Brent Barr,
whose family planted his memory in a garden he loved.

Acknowledgments

A great number of people helped to make this a practical, credible book:

Head gardener Brian Hutchinson of Castle Howard, North Yorkshire, England.

Grounds supervisor Scott Calhoun at Chicago Botanic Garden and garden designer, instructor, and volunteer Pam Duthie.

Rob Halpern of the Cincinnati Zoo and Botanical Garden.

Head gardener Sam McCracken of the Cleveland Botanical Garden.

Horticulturist Barry Burton at the Detroit Zoological Park.

Director Doug Chapman and horticulturists Chuck Martin and Dan Veresh at Dow Gardens, Midland, Michigan.

Eugene Kociba, naturalist of the gardens at Fernwood Botanic Garden in Niles, Michigan.

Walter Hunnewell of the Hunnewell Estate in Wellesley, Massachusetts.

Melissa Igoe, Gardens Director at Leila Arboretum in Battle Creek, Michigan.

Jim Querry, Supervisor of Parks and Forestry for the City of Maumee, Ohio.

Horticulturists Shirley Dommer and June Hudson and gardener Monica Hoch at the Missouri Botanical Garden.

Director of Horticulture John Morley and horticulturist Mark Stoner of the Niagara Parks Commission, Niagara Falls, Ontario.

Horticulturists Dennis Everly and Chris Graham of the Royal Botanical Gardens in Hamilton, Ontario.

Deborah Davis and Rob McCartney of the Horticulture Department at Seaworld of Ohio.

Dr. T. Richard Fisher of the Shedel Foundation, Arboretum and Gardens in Elmore, Ohio.

Michigan businesspeople Karen Bovio of Specialty Growers in Howell, Barbara Deegan of High Lair Garden Design and Services in Clarkston, and Rick Rohl of Birmingham Lawn Care in Drayton Plains, who freely shared what many would have considered proprietary information in the interests of helping other gardeners work successfully.

Horticultural Supervisor Matthew Vehr at Spring Grove Cemetery and Arboretum.

Janice Lower, horticulturist at the Toledo Botanical Garden.

Michael Williams, Assistant Director at Walpole Island Heritage Center, Ontario, and guides Mike Heath and Keith Howard.

Landscape architect Fay Langmaid, City Parks Supervisor Garry Moore, and gardeners Sharon Gough and Duane Dauncey of the Windsor (Ontario) Parks Department.

Ralph Shugert of Zelenka Nursery in Grand Haven, Michigan.

Special thanks to people in three gardens especially dear to me:

Fergus Garrett, head gardener at Christopher Lloyd's Great Dixter in East Sussex, England, showed me gardens of great beauty and complexity. I have also learned much and gained confidence from Christopher Lloyd's honest and entertaining books and articles. To those who insist that the only way to garden on a large scale is to employ an increasing number of machines, I say go to Great Dixter and see the incredible things that only innovation and thoughtful practicality can accomplish.

David Michener of Matthaei Botanical Gardens, University of Michigan, gave me not only technical but also moral support. It is a difficult task to help people see that their everyday gardening problems and triumphs are the same as those of professional gardeners and botanical garden horticulturists. Dr. Michener's candor and experience at both levels of horticulture were invaluable.

The horticultural staff of the Michigan State University Judith DeLapa Perennial Garden has my greatest respect for skill in horticulture, education, and dealing with people. Thanks to garden supervisor Doug Badgero, Laura Coit who designed the perennial beds and served as the first horticulturist, horticulturists Susan Gruber and Ann Hancock, and the entire management staff.

The experiences of all these horticulturists, gardeners, and designers convinced me that every garden has problems, even if the perception is flawless. The challenge of meeting those problems is an inescapable part of gardening and sometimes part of the attraction for an individual. I apologize if this book distracts any visitor's eye from the beauty at these institutions by giving so much attention to the problems inherent in maintenance. All the gardens I visited were beautiful and well managed. The horticultural staffs deserve only praise.

By examining horticultural problems in detail, I mean only to instruct. It is a focus as skewed toward noticing problems as a garden design book is toward showing only attractive flower beds. Both views are necessary, although neither one is whole. My hope in bringing up the workaday side of gardening is that more gardeners will recognize and adopt the kinds of sensible management strategies employed at the public parks, botanical gardens, and other institutions I have visited.

Some gardeners I met gave graciously of their time and knowledge but preferred to remain anonymous. Their reasons for this ranged from simple humility to concern that their everyday practices might no longer conform exactly to what they had learned long ago from teachers they still aim to please. Speaking to them confirmed and strengthened my conviction that gardeners are the most helpful people in the world. The anonymous gardeners in my private file have produced works of phenomenal beauty in Michigan, Minnesota, Kentucky, Pennsylvania, New York, Massachusetts, and the United Kingdom. I hope that you also will visit the botanical garden near your home and recognize the keepers' effort.

I am especially grateful to these gardening friends and associates who answered my phone calls, showed me their successes and failures, pulled facts from their libraries, gave me special tours to illustrate points, and connected me to countless other valuable sources of information: Julia Dingle, Bud Gauger, Sherry Jakubik, Judith Reiter, Erma Rhadigan, Will Strickland, Margaret Thele, Linda Thomas, Mary Walters, and Mary Wente-Lindsay.

To Deborah Hall, Ann Hancock, Marya Macunovich, Deborah Slentz, and Virginia Smith, who helped me wade through all those draft copies, thank you.

There may be others I have forgotten who helped at some point during the three years it took to produce this book. I apologize for my oversight and trust you know me well enough to understand.

It's fortunate that I am married to a fine horticultural photographer, Steven Nikkila. Without him, the points in this book would lack both illustration and life. This assignment required thoughtful observation through every minute of a year in the garden, even when there were no pictures to be taken. His excellent eye and superb technical skills produced photos that are accurate and beautiful. His experience as a horticulturist gave the photos an extra depth because they are faithful to "the way it really happens."

To my children, Sonja and Cory Nikkila, who are excellent gardeners in their own right — thanks for giving me the space, indulging my odd requests, and letting me stop at so many gardens and horticultural libraries while we were on vacation. I will always be grateful that you understand that my favorite place at the amusement park is the garden with the weeping white pine instead of the roller coaster.

The Year in a Garden

ONE OF MY CLIENTS once told me, "You sure get a lot of mileage out of a garden." That I do. As a professional gardener, I design, plant, and maintain gardens for clients from late February until early December. Throughout the year, but especially in winter, I write about gardening and give classes to professional groups, garden clubs, and individuals. When there's free time and no frost in the soil, tending my own gardens helps me to relax. At the risk of sounding irreverent — which I am not — the garden is also my church. In it I find peace, spiritual lessons, respect for all life, and a metaphor for every human experience.

There was never a time when I planned to fill every waking hour with horticulture. It just happened. Green growing things and all that goes with them have always fascinated me. Older gardeners took me in as a child-friend and apprentice. They told me stories and gave me divisions of plants, seeds, and tools. As a teenager, I gravitated toward outdoor chores, planted the vegetable garden for my mother, pruned shrubs with my father, raked leaves, and swapped yard-work tales with neighbors over the hedge.

When I became a homeowner, my own flower and shrub beds became a little larger every year and drew attention. Over-the-fence discussions with close neighbors about corn smut or lawn grubs rolled smoothly into wheeling a barrow of gift compost to Phyllis three houses down. When no new garden space was left in my backyard, the front lawn was given over to flowers. Working there by the road, I met more far-flung neighbors who walked or drove by. Taking cut flowers to my office coworkers led me to stopping on the way home to help someone decide whether to cut back a hedge or expand a perennial bed.

Now I've had the joy of gardening with my own children and watched them as teenagers sharing their love of plants with even younger children. I've introduced people to the smell of fertile soil, the life that teems on every leaf and petal, and the renewal of energy that comes from being in a garden. So I've learned that I was not the sole benefactor when as a child I visited my mentors — Mrs. Simon, Mrs. Kissinger, Mrs. Goldman — in their backyards and root cellars. They must have enjoyed the chance to share another's excitement.

One day in 1982, while I was still gardening just for fun, I was helping someone dig a new flower bed. He was basically a stranger — a neighbor to one of my coworkers. I suddenly realized that I was spending a lot of time in other people's gardens. I stopped to examine how I had come so far from my own home ground and whether I should keep traveling that route.

I decided to keep records of what I was doing — how long things took, how much they cost, and so on — to see whether professional gardening could be a viable part-time business for me. My husband, who had been home raising our son and daughter full-time, was thinking about going back to college once the kids were in school. He offered to help in any way that he could. He already knew how to pitch in with a shovel, but now he also offered his pen and notebook — he would attend classes that would be helpful to the business. Somehow that turned into an associate's degree in horticulture.

After two more years of night and weekend semipro gardening, we decided to make the part-time business a full-time affair. Over the next eight years, my maintenance records and our reputations grew, so that we were in demand to do garden-care classes for professional and homeowner groups. During this period I wrote my first book, *Easy Garden Design*.

Garden care is a broad topic. In 1993, to answer all the requests we were getting for more details, I decided to write a book about taking care of a perennial garden.

The Idea Behind Caring for Perennials

This book follows a competent gardener — myself — through all the work done during one year in a very real world-class perennial garden. You can apply the techniques and details of time required for various activities to your own garden. In doing so, you will be doing no less than the horticulturist at a botanical garden might wish to do for her own beds.

The "timesaving" promise on the back cover is true. If you follow the game plan in this book, you can have a world-class perennial garden with an average of one hour of maintenance per hundred square feet per month. Twelve years of garden maintenance records support it — data gathered in gardens of all kinds, sizes, and ages.

This book is especially for those who want a garden maintenance guide that gives specific, realistic answers within a practical schedule. It's for people who enjoy tending gardens — their own or others — but have other responsibilities, too.

That group includes professional gardeners. We all have at least one thing in common: lack of time. There are days when you and I, or the horticulturists at the Royal Botanical Gardens, have only an hour to spend in the garden. We want to spend that time wisely. We can never have all the time, all the materials, and all the conditions the way we want them. Nonetheless, we can have beautiful gardens.

What works is to focus first on what *must* be done to keep a garden going. After those basics are done, we're assured that the garden will be there and be healthy next month. With fear of catastrophe allayed, we can choose objectively between all the remaining "should-do's" and "might-do's." Failing to do one of these lower-priority jobs or botching it is not a crisis. We'll get another chance. We can even learn from our trials.

"Must-do's" are presented as maintenance priorities in each chapter of this book. Each time I worked on this trial garden, and in writing this book, all the "must's" were done before any "should's" and "might's."

So you can follow my lead in the order the book is written. Even if you're called away early from your gardening, you'll know you were getting the important stuff done if you were working on a "must." Next time in your garden, you can pick up without a hitch wherever you left off. Or you might skip the "should's" in that chapter and start at the beginning of the next, with no nagging doubts.

A Year in a Garden

This book is a narrative in real time. With one departure (Chapter 3), we'll follow a single lively garden for a year. Each bit of maintenance is explained as it's done and followed up throughout the season. You'll see how various operations fit together, how plants look and behave after being treated in particular ways, how to pick up the pieces after you've made a mistake, and how one normal person can get it all done.

The garden we'll follow is Bed Three of a university botanical garden near my home. You may recognize it because you have been there. Chances are good, however, that a botanical garden near you has a bed that could be its twin, in terms of maintenance. I have interviewed horticulturists and gardeners at almost two dozen botanical gardens to write this book. The challenges, methods, and resources related to maintaining perennial gardens are remarkably similar in most of those places.

You might wonder about my choice. Why pick a world-class, topnotch garden as an example? How can you possibly compare your garden to one that has its own staff of gardeners?

You can because the headaches are the same in all gardens, on every level. You may tend a thousand square feet of garden and shrubs as an every-Saturday-morning hobby. Though you envy the botanical garden horticulturist who has "every day, all day" to garden, that's an illusion. It's not unusual for a professional in a public garden to have sole responsibility for 5,000 square feet or more. In addition, that person often teaches classes, conducts research, and is still required to attend all the meetings necessary to coordinate the overall picture.

As for money and plants, in botanical gardens, the budget for both may be huge, but so are the needs. Every lost pair of pruning shears, broken wheelbarrow, and failed plant means as much there as in your yard. It may mean more, in that it takes not only time and money to replace or fix it, but paperwork to explain the problem and justify the expense. In comparison, it's a light sentence when the homeowner can simply drive to a hardware or garden center and buy a new tool or plant, without answering to anyone.

The dog that vexes you by crashing through your freshly staked peonies takes the form of vandals or rambunctious visitors to a public place. The argument you have with your spouse over mowing too close or not close enough to the border has its counterpart in the struggle between lawn maintenance staff and horticulturists, some of which you'll see first hand in Chapter 7 of this book. The severe weather that ruins your work just before the garden tour or graduation party hits just as hard at the botanical garden, where every day there's a crowd.

Basics Included in a Maintenance Schedule

In Chapter 14 you'll find a maintenance chart that suggests what to do in a perennial garden. It is based on the idea that certain activities are priorities at various times during the season and should be anticipated. All other tasks can be done in conjunction with a more primary concern. Here's a look at the basic flow.

During the winter, when we quit for the season, plants don't stop growing. If there's no frost in the ground, even under a blanket of snow, roots are growing, seeds are sprouting, stems and leaves are gradually dying and falling down. By early spring, we need a catch-up day, primarily to weed and clean away debris. We'll start the schedule there, with a spring clean-up. This is best tackled just before the garden inhabitants launch into really active top growth — early April in my clime.

Within the next month plants of all types hit an Olympian stride in their growth. That's the time to apply a mulch or other top dressing to replace depleted nutrients, conserve moisture, and avoid extremes of soil temperature. There will be some weeding and rearranging due at the same time. My schedule sets aside time for these things in late April.

New additions are an annual event. Since most are tender when they arrive, by virtue of genetics or acclimation to a grower's protected environment, they're best installed when spring becomes truly gentle. That's in May for me, so I pick a date for it. No, two dates, since every spring sees both planned and impulse purchases that all have to be planted.

Every Season Has Its Priority

During the summer in most parts of the country, plants need supplemental water. That need is greatest in spring and during the driest days of summer, and can usually be met with a monthly soaking in June and again in July and August. There are also going to be pests that afflict the garden to one degree or another during the season. The damage from these insects and diseases may or may not warrant control but it does bear watching. Since many pest and disease cycles seem to converge in June and those that become entrenched then make the most lasting impression through summer, I plan one or two extra visits then. These aren't usually lengthy or demanding but they're as necessary as the brief checks we make on small children playing too quietly in the next room.

In fall, to get ahead of the weeds, rearrange, redesign, and generally make spring work easier, we need one or two dates to "put the garden to bed." That's my objective during the fall visits.

This kind of schedule insures that you'll be in the garden at critical times for what I call the "must do's." Throughout the year, other tasks will occur to you and you can accommodate them within your own personal limitations. These are the "should's" and "might's," chores that are nice to do, but if missed they don't cost you the garden. Removing dead flowers, applying summer fertilizer, pinching late bloomers for bushiness are almost always "might's." Weeding, after the garden is thoroughly cleaned in spring and a mulch applied, descends to a "should" through summer and reappears as a "must" in fall. I put these secondary priorities on

the schedule in conjunction with one or more of the "must" dates. For instance, gardens can look shabby in mid-summer and appreciate a grooming, so I note my July watering date to plan on some clipping, too.

Adjusting for Individual Needs

Starting with a basic schedule, I adjust for special individual needs linked to particular species. If there are many species in a particular line-up that are in the daisy family, mid-June to mid-July bloom will probably be heavy and grooming needs may be heaviest in July. A bed that's especially full of spring bulbs and May blooming companions would need that grooming a month earlier. Certain species cannot present themselves gracefully without artificial supports. Such stakes and other devices have to be in place before spring growth is completed, so a garden full of delphiniums, biennial foxgloves, double peonies, and other such weaklings require extra time in May.

On the more serious side, some plants are predisposed to illness or highly susceptible to insect damage. These diseases and flying or crawling pests are just as predictable as the flowering of a crabapple or hydrangea. If a landscape depends on pest-prone plants, the gardener is wise who anticipates the problems rather than reacting. The chart in Chapter 14 suggests times to watch for the most common problems linked to particular species, as well as giving lists of other more unusual problems that you may need to include on your calendar.

Hustle in Spring, Coast in Summer

Every type of garden requires more time in spring than in summer. If I'm going to enlist or hire help, I start looking in January for someone to help me in spring!

The garden in this book covers 504 square feet. Using an estimate system I've developed (see page 32), I knew it would require an average of five hours and a few minutes work each month. Although I didn't focus on staying "on time," my work did add up to 35 hours over seven months.

During the first month, I spent eleven hours in the garden. Every other month required much less time (see page 153 in Chapter 13). Those heavy spring times are standard. They reflect plant life — hustle in spring, coast in summer.

If you stay with the pace that Mother Nature sets and spend extra time in spring, she'll let you lie back and enjoy time off in high summer. If you decide to slack off in spring, however, you'll pay in summer. That's a route to avoid. It is more fun to drink lemonade in August than to play catch-up in a garden.

Setting up the Schedule for This Experiment

The arrangement between myself and the staff of the botanical garden where this book takes place was that I would do all the maintenance in Bed Three as a volunteer. The horticulturist would leave that bed alone as long as I kept it up to the garden-wide standards. How often I came to work and how the work was done was my choice. The key was that the bed's appearance should match its neighbors.

Never having tended a world-class public garden before, even my tried-and-true methods of scheduling the work seemed inadequate. Would a biweekly schedule do? That's what I use for my most demanding customers, those who stop short of getting a full time gardener yet want every leaf in its place. Certainly a public garden with such a good reputation to uphold would aim to have every leaf in place. Yet there are many times when a biweekly schedule is wasteful and my goal was to present a practical, efficient way to maintain a garden.

I decided to schedule visits approximately three weeks apart. The schedule evolved from there. It was a complex hybrid — my standard routine crossed with the layout of this particular garden, back-crossed with the particular species in it.

This schedule should suit almost any high visibility garden, as long as you add one other ingredient — flexibility. Living things don't like to be predicted. As gardeners, we have to respect their right to surprise us. During the course of the season my schedule was rearranged several times to indulge this garden's wishes.

Perennial Bed Maintenance Schedule

April 7*	covered in Chapter 4
April 24	covered in Chapter 5
May 9	covered in Chapter 6
May 23	covered in Chapter 6
June 12	covered in Chapter 7
June 26	covered in Chapter 7
July 19	covered in Chapter 8
August 10	covered in Chapter 9
August 31	covered in Chapter 9
September 22	covered in Chapter 10
October 9	covered in Chapter 11
November 1*	covered in Chapter 12

*For an area with a longer growing season than USDA zone 6, extend the schedule to include one or two visits before April 7 and one or two visits after November 1.

Making the Schedule Work for You

You may live in USDA zone 4 or 8 while I garden primarily in zones 5 and 6, but you can use my basic schedule to predict the work in your garden. Don't worry that your spring may start and your fall end on different calendar dates than mine. After all, you already work with the fact that spring in a given garden may vary by a week or three from one year to the next. You probably manage by "reading" and responding to the garden's rhythm — plant development. That's more accurate than any calendar.

To make this book useful across a wider area, I've noted the "plant development date" at the beginning of each chapter. You can use that to adjust for the difference between your area and mine. For instance, in early April (Chapter 4) when I raked away Bed Three's winter coat, cornelian cherry (*Cornus mas*) and adonis (*Adonis amurensis*) were blooming, the flower buds on red maple (*Acer rubrum*) were just about to pop, and the daylilies were three inches tall. In November (Chapter 12) when I put the garden to bed, American witchhazel (*Hamamelis virginiana*) was in bloom. The wait-until-last callery pear trees (*Pyrus calleryana*) were just beginning to show fall color. For you these events may happen a few weeks earlier or later.

If you're not in USDA zone 5 or 6, here's how to set my schedule to your zone. First, check the plant development notes in the chart below. Then watch those plants in your vicinity this year to see when they reach the same stage of development. Make a note on the chapter title page so that chapter matches your calendar and your area plants. Also, use this chart to help you customize your copy of the schedule on page 163.

Don't change the whole year based on a one-month adjustment, though. Even if you find that your calendar dates for early spring and late fall work differ from my chapter titles, our summer dates will coincide. The whole country seems to hum summer's tune in synchrony, but northern areas pick up a faster beat in spring and fall.

The Truths and Joys of Gardening

This book is in story form. I tell it the way it really happened. All the drawings were done from photos of the actual work described in the book. It can be both example and pattern for your own trial of the material.

Above all, this is an honest book. All work was done and photographed without staging or touch-up. My husband (horticultural photographer Steve Nikkila) and I did not take a sabbatical from our other life to do this project. We slotted visits to the garden right into the same kind of hectic schedule that you keep. Decisions were made in real time, using the same tools and resources that are available to you, and we lived with the results. This was difficult when it meant having to admit mistakes and allow some lackluster episodes to be photographed for all the world to see. Yet it was pleasant, because we've shown the truths and joys of gardening.

Using Plant Cues to Determine Seasonal Tasks

When you see these plant development cues:	Begin tasks described in:	Zone 5/6 date:	Your calendar date:
Cornelian cherry (*Cornus mas*) and sugar maple (*Acer saccharinum*) blooming • Crocuses finished blooming • Daffodil foliage barely emerged (1"–2" tall) • First hybrid tulip leaves (2"–3" tall)	Chapter 4	April	
Forsythia and star magnolia (*Magnolia stellata*) just past peak bloom • Earliest daffodils in full bloom • Daylily (*Hemerocallis* ssp.) foliage 6"–8" tall	Chapter 5	April	
Serviceberry (*Amelanchier* spp.) and myrtle (*Vinca minor*) in bloom • Late daffodils ('King Alfred', e.g.) and grape hyacinth (*Muscari armeniacum*) in full bloom • Crabapples just beginning to show bud color	Chapter 6	May	
Ornamental onions (*Allium* spp.) in bloom • Oriental poppy (*Papaver orientale*) in bloom • Arrowwood viburnum (*Viburnum dentatum*) in full bloom • American elderberry (*Sambucus canadensis*) beginning to bloom	Chapter 7	June	
Yucca (*Yucca filamentosa*), shasta daisy, and perennial baby's breath (*Gypsophila paniculata*) in full bloom • Linden trees (*Tilia* spp.) finished blooming • Dwarf spirea (*Spirea* x *bumalda*) in full bloom	Chapter 8	July	
Fragrant white hosta (*Hosta plantaginea*) in full bloom • PeeGee hydrangea (*Hydrangea paniculata* 'Grandiflora') flower buds beginning to bloom • European mountain ash (*Sorbus aucuparia*) fruits ripen	Chapter 9	August	
Blue bush clematis (*Clematis heracleifolia*) seed pods beginning to ripen • Sweet autumn clematis (*Clematis maximowicziana*) beginning to bloom • Virginia creeper vine (*Parthenocissus quinquefolia*) and Japanese blood grass (*Imperata* 'Red Baron') beginning to turn red	Chapter 10	September	
New England aster (*Aster novae-angliae*) and fall crocus (*Colchicum autumnale*) in full bloom • Red maple (*Acer rubrum*) and serviceberry (*Amelanchier* spp.) in full fall color • Frost has killed back all but hardiest perennial foliage	Chapter 11	October/ November	

USDA HARDINESS ZONE MAP

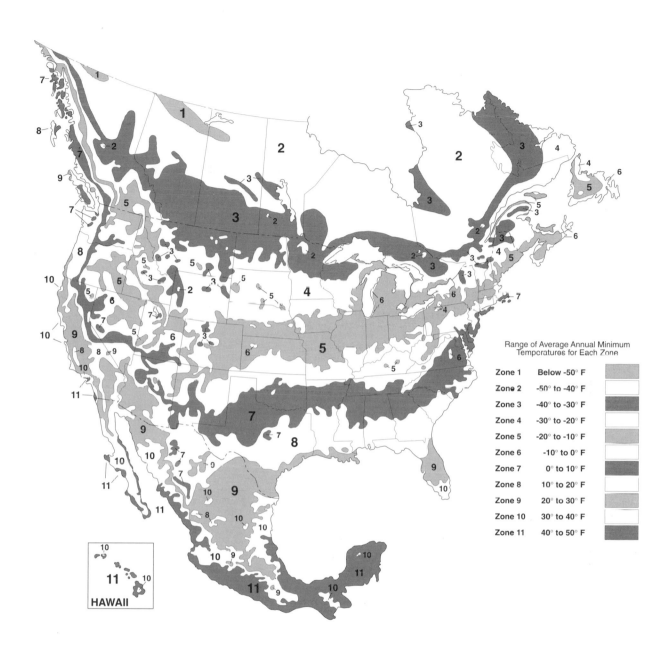

Range of Average Annual Minimum
Temperatures for Each Zone

Zone 1	Below -50° F	
Zone 2	-50° to -40° F	
Zone 3	-40° to -30° F	
Zone 4	-30° to -20° F	
Zone 5	-20° to -10° F	
Zone 6	-10° to 0° F	
Zone 7	0° to 10° F	
Zone 8	10° to 20° F	
Zone 9	20° to 30° F	
Zone 10	30° to 40° F	
Zone 11	40° to 50° F	

Hardiness zones link areas based on the average minimum temperature. Gardeners in different hardiness zones can expect to begin and end gardening on different dates, since higher number zones warm up earlier and get cold later than lower number zones. Although gardeners in various zones start their season on different calendar dates, the sequence of tasks they follow through the season is the same. You and I can use the same schedule, therefore, even if we're zones apart. Use the chart on the facing page to customize the schedules in this book to your own zone.

Planning the Season

"LIFE BEGAN IN A GARDEN." This advice, on a sundial in one of my favorite flower beds, is the message from every garden, to those who will listen. Each garden is a community of living things that grow and change. They refuse to hold still while we figure things out or tend to other concerns. It's a great part of the spell gardens weave over people like you and me. Works of art, never done, they often take the brush right out of our hands and paint their own next scene.

That's why it takes a dynamic approach to care for a bed or border. We can't keep pace if we treat maintenance as a set of disconnected events. So I'll tell you the complete, sequential story of one garden through a year. That story starts now, at New Year's, with choosing the garden, predicting its needs, and planning its care.

My own gardens, my clients' beds, and a bed in a university's botanical garden were all equal contenders to be the experimental plot that illustrates this book for you. I picked Bed Three of the botanical garden for three reasons.

First, it's open to the public and typical of most botanical garden beds I have visited. After reading this book, you will be familiar with the kind of work that goes on in such a bed. You will be able to go to a botanical garden and recognize the techniques in action.

Second, I was unfamiliar with the bed's planting, plants, and past maintenance. Given this standing start, it would be reasonable to ask even a new gardener to use my estimates of time needed to tend a known garden. Being on new ground I would also be more careful and more open to learning, which helps me make clearer explanations for you.

Third, it's such a beautiful garden. Keeping it up to a world-class standard would mean that my time and work records would be high-end. Better to give you time estimates that may be too high and let you have any leftover hours as a bonus, than to go the other way.

When I began I had no idea which species were in Bed Three, but I knew they would soon assert themselves. After some cases of mistaken identity were clarified, there was a 33-player lineup to work with. Their needs eventually ran the gamut of horticultural procedures, which means there's an example in this book of almost everything you'll run into in a garden.

THE GARDEN BED AT ITS PEAK

In July, the garden we'll follow through this book is both impressive and expressive of gardening's many dimensions. 'Fire Cup' daylilies **1** steal the show from this angle. If we step around we'll see the golden marguerite **2** recovering from the double indignity of a tumble on the lawn and restorative staking (see page 17). This worn lawn **3** is not a turf problem, but a symptom of the need to prune low tree branches that forced all traffic into one narrow lane (see Chapters 3 and 12).

THROUGHOUT THIS BOOK, you'll see diagrams of Bed Three in "Plan View" – from above. I drew up the first simple plan at the beginning of the year to figure the size of the bed, become acquainted with the species in it, and keep records simply.

I made a copy of the original for every day I planned to visit and work in the garden. On each, I wrote the scheduled date and a list of the maintenance chores that were likely to need doing. For instance, the species in this bed promised to hit a peak of bloom at the beginning of July. Thus, on the July 19 diagram I wrote "deadhead the garden."

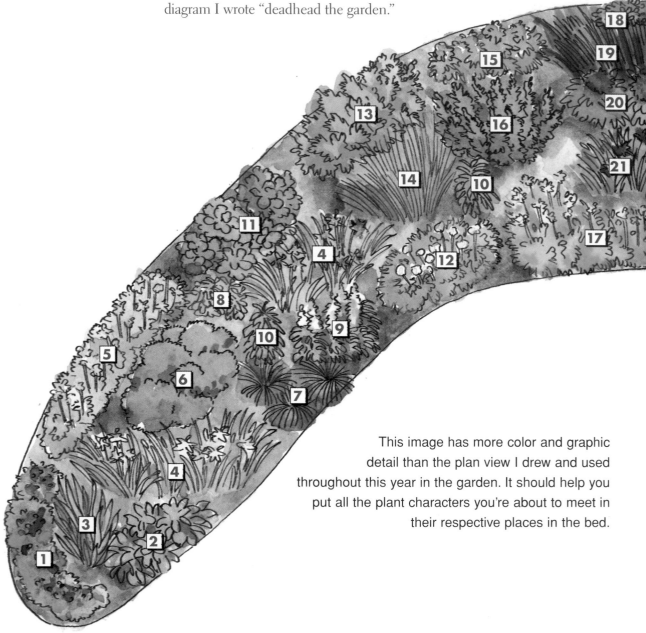

This image has more color and graphic detail than the plan view I drew and used throughout this year in the garden. It should help you put all the plant characters you're about to meet in their respective places in the bed.

As I did the work on each visit, I used that day's diagram to record what was done. My notes included thoughts that might apply to future visits, which could be transferred to the appropriate diagram as reminders.

For instance, the daylilies (*Hemerocallis* 'Fire Cup') were fantastic in bloom. It was also apparent then, though not in spring or fall, that there were too many of them. It was then easy to jot a few words on the September 22 sheet "Divide and reduce number of daylilies." It was also practical to consider "If there were fewer daylilies, what other kind of plant would look good in this company?" That question also went onto the fall schedule and became a proposed shopping list, complete with quantity needed.

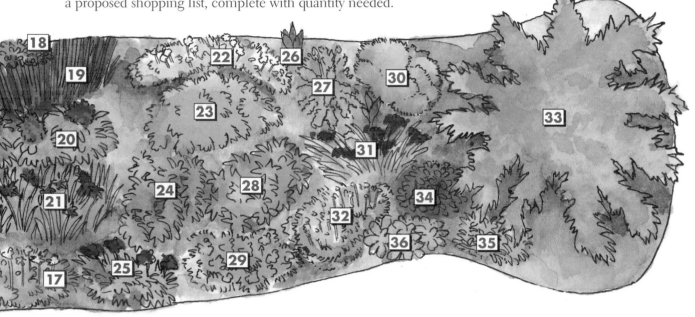

KEY

1. penstemon	13. rue	24. cardinal flower
2. lamb's ear	14. moor grass	25. lychnis
3. yellow blackberry lily	15. dianthus	26. canna
4. 'Fire Cup' daylily	16. 'Silver King' artemisia	27. oriental poppy
5. golden marguerite	17. 'Golden Showers'	28. Carolina lupine
6. 'Lambrook Silver'	coreopsis	29. rock rose
artemisia	18. potentilla	30. silver mound
7. blue fescue	19. blood grass	31. crocosmia
8. snapdragon	20. 'Orange Perfection'	32. oxeye
9. foxglove	phlox	33. swamp white oak
10. oriental lily	21. blackberry lily	34. purple leaf sedum
11. coral bells	22. 'Early Sunrise' coreopsis	35. myrtle euphorbia
12. daisy	23. monkshood	36. Missouri primrose

THE WONDER of the new gardening year is the time it affords gardeners to think and plan. Given a good look at a particular bed and the species in it, you can anticipate work that will need to be done. Walk with me through the year now.

On the pages ahead are photographs of what actually took place during the year as I tended the garden. Much of the work fulfilled my New Year's predictions, but the bed also produced surprises, both good and bad. It all added up to a typical perennial year!

CLEARING & FERTILIZING

On this first visit, I'm fertilizing the bed, after clearing away the remnants of last season and a winter's worth of blown-in debris so that emerging perennials are visible. You can see gray lamb's ear at my feet 1, the fresh green of daylilies beyond 2, gray flecks of expanding artemisia buds 3, and brown tuffets of shorn ornamental blue fescue grass 4.

Preventive Maintenance

Early Spring Garden Priorities

- ✓ Clear garden of all dead plant matter
- ✓ Weed and edge
- ✓ Fertilize
- ✓ Mulch

When I examined a weak clump of coral bells in early spring, I discovered all the coral bells in the bed had been decimated by black vine weevil grubs **1** grazing on the roots over winter. Only pieces of the plants were salvageable. It was a loss for one season, but coral bells are worth waiting for **2**, since few perennials can contribute so long and heartily to the early summer show.

REMOVING GRASS

I lifted the penstemon out of the bed in early spring, disentangled grass roots from its crown, and replanted it as bare root stock. It took its spring cure in stride, blooming well in early summer.

BY MID-SPRING, shrubs and trees in the area had begun to leaf out and the lawn was rushing into its best color, but spring wasn't firmly settled yet. Most of my time during this round of care was spent dividing and moving plants such as the daisies (opposite page) and applying mulch. I covered all exposed soil between plants with a quilt of various mulches. During the year I would evaluate each mulch in terms of appearance, effects on plant growth, weed control, and convenience of use.

MID-SPRING MULCH

A recent hard frost had killed the daylilies' leaf tips **1** and convinced more cautious species in the bed to keep their leafy growth low and slow. You can compare the early season look of shredded hardwood **2**, cocoa hulls **3**, and leaves reserved from the previous fall **4** and **5**.

MULCH, 1 MONTH LATER

After a month, mulch's job as a weed preventer was over in some parts of the bed. Daylilies **6** had formed the dense canopy that inhibits weed seed germination. Yellow blackberry lily **7** and penstemon **8** are not so self-sufficient. They arise late and cast scant shadows all summer. For them, mulch will be the only barrier against weeds at their feet. I preferred a dark fine grain mulch there, cocoa hulls.

Mid-Spring Garden Chores

✓ Divide plants and replant
✓ Stake
✓ Continue weeding
✓ Water
✓ Fertilize

Dividing Daisies

Daisies divide easily. The trick is to reset small, healthy pieces every two years in the spring. Give each enough room to grow without competition and water them in well.

A ridge of soil around each plant holds water so it soaks in where it's most needed.

By mid-summer bloom-time, the divided plants filled their space in the bed.

LAST DAYS OF SPRING: *The Color Begins*

TWO WEEKS FURTHER into the season, plants had closed over 75 percent of the bed surface. Now the designer's clever placement of gray foliage plants is apparent, causing the eye to travel from the lamb's ear **1** left to 'Lambrook Silver' artemisia **2**, then into the bed center to rest on 'Silver King' artemisia **3**. This bed was designed to provide its main show from high summer to fall, and the color was just now beginning to spark.

FLOWERS AT LAST

The foliage effects of Bed Three were striking; nevertheless, I was starved for flowers by summer. So I was glad for substantial color, beginning with the brilliant red-orange of oriental poppy **4**. Carolina lupine **5** was preparing to join the poppy—its spikes were loaded with buds. The new rock roses **6** were also budding out. Given a year or two to fill out, they would be a great accent.

A Stake in the Future

I erected various staking arrangements for the golden marguerite, a renowned flopper. Before long, however, although the plant was blooming and colorful, the stems lay all over the lawn and I had to make new staking arrangements.

I tried several different kinds of staking for the golden marguerites.

One month later the plants had outgrown both my expectations and stakes and spilled out over the lawn.

After that taste of rambling, the golden marguerite resented being restaked.

Nonetheless, the stems did straighten up and bloomed into the fall.

First Pest Problems

THE DENSE CANOPY of spring invites other living things to consider taking up residency. Rabbits, in this case, considered the newly planted dianthus their personal salad bar, mowing down those and other plants. Voles, four-lined plant bugs, and ants also had an impact on Bed Three during the season. All of the signs I needed to predict and control these presences were evident by late spring. As it so often happens, I read some signs correctly but overlooked others.

This cluster of *Dianthus* 'War Bonnet' bloomed heavily in early summer, although it had been grazed to nubs within weeks of planting (and caged after the fact!).

FALL GUY DIANTHUS

Rabbits, such as this one found hiding in the golden marguerite, preyed on the dianthus in spring. Although the plants recovered and bloomed well in early summer (above), they were too tasty for their own good. The same plants were shorn again in mid-summer (above, left) by voles operating from the dense cover provided by neighboring plants (see Chapter 8).

Herbicide Damage

WEED KILLER

You can see one of summer's first challenges here. Dying foliage on a rue plant **1** and a rock rose **2** are actually lawn care problems. Those plants probably caught errant drafts of weed killer meant for the lawn. Suspect herbicide damage if you see a quick decline — distorted and dying foliage that bears no evidence of insect feeding or any sign of gradual fungus or bacterial spread.

MID-SUMMER: *Time for "White-Glove Gardening"*

MID-SUMMER MEANS deadheading, work that doesn't dirty knees or gloves. 'Golden Showers' coreopsis **1** is a main act in July. Golden marguerite **2** is a co-star, although it began blooming two weeks before the coreopsis. I removed its spent flowers and planned to keep doing so as long as remaining stems made a contribution worthy of the spotlight.

2 VIEWS, SAME BED

Photos snapped on the same day offer very different views. A change in mental viewpoint can be just as refreshing. Don't focus solely on chores. Do enjoy the flowers.

Deadheading

**Mid-Summer
Garden Priorities**

✓ Water
✓ Weed
✓ Deadhead
✓ Stake drooping plants

I deadheaded daisies by clipping off each flower and its stem as that flower faded. After four weeks, all the flowers had bloomed and been removed.

Golden marguerites will bloom from late spring into fall if you keep up with the deadheading.

FIRST BLOOM

SECOND BLOOM

Digitalis lanata
Grecian Foxglove

When deadheaded, perennials such as this Grecian foxglove produce a second flush of flower on side shoots. At left, you can see the first and largest flower clusters. Above, secondary spikes bloom. The second bloom is never so dramatic as the first, but the continued color is worth the effort.

BY AUGUST, more than half the plants in the bed have flowered and would like to fade gradually from the scene. A certain amount of yellowing must be tolerated for the continuing health of those fading plants, but the wise gardener knows how much impact such foliage has on the late summer garden and keeps it trim.

As blackberry lily **1** finishes, cardinal flower **2** should replace it as star of the late summer show. Carolina lupine **3** is blocking that view, but a quick trim of its lax foliage clears the stage.

AN INVASIVE NEIGHBOR

This cardinal flower was undermined by Carolina lupine roots. The invading yellow roots **4** can be seen piercing this cardinal flower root ball I lifted in spring. I removed all the invaders or the cardinal flower would have been lost in a forest of Carolina lupine stems arising from those roots. By late summer, the Carolina lupine was leaning over the cardinal flower and I knew its roots were reclaiming the area, too. It's up to the gardener to continue the separation of such a pair, above and below ground.

Showstopper: Crocosmia 'Lucifer'

These crocosmia flowers drew admirers from 100 feet and were in bloom throughout July. However, the purple leaf sedum *(Sedum atropurpureum)* **1** at its feet is being crowded and shaded out, so it qualifies for a spot in the fall round of transplanting.

A SUPPORT SYSTEM

Crocosmia's not normally such a slouch. Afternoon shade from an oak may have contributed to this sprawl. Here I am lifting it and staking it to clear it out of the purple leaf sedum's space.

AUTUMN BEGINS with a few fresh bloomers as well as some post-bloom plants appreciated anew for their foliage effects. Cool days and soft light in early October work magic on many leaves, bringing out new shades of blue, red, and maroon.

At the first stroke of fall, I began to make changes.

MAKING CHANGES

Dividing and reducing the daylilies left room for purple leaf sedum to move in between the yellow blackberry lily and 'Lambrook Silver' artemisia 1. The ailing monkshood 2 would have to go, too, but I would wait until spring to remove it, so I could enjoy its final show.

The cool blue columns of monkshood flowers 2 work well with the airy plumes of moor grass seed pods 3. The ripening seed pods of yellow blackberry lily 4 and dusky foliage of purple leaf sedum 5 have as much impact as flowers on this scene. The blue shades intensified in blue-green rue 6 and blue fescue 7. Elsewhere in the bed, reds and maroons surfaced in the foliage of Japanese blood grass, cardinal flower, and *Lychnis* 'Vesuvius'. The final flowers from the cut-back golden marguerite 8 seem almost an intrusion among all these subtle variations on green.

Ailing Beauty: Monkshood

Early in spring, the clump of monkshood looked lush and green. By late spring, the leaves were beginning to die. Foliage had to be removed all summer, for appearance and to slow the spread of the disease (*Pseudomonas delphinii*).

We could still admire its fall flowers even though they were perched atop stems nearly bare of leaves.

Important Difference: Two Blackberry Lilies

The shiny black seeds that give blackberry lily (*Belamcanda chinensis*) its common name appear once the pods ripen and split in fall. They are striking, but shouldn't be allowed a winter stay. Every seed that falls into the garden over winter can become a weed to be removed in spring.

Yellow blackberry lily *(Belamcanda flabellata)*, a later-blooming cousin of blackberry lily, was a new and welcome acquaintance for me. Its seed pods have less time to ripen before frost, so it usually doesn't self-sow throughout the bed.

AS FALL SETTLED IN, I cut back unattractive faders such as daylilies and golden marguerite, to open up views and avoid visual clutter near the new stars. It's easiest for the gardener and the garden if you cut back gradually throughout fall. Each perennial species responds to its own end-of-season markers, including changing day length, completion of seed formation, and a certain degree of cold. By the time the garden has undergone its first hard freeze, many plants have already been cut back and removed as they faded.

Those blank spaces just beg for bulbs and provide a chance to plant a spring kick-start for the summer garden. Bulbs can be long-term residents, so I placed them where nearby perennials would "come on" in time to hide fading bulb foliage.

PLANTING BULBS

I planted several clusters of bulbs, each with enough color splash to catch the viewer's eye and carry it deep into the bed. I set them among the purple leaf sedum 1, daylilies 2, and 'Silver King' artemisia 3.

I could have cut back the Carolina lupine 4 earlier, since it was not striking in its own right, but it served to hide the base of the ailing monkshood 5. I was glad the Carolina lupine and other plants on the west end withstood the several frosts that preceded the monkshood's bloom.

Promising Newcomer: 'Orange Perfection' Phlox

Gardeners get attached to plants, especially those that they have watched grow from tiny starts **1**. Unfortunately this cluster of three phlox developed a problem that shouldn't be left in the garden over winter.

Early on, one plant succumbed to leaf disease (powdery mildew and leaf spot) and never shook the effects **2**. Note the sparse bloom on that plant's part of the resulting cluster **3**. I removed that weak plant and left the remaining plants to fill the void. If it had stayed, it would have continued to be a source of contagion for its more resistant neighbors.

A perennial garden can go gracefully into winter. Leave the evergreens and the strongest herbaceous perennials standing, then step back and assess the view. Clustered attractively around the moor grass in this garden are evergreen blue fescue, 'Lambrook Silver' artemisia, and rue, plus startling red blood grass.

THE UNCERTAINTY FACTOR

Winter interest is a matter of personal taste. When you try out a new species, let it stand over the first winter. Assess its sturdiness and visual appeal for yourself. If it's a winter star, you might move it in spring to fit it better into the off-season crew.

Some plants are naturals to leave standing over winter including evergreens like rue **1** and stalwarts like moor grass **2**. Yet location as much as tenacity gives a plant winter value. The rue, moor grass, and fescue **3** were well situated near the center of the bed and each other so that the bed would not look lopsided nor its tenants lonely if those three were all that remained over winter. Blood grass **4** and 'Lambrook Silver' artemisia **5** flanked the central group and gave it stability. So I cut the rest, gave the bed a final weeding, and retired for the winter with my memories and visions for next year.

Late Season Projects

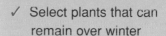

Autumn Garden Priorities

✓ Select plants that can remain over winter
✓ Cut others back
✓ Plant bulbs
✓ Do a final thorough weeding
✓ Remove all dead plant matter

Tall phlox **1**, 'Silver King' artemisia **2**, and 'Early Sunrise' coreopsis **3** are not winter stars. Left standing, however, they would mask the glow of the blood grass, so I cut them down.

I nearly ran into the overhanging oak limb **4**, trying to avoid the worn sod **5**. Fall is a good time to replace sod, but not when the cause of the trouble still exists.

I did leave cutting the coreopsis **6** and removing cannas **7** until very late, so the monkshood **8** had company while it bloomed.

AT THE END of the season, it's not the work that you remember but the glimpses of perfection for which you did the work. The best plants stand out, whether for their sturdiness, their lack of demand, their graceful foliage, or their long period of bloom.

The wheelbarrow in this photograph is loaded with my standard kit of tools: fork, spade, rake, five-gallon bucket, hand pruners, sturdy knife, and weeder. My mind and notebook are as full of plans for change.

Memories of a single startling flower like this scarlet cinquefoil *(Potentilla atrosanguinea)* can make you wish for more of the same. It's a good reason to make divisions of that plant and move it to a place with a stronger spotlight.

Best in Show: Threadleaf Coreopsis

Threadleaf coreopsis 'Golden Showers' was my pick for showiness, long season, dependability, and low care. Here it is with daisies and *Lychnis* 'Vesuvius'.

For Next Year: Astilbe 'Glut'

Astilbes are also workhorses in a perennial garden. In planning changes to compensate for increasing shade at the bed's west end, I determined to offset the abundance of yellow in this bed's July show with the saturated red of *Astilbe* 'Glut'.

After a whole season in a perennial garden, if someone asks you how you did something, can you answer completely and accurately? I can't. Not unless I keep a record, as I did for you this year.

One thing my records do is help me figure how much I can expect to accomplish. I've kept records over twelve years to establish the average time needed to care for 100 square feet of various plantings. The times shown in the chart below assume all basic maintenance is done as indicated here and in Chapter 14 of this book.

I use an average of minutes per month to figure the overall time required to tend a given area. Then I have a better idea whether I can add that maintenance work to my annual schedule, and when to hire a helper.

Estimating Time Needed to Maintain a Landscape

100 sq. ft. of:	Requires, on average:	Minutes per month vary during the season:		
		Spring	Summer	Fall
Lawn	8 minutes/month	10	5	10
Trees, shrubs, groundcover	10 minutes/month	20	5	5
Annual flowers	20 minutes/month	25	15	20
Perennial bed	60 minutes/month	95	35	30

To apply these times to a particular garden, you need an idea of the number of square feet you're tending. This is most simply figured by multiplying the area's length times width. For irregularly shaped areas, you can imagine the space as a number of separate areas, such as breaking a tear-drop bed into a circle connected to a triangle. Then estimate the area of each component.

Alternately, if you have a scale drawing of the area, overlay it with graph paper, count the squares that fall within the area's outline, and multiply by the number of feet each square represents. For instance, if every inch on the drawing represents eight feet, each square of quarter-inch graph paper covers a square two feet on a side, or four square feet. When I count 25 squares within my graph paper overlay, the garden is 25 times 4 square feet — 100 square feet. A perennial bed of that size will ask for about an hour of my time each month.

Finding Plants and Tools

THE MIDDLE OF WINTER is a difficult time of year for many gardeners. Trees have no swollen buds. They give no outward sign that spring is around the corner. Sometime during this period (February, for me in zone 5–6) there's a thaw for several days. Walk the paths in the garden then and find noses of early bulbs just breaking the surface — not up, not green yet, just little nubs sitting at soil level.

It's above 40°F during the thaw, pleasant for working outside. Orchardists start pruning apple trees. Other signs and outdoor inhabitants reappear, some you may not have missed until they return: a raccoon in the headlights, an opossum scurrying away, or a whiff of skunk scent. By the end of the month, the first brave male birds of migrating species call at the feeder.

Using Catalogs Carefully

The catalogs started coming in December and January. My strategy is to avoid looking at them until my scheme for the coming season in the garden has had a chance to gel. Otherwise, those slick photos and tempting phrases tend to drive my plans rather than support them.

Many times in spring the mail has brought me bundles and packages from forgotten orders. Not once did any of those packages include a note from my ambitious December or January self advising my more realistic April self what to do with the stuff. More than once the enclosed plants languished or nifty new tools got shuffled into the twilight zone unused.

Given specific items to find, catalogs can be fun. Let's say you know eight plants in the bed need stakes and you've had a frustrating experience with plant supports such as the one I'll describe later. In that case, it's delightful to order hoops of the right size, in the correct number, all to be on hand by May.

Wait to open catalogs until you've finished sifting through your notes or photographs from the previous year. Then you'll be aware that some miserable, mildew-prone phlox finally bit the dust last fall, or that its sad remnant must be removed in spring. You can browse catalogs for possible replacements, remembering to avoid plants that need great air circulation, since lack of such circulation was partially responsible for the phlox's demise. Color, height, and quantity of a suitable replacement will be obvious. This will narrow your choices in species and variety from about ten thousand to one hundred — much fairer odds of spending well and enjoying the results.

Creating Stellar Displays

All warnings in place, consider the fact that February catalog orders may be your best chance to make some superb perennial match-ups. These are the type you carry a notebook to record at botanical parks, on garden tours, or when reading magazines. Bellflower and coreopsis generally go well together, but after seeing *Campanula glomerata* 'Joan Elliot' with *Coreopsis* 'Goldfink', the impact of any other pair may pale in your eyes. Catalogs from many different growers will help you arrange these visual feasts.

Reduce Search Time

To streamline the search for mail-order sources, check your library for a copy of The Andersen Horticultural Library's *Source List of Plants and Seeds,* the single best reference for determining which grower offers the annual, perennial, bulb, shrub, or tree cultivar you want. Species and varieties are listed alphabetically and cross-referenced to growers. Nurseries' addresses and telephone numbers are included, so you can write for a catalog or call to place an order.

If your local library doesn't have a copy of this book, think about buying one and donating it to the library. You may use it only in February, so why not share? For information, write to Andersen Horticultural Library, Minnesota Landscape Arboretum, 3675 Arboretum Drive, Box 39, Chanhassen, MN 55317-0039.

Integrating Annuals and Perennials

If the elusive cultivar you're after is an annual and you intend to add it to a perennial garden or vice versa, go beyond the catalog and consult a plant encyclopedia to plan the matches. Although annuals and perennials can mix well, it's a good idea to avoid combining them solely on the basis of flower. The annual may bloom all summer, but the perennial won't. Despite every catalog claim, no perennial looks like its promotional picture for more than two weeks.

Consider the shapes, textures, and foliage of your selections. If you don't, an annual-perennial pair may be mismatched before and after the perennial blooms. For instance, in late spring I determined to add cannas near the oriental poppies in Bed Three. The attraction was not the canna's red flowers but its huge leaves, especially if they were maroon (*Canna* 'Black Knight') or yellow-variegated (*Canna* 'Pretoria'). With or without flowers, the cannas would provide textural and foliar color contrast. Regrettably, the only cannas available at that time were green-leaf varieties. They did add texture, but my desired vision of striking foliage color would have to wait until the next February catalog order.

Floral close-ups are the hallmark — and the limitation — of mail-order plant lists. To help you become familiar with the whole-plant view, I recommend several plant encyclopedias in the Appendix, "References and Tools" to take you beyond the flower.

Finding the Right Tools

The need for tools and accessories is clearest in winter, after you have revisited the season just passed and set goals for the coming year. Yet I caution you against diving into the catalogs to replace a favorite spade or to buy an additional hoe. Gardeners rarely need many tools, but we tend to amass impressive collections in our search for the "right" ones. Clattering around in my garage are several different styles of hoe, five kinds of spade, and a gaggle of rakes.

Many of these tools are never used. A surprising number were acquired by mail in the off-season. In field tests months later, the handles didn't sit right in my hand, the blade was too long or too short, the tool was too bulky to lug around, or it just didn't get the job done effectively. Now my new purchases are limited to implements I can evaluate in person — lift, snap open and shut, or test for fit in my pocket.

The opportunities to do this are more numerous than you may think. Friends allow me to pick up their tools and make swipes at phantom shrubs and weeds. Several local hardware stores are on my regular rainy-day route. I visit annual garden and home shows, and make sure to see their tool displays.

The annual trade shows of the landscape and nursery industry also feature scores of tools attended by knowledgeable people with time to talk. Trade shows are often open to anyone who pays the fee for a pass, usually just a few dollars. Most of these professional events are held during January and February. As a bonus, for an additional fee you may be able to attend horticultural lectures going on in conjunction with the show.

Contact local professional landscape organizations for information about their conventions. You can find the names of local groups by calling your local Cooperative Extension Service office. Or visit your local library's reference section, where you'll find directories of associations such as *The Encyclopedia of Associations*. Consult listings for "Gardening," "Horticulture," "Landscape," and "Agriculture."

My favorite tools and tool suppliers are listed in the Appendix, "References and Tools."

Observing What Trees and Shrubs Need

It's not a bad idea to stroll the yard in late winter and take a critical look at the woody plants. Pale needles on pines, sooty mold on a linden's limbs, or thickened twigs on a crabapple have a way of jumping out at us when the stage is clear of most foliage.

The pine may be gasping for fertilizer. That's best applied just as active growth is starting in early spring.

An insect infestation may have built to harmful proportions on the linden last year, coating the wood with insect excrement and inviting a sooty layer of fungus to grow on the accumulation. The fungus itself is not a danger, but it's a sign that you should crack the books or consult the experts about what insect developments to watch for and when.

Egg masses can make the twigs look thick — perhaps you've found eggs of those annoying tent caterpillars, waiting to invade the crabapple. The damage these moth larvae do might defoliate whole limbs or even the entire tree. You can avoid the damage by clipping that twig now or scraping off the eggs.

Occasionally, only in winter will you notice that trees have reached out to cover gardens once flooded with sun. Maybe our eyes are open to discovery in the increasing light at the end of winter. Perhaps the bare-bones landscape is easier to read.

By midsummer, our attention is on the ground-level plants, and we wonder: Why are plants in that area not blooming as well as in previous years? Why are they developing so slowly and showing weak stems? In winter, the answers were already there. That's when I noticed the overhanging oak in Bed Three. You'll meet that tree in the next chapter and again in fall.

Tree and shrub skeletons are now open to inspection. You'll see broken branches, cluttered frames, and accumulated deadwood. March offers ample time for cutting, but any pruning you can do now is a jump on spring. The plants are amenable during a midwinter thaw as long as temperatures stay above freezing for at least a day after the work.

My focus on winter pruning began when I noticed the annual carnage at orchards during midwinter thaws. It became fixed in my routine when a Japanese maple grower mentioned that he always prunes during winter thaws. The reason? The trees are fully dormant at that time. Bleeding (loss of sap) is minimal.

Ah, sap flowing! Maple-sugaring time means spring must be here.

Pruning

AT LAST, A HINT OF SPRING! We know it's late winter or early spring when snowdrops *(Galanthus nivalis)*, snow crocus *(Crocus minimus)*, and winter aconite *(Eranthis hyemalis)* are blooming, along with the fragrant spring witchhazels *(Hamamelis vernalis* and *H. mollis* hybrids). The names tell it all: spring, with winter and snow not quite out of the picture.

Don't let this time pass by without thinking about pruning woody plants that share your garden's sun, soil, water, and spotlight. Very soon leaves, flowers, and other garden diversions will muddy the picture.

Get trees and shrubs in shape now so they won't block the spring sun or become overbearing by summer. If they do steal the light, the size and showiness of your annuals or perennials will suffer. If you overlook a shrub's size now and take exception to it later, you may have to wade into the bed to prune the offenders in July. In the process, you're likely to trample some of the very plants you hoped to bring out of the shadows. Do that pruning in late winter or early spring, before the perennials' foliage breaks the surface.

What to Prune

Many people are uncertain about what to prune and when. After receiving confusing or conflicting information from credible sources they're tempted to avoid the whole issue. As a result, evergreens get too big for their spaces along the house front, flowering shrubs get twiggier and less floriferous, and trees develop crowded canopies that eventually call for major surgery.

The key is to understand your personal objectives. I'm often asked for pruning advice. Two people may ask about pruning the same type of shrub, but I'll give each a different answer. This reflects individual circumstances — whether the plant is growing in a shrub border, doing nothing except supplying flowers and privacy, or poking mower operators in the eye and blocking a doorway.

When to Prune

One arboriculture textbook recommends pruning in late winter and early spring because trees grow over pruning wounds most quickly in spring and early summer. This speeds the process that blocks opportunistic insects and decay.

A second author warns against pruning while leaves are forming from mid- to late spring and falling in autumn. The tree's reserves are low in late spring — all tied up in producing foliage. Once the leaves mature, the plant will have a net gain in energy from photosynthesis and can restock the reserves. In fall, energy in the form of starches descends from dying leaves to roots, passing cell by cell through the tree. Removing a limb while either process is under way will result in some reduction of energy stored for the following year.

Both textbooks present valid arguments, but only if the main objective in pruning is to maintain the tree's health. Ask either expert about the best time to prune an oak that gets into visitors' faces, and you're likely to be told, "Before someone knocks himself on the head!"

When people and cultivated plants are both at risk, it should be clear that both are losers if the people lose. So if one of Bed Three's oaks did have an unsafe branch, removal timing would not have been an issue. It would have been pruned as soon as it was identified, even in June while leaves were forming or in October as they fell.

I recommend using the following problem-solving process to clarify your objective and map out pruning strategies. First, identify a specific problem. Second, set a desirable outcome. Third, develop several methods to achieve the objective. Fourth, evaluate each method for possible disadvantages. Finally, set an acceptable course of action.

Let me step you through this.

When Bloom Is an Issue

Timing is certainly an issue when the plant is being grown primarily for flowers. Still, there is leeway even then.

Use the process I recommend in the case of a cornelian cherry (Cornus mas) adjacent to Bed Three, which will bloom soon. It's not dangerous to anyone; it's healthy and blooms well each year. The concern is that it's becoming lopsided. This is evident while it's leafless and even more so when yellow flowers outline its bare form in early spring.

Maybe it was always a little fuller on its north side, but it has become more so as trees to the south cast increasing shade and slow growth within their shadow. Seen from due north, it's symmetrical. Seen from Bed Three to the west, it's not.

What's the problem? Its shape is not pleasing when seen from our viewing angle.

Goals. The most desirable outcome will give us a balanced tree without sacrificing any of this year's yellow flowers. We also might aim to sustain or improve its flowering in future years.

Possible actions. Prune the cornelian cherry, now or later. Remove or thin some of the shading trees on its south side. Ignore the situation until summer foliage masks it, or look at the tree only from the north.

Disadvantages to the possibilities. Pruning now will reduce the flower show that's about to start by the number of branches removed. That's a disadvantage to any gardener starved in March for flowers. Deciding to prune later is risky. It means we may not do it at all. This is a real concern for gardeners with other lives to lead and deadlines to meet. The third option, ignoring the situation, isn't satisfactory. The tree makes a splash every March, and we'll certainly be drawn to look at an unbalanced yellow mass again next spring.

What to do? I'm a follower of Christopher Lloyd's advice: "The time to do something in the garden is when you think of it." That's why in such situations I tend to pull out my saw right away.

In an ideal world, I'd wait until after the tree blooms and then prune. That would give me the best possible show this spring plus a correctly shaped specimen. It's also in accordance with the most often-quoted advice for preserving a floral show: "Prune spring-blooming shrubs and trees in spring immediately after they flower."

Allow Three Months to Set Flower Buds

That rule has its corollary: "Prune summer-blooming woody plants in fall or before they leaf out in early spring." The summer show comes on wood that grew and set buds after spring. We leave them alone while they're working on those buds.

Sometimes these rules make gardeners nervous. Did we wait too long to trim the forsythia if we pruned in June rather than immediately after it flowered in April? Will that rose of Sharon (Hibiscus syriacus) really recover from its October or April clip and bloom next August?

Give the plant three months of good growing between the time you cut it and when you expect to see it bloom. Months when leaves are dropping or the plant is dormant don't count. Forsythia pruned in early

June still has part of June, all of July and August, and at least a little of September to finish this year's branches. It should bloom next April.

I cut my own forsythia back by almost three feet every May. Then I let it grow until June and give it a once-over to tidy the crowd of branches that developed since May. It blooms well every spring.

My peegee hydrangea (*Hydrangea paniculata* 'Grandiflora') is cut back in March or early April to 12 to 18 inches tall. It has a portion of April, all of May and June, and at least part of July to grow and prepare to flower. It's 4 feet tall when it reaches and keeps the normal late July or early August appointment to bloom.

Exceptions to Every Rule

There are exceptions, such as flowering quince (*Chaenomeles speciosa*) and mophead hydrangea (*Hydrangea macrophylla*). These bloom on wood that's been developing for two years so any one-year wood is expendable.

Some exceptions apply not by species but by gardener intention. One is when you don't care about the flowers. Then you can prune whenever you like.

Golden vicary privet (*Ligustrum* × *vicaryi*) and barberry (*Berberis thunbergii*) are flowering shrubs. Privet blooms in summer, barberry in spring. Yet most people prune them with abandon because they're being grown for foliage effect alone. Niagara Falls Botanical Park horticulturists clip both to within inches of the ground early each spring. The clippers come out again whenever these shrubs get out of bounds.

Another objective, pruning to remove unwanted wood, steps right around most rules. This type of pruning is meant to take out whole branches because they're cracked, in the way, or cluttering an otherwise beautiful branching arrangement. Since the idea is to get rid of the branch entirely, flower buds and all, it doesn't matter when it comes off.

The Cost of Lifelong Pruning

Most of us have visions of our shrubs and trees that involve restricting the plant's size, maintaining a certain shape, encouraging a better show, and/or keeping the plant healthy. Of these, keeping a woody plant within set size bounds is the most common objective. It's also the costliest one for both plant and gardener.

You may not think so if you simply unsheathe the shears and whack away every June. Yet over the long haul, the practice shortens the plant's effective life. If you could avoid replacing foundation shrubs every fifteen to twenty years, would you?

Problem solving and personal objectives come into play. You may not have known that your pruning method could shorten your plant's life expectancy. Now you can consider it.

Most shrubs and trees put a disproportionately large amount of energy into lengthening their branch tips. That's how a tree manages to grow ever taller and a shrub to spread up and out. If we repeatedly remove branch tips, splitting each tip's energy among its several close followers, the result is a twiggier branch end.

After one shearing, each branch on the shrub has four or five tip buds where it would have had one. After another year of clipping, the five become twenty-five. As the outermost layer of foliage becomes more crowded with twigs, less light and air reach the middle of the plant to stimulate new growth and help fend off disease. Thus shearing promotes an ever-thinner layer of leaf surrounding a leafless, weakened center.

Given that most foundation shrubs have the potential to be larger than we want them to be, shearing goes on indefinitely; the geometric increase of branch ends can't. A branch or two finally succumbs to the boring of insects, the weight of snow or ice, or a slip of the shears, and an unsightly hole appears. Adjacent branch tips, weakened by the division of energy and programmed to grow out toward open air and light, make little progress toward filling space laterally.

On a healthy shrub, we could rely on interior wood to release a few dormant buds, grow them into branches, and fill the hole. On our continuously sheared plant, wood in the interior is deprived of light that can stimulate the production of new branches (see branch A on drawing, page 40). Limbs are also worn out by producing a few dozen tip buds where once they would have spawned just a few. It's understandable when they fail to push out dormant buds that could become stop-gap branches. On the outer edge, holes remain and increase. The overall appearance of the shrub declines.

Shearing, Replacing, or Modified Pruning

What's the problem? How to keep the plants small and neat. *What's the most desirable situation?* Minimal time and bother in pruning or replacing, plus maximum visual appeal.

Possible routes to the goal. Keep shearing annually and replace shrubs as needed. Learn a modified pruning method that avoids the problem just described. Replace the shrubs with some that will mature at the desired size, so that pruning will be eliminated or reduced.

Disadvantages. Both wholesale replacement and shearing require time and money, a substantial amount of both in some cases. Replacing as needed may mean living with the unbalanced look of a planting with one or more unmatched members. This can be especially vexing if the gardener is unaware that the whole group is "on the edge." He or she may replace one at a time, nursing each for several years until it matches the others, only to face another loss.

Sustainable Pruning

Learning a modified pruning technique also involves time. However, it can save you money, since through its use yews, junipers, and many common landscape plants can remain attractive for more than one hundred years.

Here's the trick to sustainable pruning. Leave the shears sheathed to start. Go out now, before the buds break, and thin the branch ends. It's easiest to see how to do this on a deciduous shrub like burning bush or privet, but the technique is the same on evergreens. Go over the plant with a pair of sharp hand pruners, clipping up to one-third of the branch ends out of each cluster. Remove the twiggy branch end completely, plus a few inches. Then shear, also in late winter or early spring. You may see a few holes or depressions, but you'll also see tremendous new growth within a few weeks as the unmatchable combination of spring energy and sun on bare twigs causes dormant buds to break.

Each cut branch will sprout a new tip that can be shorn for several years before it needs to be thinned again. Evergreen juniper, spruce, pine, and arborvitae will not usually generate new leafy growth from wood that has been cut so far as to remove all green. If you're pruning one of these, restrict your thinning cuts to leave at least some leaf (needle) on each branch or remove the branch entirely.

If the shrub you're restricting in size is a deciduous species that wants so badly to be big that it requires three or four clippings a year, cut it back hard in late winter or early spring. Shorten it by the number of inches you know it will put out this season. Dwarf burning bush (*Euonymus alata* 'Compacta'), for instance, can add 12 to 18 inches each year. I shorten mine by 15 inches every March, using hand pruners, and touch them up just once in early summer if necessary to remove uneven ends.

A sun-grown dwarf spirea (*Spirea bumalda* 'Gold Flame' and others) can grow 24 to 36 inches every season. Shrubby potentilla (*Potentilla fruticosa*) is its match. Since they're both species that bloom after June 21, they can be cut right to the ground in March ("stooled") without hampering bloom. They're so neat in habit that there is generally no need to even the ends in June. The next time they see the scissors is in July, when I deadhead them to promote continued bloom. (See drawings next page.)

Standard forsythia (*Forsythia* × *intermedia*) can grow 4 or 5 feet in a year. It often outgrows the space we give it and qualifies for hard cutting back. However, it blooms in spring from buds that formed the previous June, so wait until later in the spring to prune if flower is a priority. Cut it back hard immediately after the golden show finishes.

No Time Saved in Shearing

Sustainable pruning has kept ancient hedges and topiary in good trim for a century or more. There's no other way to keep a wall shrub lush and flowering for decades even though it's no thicker than a plush tapestry on that wall. I've pruned my own and clients' shrubs this way for twenty years. It may surprise you to hear that it requires no more time in a season than shearing.

Three Years of Conventional Shearing

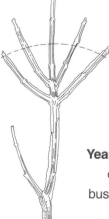

Year One. In early spring of Year One, dotted line indicates where burning bush branch will be cut when it begins to outgrow its given area.

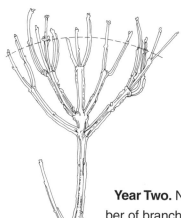

Year Two. Notice the larger number of branch tips compared to the first year. Dotted line indicates where it will be cut in mid-summer.

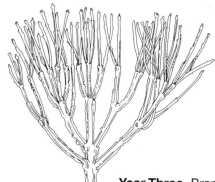

Branch A

Year Three. Branching is restricted to the extremities and is so dense that the bush's shade has curtailed new growth from the interior. Note Branch A has not grown; eventually it will die out.

Three Years of Sustainable Pruning

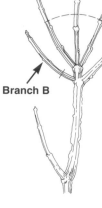

Branch B

Year One. Bar indicates where burning bush Branch B will be cut back in early spring. Dotted line indicates where plant will be sheared. All pruning is done in early spring.

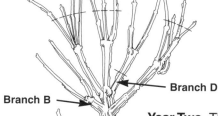

Branch D

Branch B

Branch C

Year Two. The new branches from Branch B have grown to the dotted shearing line and interior growth was stimulated on Branch C. Bar indicates where Branch D will be cut back. All pruning is done in early spring.

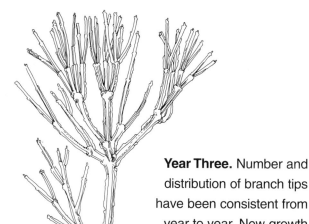

Branch C

Year Three. Number and distribution of branch tips have been consistent from year to year. New growth extends deep into the interior. Compare Branch C to Branch A on the sheared bush at left.

If we could stage a contest, cumulative times for the season would have to count, including clean-up. One simple shearing can be finished quicker than a thinning and shearing, but the latter leads to fewer summer touch-ups.

Debris is often simpler to pick up after hand-clipping. Every piece large enough to need removal is in hand when cut and can be tossed onto a rake-able surface or tarp for collection.

Shearing would actually lose points if there was an impartial judge to rate the jobs for finished looks and assign an irritation factor for noise. Sustainable pruning rarely leaves dried bits of shrubbery hanging and requires no ear-splitting leaf blowers to clean up fallen debris.

Pruning for Plant Health

Even if all your shrubs and trees are the right size and shape, they stand to gain from early spring attention. Take a stroll and give them a critical look.

Has a particular shrub's flowering or foliage been substandard? Check to see whether the branches are densely packed, with few leaf or flower buds within the interior of the plant. Thinning out the canes on that shrub can lengthen its life and improve its appearance. Right now, in early spring, you can take out up to one-third of the oldest, thickest canes at ground level without unduly stressing the plant. Even if it's a spring-blooming species, it will still bloom on every branch you left intact.

Examples of Unpruned and "Stooled" Spireas

Early Spring

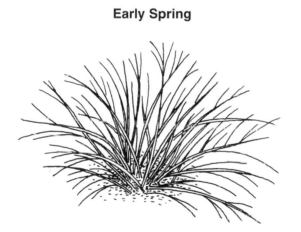

Fall

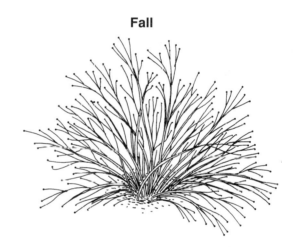

Dwarf spirea can simply be left to grow unchecked. Compare this spirea to that in the drawings below.

Fall

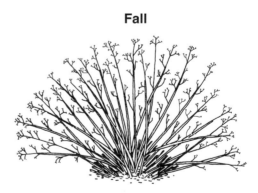

Early Spring

This dwarf spirea was cut to the ground in late winter or early spring. New stems grew rapidly from the roots and stem buds below the cut. It bloomed a bit later in July than its unchecked counterpart above, but its bloom was more dense and its height and twigginess less. Many other fast-growing summer-blooming species can be stooled in this manner.

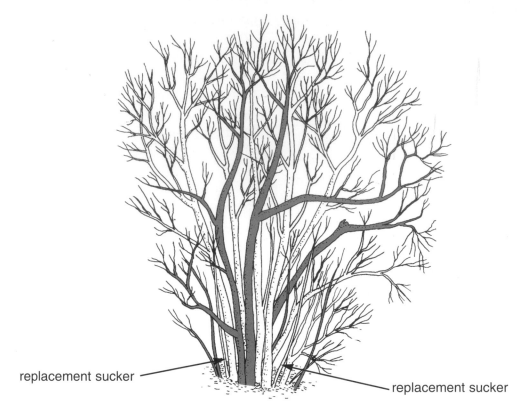

replacement sucker   replacement sucker

An older shrub can be rejuvenated by removing the oldest canes in late winter. Shaded limbs will be removed from this lilac. Arrows point to suckers that will remain to replace old wood.

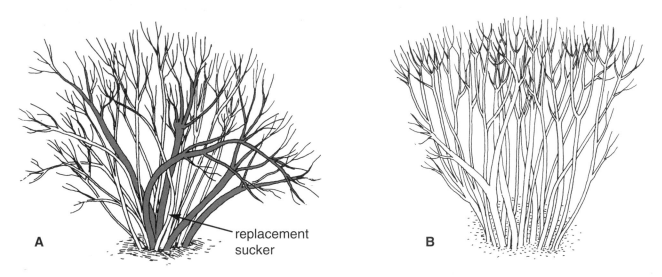

A

replacement sucker

B

Fast-growing shrubs such as redtwig dogwood and forsythia can be thinned annually in late winter or early spring. On the redtwig dogwood (A), the oldest third of the canes (shaded limbs) are removed. Arrow indicates one-year-old replacement sucker that will sport brightest red bark for two winters before its own removal. Another redtwig dogwood (B) has been simply sheared each year. It becomes twiggier at the tips and bare in its center. As interior wood ages, it becomes less and less colorful.

Are there a lot of very old stems and few young ones? Most plants flower best and grow most vigorously on young wood. Many with attractive bark color, such as redtwig dogwood *(Cornus alba sibirica)* and Japanese kerria *(Kerria japonica)*, have the brightest bark on stems just one or two years old. These are most attractive when the oldest stems — one-quarter to one-third of the shrub's wood — are cut back to the ground in late winter.

Are suckers ruining the appearance of a grafted plant? Are there suckers coming from the roots or trunk below the graft union? Such wood will be different from the plant you bought in flower, leaf, or form. Often, it will grow much faster than the desired plant, shading out its top partner and eventually taking over.

In late winter, it's simple to pick out a straight branch that can ruin the habit of a weeping tree — cherry, crabapple, spruce, etc. Trace it to the spot on the trunk or roots where it originates and cut it off.

At this bare time of year, a contorted hazel *(Corylus avellana contorta)* may look like one gnarly trunk in a young forest of saplings. That's the desirable plant's corkscrew trunk surrounded by straight root suckers. Cut out undesirable straight sprouts as low as you can manage.

Do branches cross each other? Crossing limbs often muddle the outline of a woody plant. Worse, bark wears off at the rub. Bark is a plant's greatest defense against infection. When the plant loses bark, the cambium beneath is at the mercy of diseases and insects. It's better to remove one or both of the rubbing branches than to lose them to a pest.

Do all the branches have live buds, or are there dead limbs? Deadwood can harbor diseases and pests, even offering a route for their entry into live wood that would otherwise resist infection.

Four Cutting Steps

You probably have shrubs that require pruning for many reasons. No matter how few or many things there are that should be done in a garden, a few always get overlooked, postponed, or wished into temporary invisibility.

Faced with a plant that has deadwood, crossing branches, a crying need to be thinned, and who knows what else, I fall back on the four-step approach to pruning:

1. Remove the dead and diseased wood.
2. Cut out suckers and water sprouts.
3. Take out any crossing wood.
4. Prune for aesthetics.

You can do the first three steps at any time, to any plant, without concern for flower. Dead or diseased wood and water sprouts — lank, vertical growth that blasts off from more horizontal limbs of crabapples and other trees — are unlikely to bloom.

After all the harmful and useless wood is out of the way, the fourth step is a snap. Prune for aesthetics now, including thinning. You'll be looking at a healthy framework and have a clear field of vision. It will be simpler to select for the best-distributed stems or those with the most grace.

Pruning a Weeping Cherry

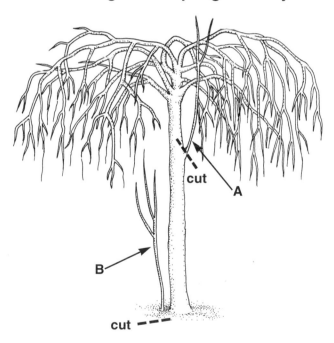

In early spring it's simple to pick out the straight stem sucker (A) and root sucker (B) that will ruin the weeping cherry's form. Bars indicate where the stem sucker will be cut and root sucker severed at its point of origin.

Four Steps to Rejuvenate a Neglected Crabapple

1. Remove the deadwood.

2. Remove the suckers . . .

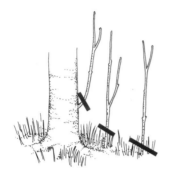

. . . and water sprouts.

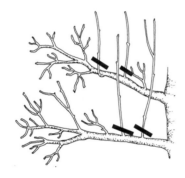

3. Remove the crossing wood to prevent rubbing wounds and a cluttered profile.

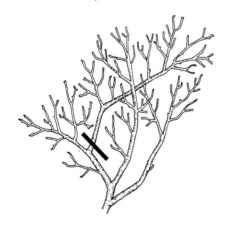

4. Prune for aesthetics, to balance the tree's profile. This last step can wait until after bloom.

BEFORE

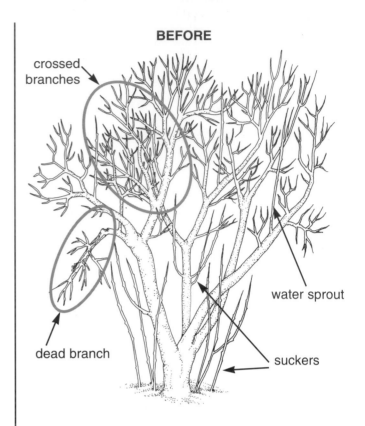

crossed branches

dead branch

water sprout

suckers

AFTER

Keep an eye on the pile of branches you remove, and compare the total number of leaf buds they represent to the number left on the tree or shrub. Try to limit your pruning in any one season to one-third or less of the total leaf surface. There are exceptions, as in stumping back, or "stooling," spirea, potentilla, and the like. If you don't know whether the plant will respond well to hard pruning, let it keep two-thirds of its leaf buds and finish the pruning the next season.

Letting Losers Go

Sometimes when the objective is to restrict a plant's size, hard pruning is required to accomplish this goal. Why not go for broke? The worst thing that can happen is that the plant will die. This will be no great loss, since it will prove that the plant couldn't live with your size limitations.

Occasionally, I've arrived at Step Four and realized that there wasn't enough plant left to work with. One crabapple comes to mind. It had been long overgrown by suckers. After those and the deadwood were gone, it was apparent that the original plant had dwindled to a bare frame.

What remained was sad to see, and probably doomed to defeat by the fire blight that had marked most of its limbs for Step One removal. I took the whole tree out and planted a new shrub. The response was surprising. At least one person familiar with the property didn't even notice that the tree was gone. That's one great advantage to working in late winter or early spring — leafless plants tend to take up a lot less room in the shredder and in the mind's eye.

All Done in Fifteen Minutes

All of this can be done in quarter-hour expeditions, a good way to build up your stamina. Whacking back a dwarf spirea, potentilla, butterfly bush (*Buddleia davidii*), or blue mist (*Caryopteris × clandonensis*) is a matter of ten minutes, tops. Removing three of the oldest canes from a lilac may take only one or two trips.

Between outings, you can assess what you've done and change any of your plans according to what you see. An old friend told me one year, with a grin, "You know, I feel older and creakier every spring. Makes me wonder why I didn't tackle all this work last fall when I was younger and in better shape." That's a practical argument for getting beds ready for planting in the fall and pruning shrubs in the spring. We're so often better fit for digging in the fall and need a more gradual initiation in the spring. Pruning is the perfect "vehicle."

Tools and Techniques for the Perfect Cut

My basic tool kit for early spring consists of bypass pruning shears, long-handled loppers, a folding pruning saw, a curved-blade pruning saw, and a ball of twine. The curved-blade saw usually stays in the garage or in my van. One of the basic tenets of pruning is to cut and train young, flexible wood, rather than waiting to do corrective pruning. Thus, that saw suitable for larger branches is my least used item.

The pruners and folding saw fit in my pocket, the twine fits nicely on the handle of the loppers, and

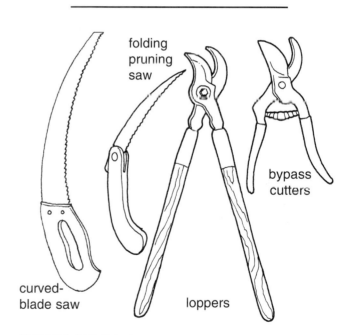

folding pruning saw

curved-blade saw

loppers

bypass cutters

BYPASS CUTTERS, with blades that cut with a scissor motion, are indispensable for branches ½" in diameter or less. LOPPERS can do rough pruning on branches up to 1" in diameter. Long handles provide the best leverage. A FOLDING PRUNING SAW is handy for larger limbs. A CURVED-BLADE SAW is my preferred tool for the largest limbs.

that leaves me with at least one hand free to swing as I walk, wave to neighbors, and grab the next branch up when I'm climbing to prune. How great it is to be back outdoors!

Surgically Sharp and Clean

When you cut your fingernails, do you snip them so that they're smooth, or do you leave serrated and jagged edges? I thought so. Give your trees and shrubs the same consideration, since they suffer the same or greater trauma if a rough edge gets caught and peeled back. Always use sharp, clean tools and cut so that the stubs and stumps have smooth edges.

I admit to laziness, a tendency to buy new saw blades rather than hunt up someone who can sharpen the old ones properly. I've also been known to put a new blade on my hand pruners rather than figure out where the honing stone is stashed. Take whatever path you have to take, but leave those clean cuts.

If you have any concern about spreading diseases or pest insects between plants, keep a rag and a jar of rubbing alcohol or 10 percent bleach solution on hand when you're pruning. I can assure you that those who know the risk take the time to clean their tools before moving on to the next plant.

I once interviewed a grower of junipers. He grows them dense and bushy, which is the way most of his customers think they should look. This calls for annual shearing. Since many junipers are susceptible to twig blight, a fungus adept at entering the plant through broken twigs, he sterilizes his blade with chlorine bleach between plants — all four or five thousand of them. One dip into the bleach solution and one pass over the rag hanging from his belt is all it takes.

For me, sterilizing my pruning equipment is not quite a daily routine. Perhaps that's because I'm still learning and am mistaken in thinking that most of the plants I deal with are healthy. When I am aware of the existence or possibility of disease, it's a different matter. Last year I helped a friend remove dead and dying wood from an Amur maple (*Acer ginnala*) that looked very much as if it were infected with verticillium wilt, a fungus that can live in hundreds of plant species. In another yard, I cut out vine euonymus (*Euonymus for-*

tunei) branches that were deformed by crown gall. This is a bacterial problem capable of taking up residence in many plants. On both occasions, I dipped my tools into rubbing alcohol and wiped them dry right away.

Three Cuts to Drop That Limb

Even sharp, sterile tools aren't enough to remove large or heavy limbs safely. Whenever a limb an inch or more in diameter has to come off, there's a good chance that it has enough weight to get away from you. If so, it may drop down when it's half-severed and rip a section of the trunk's bark off in the process.

This is a situation to avoid. Woody plants have natural internal barrier layers between trunk and branch, branch and twig. These allow the passage of water and nutrients but block the transmission of most diseases and decay organisms. If the barrier layer and its bark are left when an offending limb is removed, the remaining wood is guarded against infection. Within several years, healthy wood will grow over the stub.

The branch bark collar is a barrier layer, a thickened ring of bark at the junction of branch and trunk, or branch and larger branch. Sometimes it resembles a turtleneck; other times it's harder to distinguish. Years ago, arborists thought that the best pruning technique was flush cutting — taking the stub off completely. As a result of the work of Alex Shigo and Associates and others, we now know that letting the branch bark collar stay can make a life-or-death difference by preventing decay within the trunk.

To leave the collar and avoid tearing the bark, make three cuts to drop the limb. First, cut halfway through the underside of the limb, 6 to 12 inches out from the branch bark collar. Then make a second cut, a few inches farther out than the first, cutting from the top of the branch down into the center. This will make the branch cant sharply down from the second cut and crack off at the first cut. Finally, make a third cut to remove the stub just to the branch bark collar.

The same researchers who dissected thousands of trees to prove the value of leaving collars intact have done tests showing that pruning paint isn't necessary. In some cases it proved to be counterproductive, damaging the wood or trapping moisture that harbors

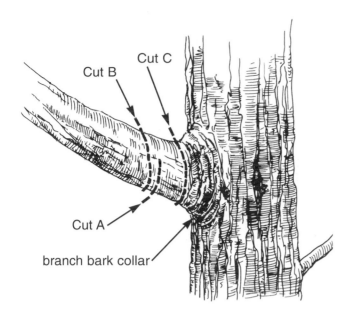

Three cuts to drop the limb:
Cut A prevents tearing.
Cut B removes the weighty end of the limb.
Cut C removes the stub, leaving the collar intact.

---

pests. It's taken a long time for this message to take hold among professional arborists, and it may take longer still to be accepted by private gardeners. Be a trendsetter — throw out those asphalt paints and fungicidal dressings.

Be Careful of the Soil

The soil may be cold, wet, and vulnerable in late winter or early spring. It's easily pressed down to an airless, compacted state but slow to repair itself. Soil without any air spaces is dead soil, and the roots in it die, too. Most of us want to leave green footprints behind, not lifeless tracks, so stay off bare soil in late winter and early spring. You'll see the wreckage of good soil wherever your kids, meter readers, or pets have established cold-season shortcuts through your beds. It's especially shocking to see the impressions left where pruning was done with all the pruner's weight concentrated on tiptoe.

In trials conducted to test the effectiveness of different techniques for preventing soil compaction on new building sites, an 8-inch layer of bark mulch effectively protected the soil against several passes with a bulldozer. Even I don't gain that much weight over the winter! A layer of mulch 4 to 5 inches thick, a sheet of plywood, or even a blanket of twigs is enough to pad the plants against the pruner's boot.

The sandy loam in my own sunny bed drains freely and warms up early in spring. By the end of March, bulb foliage has emerged and begun to grow rapidly. The danger of ruining the soil structure is past, and it's finally time to dig into the garden!

Edging and Weeding

EARLY SPRING PROVIDES a grand opportunity to set weeds and pests back so far they won't be a presence again until summer. Perennials are so forgiving now that after being dug, left out of the ground for extended periods, chopped up, and put back into new territory, they won't even sniffle at you, let alone tell anyone else what you've done.

There are three things on an early spring's "must-do" list: edge, weed, and mulch. There's only one "should" and a "might" in the wings — dividing and fertilizing, respectively. How much simpler can it get?

The only trouble is getting started.

What I describe here begins for me around April 1. For you it may start a bit earlier or later. Soil condition, not a calendar, marks time in a perennial garden. My far southern friends start watching for the signs in early March. My aunt in zone 4 doesn't get antsy until the third week of April. We all know when the soil is awake by reading the plants' reactions.

You'll notice indicators of this season, such as the blooming of cornelian cherry (*Cornus mas*) and sugar maple (*Acer saccharum*). Crocuses have finished flowering, daffodils have broken the surface, and some tulip leaves are 2 inches above the ground. Let other people nurse calendar fixations, curse weather reports, and groan about spring not coming — you watch the plants for the good news, because they never fail to advise.

Self-Starters Have the Edge

When spring does come, most of us are at least a little bit out of shape, out of sorts, and not accustomed to working out in the weather. Even after limbering up with some late-winter pruning, it's tough to contemplate putting knee to ground. The weather report on any given day in April may repeat the numbers from a day last November. We may have worked outside in shirt sleeves on that November day but recoil from the same conditions now. We wait, assuring ourselves that all of spring is yet to come, lots of time to whip the yard into shape.

Plants are not so fickle. On frostless days in late winter, roots grow, sap rises, and new vegetative buds prime for action. In early spring, green swells and builds like cumulus clouds stacking up on a front. Trees, shrubs, perennials, and weeds are all included. The gardener who misses a ride on the crest of this weather system risks a whole season of catch-up.

Most of my records of garden work begin in April. When I couldn't or didn't start work on a particular garden until later in the season, my standards for its appearance and performance had to slide. I had to tolerate plants that could have looked better, kill and mask pest problems rather than prevent them, and do without that joyful abandon plants can radiate in May and early June. It also meant I had to work harder and longer in August's heat.

No Place for the Fashion Conscious

It wasn't snowing on my first visit in early spring, or raining. It was certainly cool, but not cold. I dressed for a typical unpredictable spring day — no bulky clothes that hinder movement, but comfortable, easily shed layers. That meant a long johns lining, sweatshirt under jacket, hat under hood, and numerous extra gloves put by so that I could change every time a pair got wet. Wet, cold fingers can bench me more quickly than anything, and wet knees are almost as bad. That's why the knee-pad pockets on my gardening pants have a waterproof lining.

I'm not one of those people sometimes pictured in gardening books — the ones in shorts, short sleeves, tennis shoes or sandals, and bare hands. There's marketing power in that image — the carefree gardener enjoying quality time among the greenery. But I can't endorse it.

The gardeners I know have one or more articles they swear by that ruins that blithe image. One always wears boots, having once lost a gardening month to an infection from a thorn. Another shuns shorts since discovering how sensitive the backs of his legs are to the oils of certain plants. He's found that those substances have no immediate effect but can combine with sunlight over several hours to produce deep and painful burns. (For more on this, look into the books listed in the Appendix, "References and Tools." Check under "Dermatitis" and "Phyto-Photo Toxicity" in the poisonous plants books listed there.)

More and more of us also are covering our heads and arms against the sun. People like me whose hands have become hypersensitive to abrasion and dehydration are rarely seen without gloves.

Back to my plunge into the open air after months spent next to a heat register. I felt a chill for only a few minutes, started peeling layers within an hour, and was in shirt sleeves at lunchtime. I was glad to have overcome that initial inclination to stay inside.

A Single Load of Tools

My first step "on the clock" in this project was loading my tools into a wheelbarrow for the walk out to the bed. I brought my standard spring kit. (Sources for these tools are listed in the Appendix, "References and Tools.")

- Spade with sharp, squared blade
- Spading fork
- Metal-tine leaf rake, adjustable for raking a wide or narrow path
- Five-gallon bucket
- Short-handled weeder — something for close work
- Hand pruners
- Sturdy knife

I also had five pounds of slow-release 14-14-14 fertilizer in a one-gallon plastic bag, and a garden diagram and pencil inside a clear plastic page protector.

Long-handled tools go into the wheelbarrow, smaller things into the bucket. I consider it a challenge to transport everything I need in one trip, especially when it's a long hike. This is even more important when I'm in my own garden. Even though I'm never more than 100 feet from the garage and its tool bin, every walk I take is likely to turn up at least one distraction.

Wandering is a common affliction among gardeners. Catch one of us in the garden, and you're likely to find a wheelbarrow here, a spade propped up over there, hand pruners on that far bench, a rake lying on the lawn halfway to the target bed, and the gardener herself leaning on the fence, talking to a neighbor. It's fun, but not the best way to get things done.

Clearing the Debris

The beauty of early spring is the uncluttered playing field — just you, the barely sprouted perennials, and the weeds. Clear away the debris, and there's nowhere an interloper or problem can hide.

If the bed was well tended last year, cutting and clearing old plant parts is a breeze. This bed was in good shape in that respect. Only evergreens had been left untouched in the fall clean-up. Of the others, basal rosettes, 6-inch stubble, and stray stalks remained.

That had been enough to trap leaves and other windblown chaff over the winter. The stubble had to go so that I could rake everything clean. The evergreens needed cutting back to remove winter-killed branches, improve their shape, and encourage denser growth. I started at one end of the bed and began excising dead pieces, one plant at a time.

Cut Out Old Growth

Yellow blackberry lily (*Belamcanda flabellata* 'Halo Yellow'), penstemon (*Penstemon barbatus* 'Prairie Fire'), and lamb's ear (*Stachys lanata*) were the first to be groomed. The basal leaves of penstemon and lamb's ear are semi-evergreen, but new growth was already sprouting among the tattered old foliage. I cut out leaves that spread beyond the new shoots but didn't nip the grass that had insinuated itself in the crowns. I did not want to overlook that later, so it and all the other weeds stayed intact for visibility.

Straggler stalks and leaves of last year's blackberry lilies had splayed out across this end of the bed, but the only signs of life were tight pinpoints of green at ground level. The dead foliage tugged away cleanly, and I snipped off the stalks.

The daylilies were in the same state as the blackberry lilies and needed the same tugging and snipping. Since their new growth was more advanced than the blackberry lilies, I didn't cut as far down when removing the old foliage.

There's no need to tease every old leaf base away from new shoots and snip it. Just cut all the remains to the height of the new green. Remember, the purpose of this cutting is to clear the field of vision for weed hunting. If indispensable new shoots are 3 inches tall, that will be an unavoidable 3-inch obstruction, whether old leaves are removed from the mound or not.

Here's an insight into daylilies and their springtime rush. Daylilies are always so eager to be up that their early spring foliage may be pale yellow-green, even golden. The color is probably a result of their pushing up fast while the soil is very cool, microbial activity is still low, and so nitrogen is not readily available. They'll green up later on their own.

Wait for Slow-Risers

What if you don't see any new growth coming? Are the old stalks dry and brown — no moist, green pith when you cut into them? If so, cut them down.

If you scratch gently in the soil around the base of old stalks, do you see any sprouts coming? If so, you know it's an herbaceous perennial just about to emerge.

Sometimes you can't find any shoots subtending those withered remains, even when you scratch away the soil. Nevertheless, don't give up or pull out the plant. Many perennials are slow-risers.

A good thing, too, since the appearance of the late-summer and fall garden depends on fresh faces like balloon flower *(Platycodon grandiflorus)*, perennial ageratum *(Eupatorium coelestinum)*, hardy hibiscus *(Hibiscus moscheutos)*, and Japanese anemone *(Anemone x hybrida)*. Just cut back any unsightly or concealing old foliage, mark the spot, and wait three weeks for them to make their entrance.

Stay Focused on the Task

The golden marguerite was as ratty looking as it always is in spring. It grows so fast and spends so much energy blooming every year that the center of the plant dies. Brown stalks lean higgledy-piggledy from that lifeless bull's-eye, surrounded by a ring of fresh green shoots from offsets. I cut these old stalks. Pulling will not do — I have learned that this shallow-rooted plant can be dislodged by a sharp tug. Dead parts and living may peel up together as easily and messily as a tangle of paper clips emerging from a bin.

This species also sets large amounts of very willing seed, so the whole area and adjoining spaces were carpeted with seedling marguerites. I live by the adage "A weed is simply a plant growing out of place." Thus, I viewed all but three or four of this seedling mob as weeds. A strong desire to start culling rose in me and got as far as my shoulders, but I stuck with cutting back. I knew that once the cutting was done and the area raked over, even more weeds would be visible. I'd have to revisit this area after raking. Sometimes waiting saves time in the long run.

Cutting Perennials with Abandon

The overwhelming majority of perennials can be cut with impudence in early spring, relieved of all their above-ground parts. I'm going to tell you how to know which should not be cut so hard and how to handle those few.

As you examine a plant in early spring, look for the newest foliage and/or growing points that will become leaves. You're unlikely to find any green swellings on dry, brown stems or limp remains radiating from the center of the plant. Most often, new leaves will be coming tightly-curled from ground level, or spears of varied colors will be just breaking the surface. If that's what you see, you're definitely looking at an herbaceous perennial — one in which all above-ground parts die and new growth arises from some underground part. Go ahead and cut away all the old material. Just take care not to smash or cut the new growth.

The ease in working around such low-profile new buds is one advantage to cleaning and weeding beds

---

Be Bold

Many people are very reluctant to cut down perennials in fall or early spring for fear they'll kill them. Overcome your reluctance and keep cutting. It's unproductive to hesitate and second-guess every stalk you remove.

---

in early spring. There's no need to tease debris from within an expansive crop of new foliage and as much room to maneuver as there will ever be without fear of trampling the new plants. Given the fast, relentless pace of spring growth, in two weeks you might find that you'll need double the time and patience to do the same job.

Recognize Evergreen Perennials

With some plants, you'll find a crowd of live green leaves linked directly to the crown. Or you'll discover stems that are woody and moist, often with leaves or leaf remnants still clinging to them. These stems will have buds swelling and greening somewhere along their length.

These are evergreen perennials. They come in two types — those with evergreen leaves on woody stems, and those with evergreen leaves that arise directly from the crown of the plant. I ran into three evergreens in this first part of the garden. Two were woody (rue and 'Lambrook Silver' artemisia), and one was without wood (little blue fescue). When it comes to cutting, there's a big difference between the two.

Woody perennials set new growth buds on the wood. Nonwoody perennials grow back right from the crown. If you cut off all the above-ground parts of a woody like rue or 'Lambrook Silver' artemisia, you've removed all the growing points, and the plant may die. If you mow the fescue to the ground, you've cut only the leaves. More were ready to grow from the crown anyway, so there's very little setback.

Nonwoody Evergreens and Grasses

For both kinds of evergreens, my objective was to take out the dead stems and foliage and improve the shape of the plant if possible. For blue fescue, the simplest way to eliminate the tattered foliage was by shaving the whole clump off at ground level.

Most of the ornamental grasses aren't evergreen like blue fescue. They're dried husks in winter, no different from the moor grass (*Molinia Caerulea* 'Sky Racer') in our test bed. I treat them as I do blackberry lily, shearing off the old before the new growth starts. Yet people are often in a quandary about cutting them.

After fielding many questions and as many conflicting reports about how close to cut and whether burning off a grass's old growth has advantages over cutting, I experimented with different spring clean-ups on fescue and other grasses.

I chose gardens where three or more clumps of the same type of ornamental grass were growing. *Pennisetum, Miscanthus, Calamagrostis, Erianthus, Helictotrichon, Phalaris,* and *Chasmanthium* species were involved. In these gardens, I burned one of each clump, cut one to 6 inches, and shaved one. Watching them throughout the following season, I saw only one significant difference in growth: the closer the shave, the less tendency the grass had to develop a dead center.

Fescue has grassy leaves, but some nonwoody evergreen species have broad leaves. Bed Three's coralbells (*Heuchera* spp.) are prime examples. These can be handled like the fescue, but I generally remove only the oldest, most unsightly leaves. Usually this culls the widest, lowest, and sloppiest foliage. With this trimming done, the soil around the base of the plant becomes visible. Good, because that's where the worst weeds hide.

Incidentally, trimming improves the plant's appearance and makes a better backdrop for the flowers on early-blooming species such as *Bergenia, Hepatica, Helleborus,* and *Tiarella.* Already in early spring you can see some of their flower stalks and buds coming.

Woody Evergreens

I cut back the woody evergreen species to remove deadwood and even up stems to give the plants better shape. I just made sure each remaining branch had some leaves or leaf buds on it.

In addition to 'Lambrook Silver' artemisia and rue, this bed has woody silvermound artemisia in it. On both artemisia species, I reduced the branches by about one-half before I was satisfied with them. The rue had been so badly winter-killed that removing the deadwood left it with only branch bases and a few tiny buds. I made a note on my garden diagram to buy some replacement rue before my next visit. I wanted to be prepared in case these plants failed.

Other common woody perennials are lavender (*Lavandula* spp.), cotton lavender (*Santolina* spp.),

Cutting Back Ornamental Grass

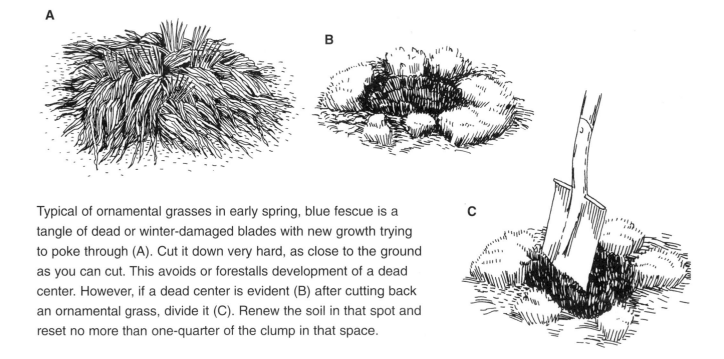

A

B

C

Typical of ornamental grasses in early spring, blue fescue is a tangle of dead or winter-damaged blades with new growth trying to poke through (A). Cut it down very hard, as close to the ground as you can cut. This avoids or forestalls development of a dead center. However, if a dead center is evident (B) after cutting back an ornamental grass, divide it (C). Renew the soil in that spot and reset no more than one-quarter of the clump in that space.

thyme (*Thymus* spp.), perennial candytuft (*Iberis sempervirens*), germander (*Teucrium chamaedrys*), false rock cress (*Aubrieta deltoidea*), snow-in-summer (*Cerastium tomentosum*), and perennial alyssum (*Aurinia saxatilis*). Each of these should be pruned to removed deadwood, but remember to leave some leaf buds on each remaining branch.

Now that you've read my pointers for cutting herbaceous and woody perennials, look at the diagram on the next page. I started cutting in the penstemon and blackberry lily areas, where indicated. I told you that the penstemon has a semi-evergreen basal rosette, which I cut except for the new growth. On the diagram, its space is crosshatched, and so is that for every other plant I treated that way.

The blackberry lily remains can be cut entirely, as long as new growing points are not molested. On the diagram, the blackberry lily's space is white, as is the daylily space and that of every other herbaceous perennial. They all fall into this treatment category.

Light shading indicates nonwoody evergreens that were groomed as needed, even to the ground as for blue fescue.

Dark shading marks the woody evergreens whose stems were shortened to live wood above green buds — rue and the like.

Raking

Once an area is cut back, rake it lightly to pull all the loose duff off the bed. There's no need to scrape deep or remove the mulch; just peel all the loose debris off the surface.

Some people pitch their cuttings onto a tarp; I threw mine out to the lawn as I worked. Even so, I had to rake the beds as I didn't pick up and throw every loose leaf and twig. That's too much plucking and tossing for me, and I look to raking as a much-needed break from cutting.

A Healthy Variety of Motion

I've heard arguments for specialization as a means to getting more work done in a garden. For instance, when all this cutting has to be done, the gardener is

Trimming a Woody Evergreen

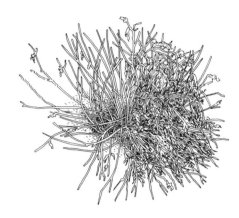

1. 'Lambrook Silver' artemisia as the debris was being cleared from Bed Three. First, the clutter of dead foliage and stems is removed, as has been done to the left side of this plant.

2. The remaining stems are shortened as desired. I cut Bed Three's plants to 6". Each remaining stem has a moist, green center and several live leaf buds. It is best if the tip buds on remaining stems face out, away from the center. This directs new growth into a wide, graceful spread.

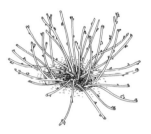

3. 'Lambrook Silver' artemisia one month after it was cut back. After an additional two weeks, all stems were invisible, hidden beneath dense silver foliage. By mid-summer it was an 18 inch mound of new stems and foliage.

to take the appropriate tool in hand and keep at it until there's nothing left to clip. I even admonished you along these lines in mentioning my urge to weed the marguerite.

The danger in overdoing this approach is in muscle strain and boredom. Especially in spring, but also in light of the increasing number of repetitive motion injuries that people are incurring, you should vary your activities as much as possible. It's best to let bending over a spade give way to kneeling to weed, then standing to rake or scoop mulch into a wheelbarrow.

I've had problems with carpal tunnel syndrome, tennis elbow, and back strain during my time as a gardener, but not in the past six or seven years. That's how long it's been since I realized the importance of

varying motions, stances, and tools. After about twenty strokes on a rake with my right hand above the left, I switch hands. I use one foot on the shovel for a few minutes, then the other, which evens out the wear on my feet, legs, and back. Being strongly right-handed, it was difficult for me to teach my left hand to weed, but now it does equal time. I spend more time maintaining gardens now than ever before, yet I have fewer aches and pains.

I divide a garden like this into sections of 100 or 200 square feet — that's 10 feet by 10 feet, or 10 by 20. I do all the cutting in one section, then stand to rake. That's about ten minutes of clipping followed by ten minutes of raking. This rhythm of changing stance and motion can become a habit — one worth keeping.

Cutting Herbaceous and Woody Perennials

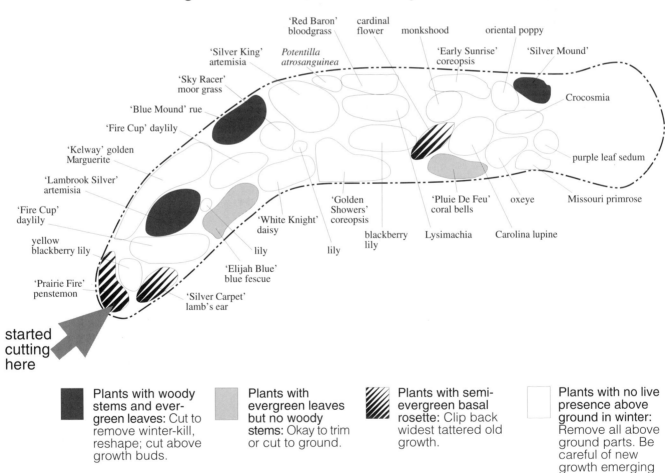

Plants with woody stems and ever-green leaves: Cut to remove winter-kill, reshape; cut above growth buds.

Plants with evergreen leaves but no woody stems: Okay to trim or cut to ground.

Plants with semi-evergreen basal rosette: Clip back widest tattered old growth.

Plants with no live presence above ground in winter: Remove all above ground parts. Be careful of new growth emerging from soil.

Step One, Done

An hour and a half after I arrived, all was cut down and raked out. Excluding wheelbarrow and get-my-bearings time, I had alternated cutting and raking for seventy-five minutes.

Stay Alert for Water Needs

In a dry year, it's helpful to water before weeding. On this visit, the soil was cool, slightly moist, and crumbly. That's called "in perfect tilth." If water had been needed, supplying it would have been a simple third step in my dance. I would have cut, raked, and then set or moved a sprinkler to the 100 square feet just completed.

Like most botanical gardens, this one does not have an automatic watering system. Gardeners gauge the needs of individual areas or even individual plants and water each when appropriate. The water supply for this garden comes from taps on the system that also waters the lawn, which had yet to be activated for the season. I thanked goodness it wasn't a droughty spring, or I'd have been obliged to carry buckets of water to thirsty plants.

Nothing fuels a summer perennial display like a steadily moist spring. Although watering doesn't become a priority until summer, when deficits are more likely, I keep an eye on soil moisture all season and am quicker with a hose in spring than at any other time.

Weeding Starts with Edging

The worst weed in any garden is the one that shares the garden's edge. That's often lawn grass, but it may be groundcovers, vines, shrubs, and trees. We encourage all of these to be as large and vigorous as possible, which sets them far apart from species more readily recognized as weeds.

Picture the most irksome weed on your list. If you can't think of one of your own, take one of mine. Quack grass, thistle, nut sedge, scouring rush, and bindweed are all on my top ten list. Now imagine that weed coddled, watered, fed, aerated, even given help against diseases and pests. Wouldn't it be a monster of unthinkable proportions?

A client of mine, a lifelong student of the scientific approach, nurtured a quack grass plant to see what it could do. He measured the growth of a single root on the resulting plant at more than 12 inches in twenty-four hours. That's enough to keep me awake at night.

So you can see why, now that it was time to start weeding, I aimed first to beat back the tide of lawn lapping at every edge of the bed. It's not unusual for a cool-season plant like Kentucky bluegrass to send roots 18 inches into a perennial bed between November and April. If this bed had been surrounded by groundcover or trees, I would have been no less compelled. Pachysandra can surge 8 to 12 inches, and Siberian elm or silver maple roots can creep 3 feet during a gardener's off-season.

That's why most gardens have either a cut edge or a root barrier installed along the perimeter. I'll start with cut edges, since that's what surrounds this bed and most of my other gardens.

Edging Tools and Techniques

Fortifying the edge was simply a matter of slicing down along the outline of the bed, cutting as deep as the weed roots were growing, loosening that soil just inside the bed, and lifting out all the invading roots. I did most of this in a one-two motion with a sharp, rectangular-bladed spade.

Here's the drill: Stand outside the bed. Insert the spade to its full 9-inch depth. With the blade fully in the ground, lean back and force the spade's handle down toward the lawn. This heaves the blade end up. The edge line is cut, and the soil 9 inches deep and 9 inches into the bed is loosened. Pull out the spade, move left or right, and make the next slice. Remember to change feet occasionally.

Half-moon edgers are popular tools, but they've never satisfied me for this operation. I want the blade to go deep enough to sever the invading roots and move far enough laterally to loosen a reasonable amount of soil. Even bluegrass rhizomes (the running roots on a grass plant) go 5 or 6 inches deep when offered the loose, rich soil of a perennial bed. Half-moon edgers might cut 6 inches deep at the center of the blade. However, that only happens where the perennial bed soil is even with the sod and the gardener sinks the edger to its hilt.

But there's no sense quibbling over tools. Grab whatever you're comfortable using to cut and fluff the edge.

Weeding and Renewing a Cut Edge around Your Garden

Stand outside the bed. Insert the spade to its full depth, removing a bare sliver of sod. Force the spade's handle down toward the lawn. This causes the soil within the bed to loosen and pop up. Repeat.

Grasp the sliver of sod, lift, and tease out all the attached roots that have invaded the bed.

Add a Sliver of Lawn

After slicing the edge for a distance, I crouch down, get my hands into the fray and go back over the same ground.

Since this bed is surrounded by lawn grass, I'll be repeating terms such as *lawn*, *sod*, and *turf* to describe what I did next. Just remember, everything applies equally to snow-on-the-mountain, vinca, pachysandra, or tree roots if they surround a bed.

In early spring, each slice along the edge separates a sliver of invading sod from the lawn proper. Some people fret that this makes the bed bigger every year, but if you restrain yourself, you'll be cutting only sod that's recently expanded into the bed.

It's desirable to produce this sliver because it gives you something to grab hold of, a single source from which to trace penetrating roots. My next move was to lift each sliver of turf, making sure to tease out all its attached roots on the bed side of the cut.

Extract Entire Roots

Some of those roots went farther than 9 inches into the bed, into firm soil beyond what was loosened in popping the spade blade. They teased out just so far and then held fast. It was apparent by the tension that if I pulled any harder, they'd snap. I keep my spading fork next to me to deal with these die-hards. Holding the offending bit of sod and its roots like reins in one hand, I inserted the fork's tines into the firm ground beneath the far end of the roots and popped the tines to loosen it. Then I could tug and free the roots 6 inches farther into the bed.

Sometimes I've chased grass roots 2 feet or more into a bed. This bed was like most, however. One extra lift with the fork was enough. 9- to 12-inch grass roots slid out whole, and I tossed them over my shoulder onto the lawn or into my wheelbarrow.

When roots snapped in this process, or when I saw telltale white cords wink out and then settle back into the bed as I first lifted the sliver of sod, I went back to get them. If they were thick enough to catch my eye, they had enough substance to sprout. In a month or less, they would be sprouting up all over the edge and would be difficult to trace and lift out.

My hand weeder or the fork works to dip down into the bed edge, get under such root ends, and lift up like a strainer. All I needed was enough to latch onto, then I could work those stragglers loose.

Create a Trenched Boundary

Once all the trespassing rhizomes were out, I used my hand weeder to make a trench that would prevent the lawn's roots from marching right back into the bed. This trench has one side that's straight up and down like a cliff — that's the side butting up against the lawn. The cliff already existed, from my original spade cut; it just needed to be defined.

The bed side of such a trench describes a very gradual slope up to the perennials. I used my weeding tool to drag the material cut from the cliff up the slope and into the bed. The trench works best if it's as deep along the lawn edge as the majority of offending roots run.

To a root, this trench is an impassable barrier. Roots can't grow out into dry air any more than they can grow through thick plastic, metal, or stone. To confine a genteel, closely mown lawn, the trench may be only 2 inches deep. In my backyard, it's 4 inches deep. In our trial bed in the midst of good Spartan turf, I made it about 3 inches deep.

Take a look at the edge of one of those luscious English borders next time you visit England or see a detailed photograph. You'll see that the edge is cut and trenched in just this way. The shadow cast into the bed by the lawn-side "cliff" adds to the appearance. It makes the edge stand out in even greater relief. The edge will usually stay quite clean if cut twice a year, and it doesn't take even as long to do this edging as it does to describe it. I cut, weeded, and raked 120 feet of edge in ninety minutes. The same bed would have taken even less time to edge, if it had been edged in this fashion the previous fall.

If this edging sounds like too much work, follow my lead and recognize it as work prevention. It's attending to a detail in spring that would haunt you all summer if left undone.

A Few Blades of Grass Just the Tip of the Iceberg

Sometimes only a few blades of grass are visible in that strip just inside the bed. Don't kid yourself that such an edge can go without a spring recutting.

Try my technique on a short stretch, then lift out all the roots that are attached to one of those slivers of sod. One sod that I lifted from the test bed had just seven blades showing. However, it was attached to a total of 36 inches of new rhizomes positioned under more than a square foot of bed. Those rhizomes were armed with twenty-two growing tips.

All this from a reasonably well-mannered lawn. Imagine the power of the half-tamed, mixed-bag turf many of us grow at home. Just seven blades fueled the invasion I saw. How much more grass would be showing and foraging farther into the bed by the end of that prime grass-growing season, spring?

Using Commercial Edging

By now, you may be running for the nearest landscape supply outlet to stock up on plastic edging. Good thought, because a permanent edge can come close to

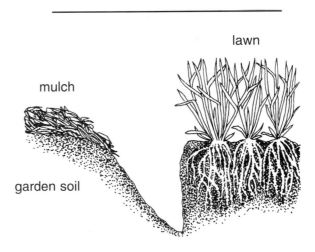

In a trenched edge, the lawn side of the trench is sharply vertical and as deep as invading roots tend to run. The bed side of the trench slopes gradually up into the bed. This trench is an effective air barrier against root growth into the bed.

eliminating the edging chore. It just has to be chosen to suit the specific need and installed well.

Our test bed doesn't and won't have such an edging, for several reasons. One reason is expense — all 15,000 square feet of bed in that botanical garden would have to be edged for consistency of appearance. Another reason is for the sake of the trees; you'll hear about that come fall. Finally, the garden's designer may have felt, as I do, that a well-cut edge is the most attractive and flexible option.

In fact, I took advantage of the cut edge's flexibility on this date. As I edged, I smoothed out a curve near the blue fescue and enlarged the bed slightly near the monkshood to give the 'Early Sunrise' coreopsis just a bit more breathing room.

Now I'm going to depart temporarily from the work done in this bed to help you install that edging material you've bought.

Select Edging Material for Depth

Make sure edging material is at least as deep as invading roots tend to run. Standard black polyvinyl, steel, and aluminum strips sit just deep enough to keep out refined sod. Many roots run deeper and can duck right under that barrier. Such edging is not only inadequate, but it also becomes an impediment to easy removal of the invaders that undermine it.

I've sliced miles of edge and checked root depth on dozens of plant species that have to be excluded. I have

Surface-rooting plants can reach over vertical root barriers.

come to think in terms of surface level, 5-inch-, 9-inch-, and 12-inch-deep edges. Once in a while, there are deeper roots, but the running roots are closer to the surface. Thistle and bindweed run primarily in the top 12 inches of soil, most invasive tree roots in the top 8 to 12 inches, quack grass in 5 to 9 inches, bishop's weed in 3 to 6 inches, and so on.

In the case of surface-level rooters to be excluded — ajuga, ground ivy, moneywort — I discard the idea of vertically installed edging. A cut edge and containment via close mowing along the boundary are best for this bunch. Then they can't stretch an "arm" over the top, touch down, and root within the bed.

To bar really deep rooters, I buy carpet runner — thick, clear plastic sold in rolls to protect carpet in heavily trafficked hallways. It comes 27 inches wide, and I slice the roll into two or three narrower rolls. Then I use it as if it were ready-made black polyvinyl edging with greater depth potential.

Greater depth isn't the only advantage of carpet runner over prefabricated edging. Even when I have to buy anchors separately, it's less expensive than a similar installed length of conventional material. It's also nearly invisible. I can simulate the look of a cut edge or use it on a single, problem area without making that area look odd among adjacent beds that have no permanent edging.

Wood and Stone Edges

Wood doesn't work well as an edge because there's no such thing as a continuous, solid-wood edge. Grass roots just love sidling between boards. It's necessary to cover the seams with plastic that overlaps a foot of board on either side.

Use an impenetrable material such as heavy plastic carpet runner or the metal flashing used in roofing.

Stone and brick don't usually sit deep enough to stop grass roots. In addition, the spaces between the stones or bricks have to be covered with an unbroken material to intercept rhizomes. Setting the stones or bricks into a poured concrete footing would work, but it also would be a hefty investment.

Cobblestone or fieldstone edges can be infuriating if they have a high profile that prevents the mower from cutting close along the bed edge. Then you're obliged to trim the ragged verge with a weed whip or shears.

Install Edging Correctly

To install either carpet runner or bona fide edging, cut and clean the bed edge as I've already described. Use a spade to make the trench, digging the cliff side as deep as the edging you'll install. Make it wide enough that it will stay open while you position the edging material. Trench as far as a full section of edging material is long, install it, and then trench farther. This can involve sizable excavations. You may have to pile extra soil within the bed proper for the time being.

Don't try to make a narrow slit in the soil and force the edging down. In a minute, you'll see why this isn't a good idea.

The real secret to installing a permanent edge is to cut the lawn side of the trench so that it's straight up and down, perpendicular to the plane of the lawn. Unless you pay attention, a trench dug with a spade tends to slope down and in toward the bed.

Avoid Gaps and Pockets

In elementary sewing classes, tailors learn to clip the fabric along a curving seam, or it won't lie flat. We love curves in our bed lines. Edging wants to stand straight up around curves just like that tailor's seam, even if the top of the trench slopes away. It would defeat the purpose of a root barrier to clip it and let it spread around sloping curves — this would offer wide open spaces for weed roots to enter. But between the edging and the slope there's an air pocket. That's the death of most edging.

The pocket tends to collect water. In late fall and winter, that water freezes and pushes out against the edging. Think now about those anchors that come with prefabricated edging. They're supposed to be pounded through the base of the edging, at an angle, and down into the undisturbed soil under the sod. Pressure from expanding ice loosens the anchors and lets the edging gap a little farther from the lawn.

Now there's a wider gap between soil and edging, which fills with more water that freezes and expands. This cycle continues. One spring, the edging is loose

---

Edging Installation Issues

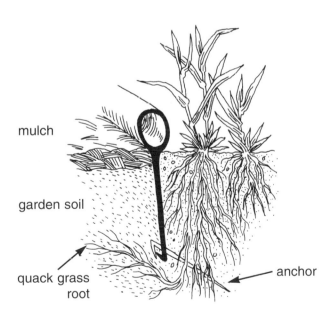

Vertical root barriers must be at least as deep as the roots to be excluded. Here, standard 5" plastic edging does not exclude quack grass which can forage deeply to find rich garden soil.

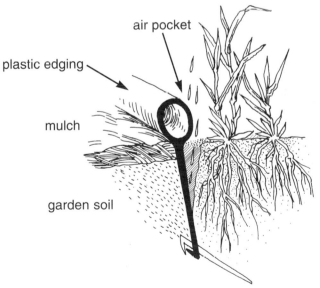

This improperly angled edge creates a pocket that can accumulate moisture. In alternating freeze-thaw conditions, the edging will become loosened.

enough that it pops up. Gleeful roots slip under and in. Jutting high above the sod, the edging tangles with the mower and gets frayed, pulled even looser, or both.

That spring, you saunter out with no intention of recutting any edges. You installed that root barrier to eliminate that chore. Thus it's doubly frustrating to find that you have to clear weed roots from the bed's perimeter and reset your edging.

So cut the trench straight up and down and use anchors. On custom-cut carpet runner edges 6 inches deep or less, I anchor with 5-inch rust-resistant spikes from the local hardware store. Edging material that extends deeper tends to stay put without anchors.

Observing at Every Opportunity

As I edged, I did more than complete the first task on early spring's "must" list. By loosening and removing weed roots 9 inches or so into the bed, I got a huge start on the second "must" — weeding. Almost 100 of the 504 square feet in this bed were now weed-free. In addition, my use of hand pruners to do the preliminary clean-up prepared me well for both weeding and a number of potential "should-do" and "might-do" items.

What hand-cutting did was get me close to the plants. Every second that I spent on this routine maneuver, my gardener's eye was observing, plotting the location of each weed, and filing away clues about each plant's health. That eye also noticed the impressive differences between compact early spring crowns and outspread remains. It figured from these remains how crowded the bed might be by summer. It even visualized changes.

If I gained nothing else from this semiconscious study, I did a more thorough job of weeding than I otherwise would. If quizzed on where the weeds were, in what quantity, I probably would have failed the test. Yet my hands and subconscious had memorized the bed. Every weed I'd seen was recalled in its turn and dispatched.

This is probably why so many people claim that hand-weeding is a great way to meditate. You can set yourself on automatic and let your mind run on other matters. There's also evidence suggesting that people are generally more creative when relaxed and in the presence of plants. What a great combination in early spring, when we're thinking about what we want the garden to look like and planning how to achieve it. Being close to the plants has benefits that make a strong argument against using long-handled power tools to clear the previous year's debris.

Fertilizing

I find it helpful to take short breaks — momentary stretches of muscle and mind. The interval between finishing one priority job and starting another is a good time to assess what's been done and what's left to do and to pat yourself on the back for getting so far.

During one such break, I thought about the soil test results I'd seen for this garden and recalled the fertilizer I'd brought with me.

Consider Your Mulch

Fertilizer is not a priority in the average perennial garden. This bed is no exception. The soil test showed that all nutrient levels were adequate. However, I decided to bump fertilizing up from its usual "might-do" category to "should-do" status, based on what I knew about the mulch I'd be using.

That mulch has a significant amount of wood in it, and the decomposition of wood can be a drain on available nitrogen in the soil. Some perennials develop chronic nitrogen deficiencies in worst-case wood-mulch situations. Such plants are pale and stunted to one degree or another. The name for the condition is *chlorosis*. It's the botanical equivalent of anemia. Some studies show that extra nitrogen in the form of fertilizer can correct the problem, others raise doubts.

Why would I use a mulch that might cause problems? There were benefits to outweigh the risks. That subject is covered in the next chapter and on page 151. Now, faced with a possible problem and a possible solution, I opted to play it safe and fertilize.

Use Fertilizers with Care

The time may come when American gardeners and the U.S. public accept the ripe, sweet smell of composted chicken droppings and other manures so common in Old World spring gardens. My own family objects to the smell of composted sludge products such as Milorganite and Fertrell. I've been told to use them as slow-release fertilizer or mulch only in the fall so that the faint odor dissipates by spring. For this project in a public place, I opted to avoid any extra attention that odor might bring by using a granular fertilizer.

One problem with granular products is that the nutrients in them are in salt form. They can cause burns — actually severe dehydration of cells — if they have prolonged, direct contact with foliage. It's best to apply them at times and in ways that keep them off the leaf surfaces.

Incidentally, roots burn from an excess of soluble salts, too. It's hard to brush fertilizer off roots, so apply these fertilizers according to label directions.

Another drawback to granular products is that they are not very effective unless mixed into the top few inches of soil. In full contact with moist soil, they dissolve, and the elements they contain become part of a solution that roots can absorb. Left on top of the soil, fertilizer bits are much less likely to melt.

Putting down granular fertilizer requires brushing it off leaves and scratching it into the soil. This is time-consuming and tedious. I've learned instead to scatter the granules before I start to weed so that they'll be mixed into the soil as I hoe, fork, and dig. There is also very little foliage cleaning to do if fertilizer is applied in early spring when the plants have little leaf showing. It took me less than five minutes to spread half the season's fertilizer on the bed. That was five pounds of 14-14-14 in slow-release form. I concentrated it in areas where plants were already in active growth.

Categorizing Weeds

While I was cutting, I saw three types of weeds — well-known weeds, question-mark weeds, and nice plants gone bad. Most of these weeds were around the edge, as is often the case. The well-known weeds occupy the bulk of my time during the first maintenance visit of each season.

Well-Known Weeds

Well-known weeds are the ones I know without pause. Some are recognizable because they're so distinctive. Dandelion and thistle are two. Others might not be well-known to everyone, but they are to you or me as the result of long or emotionally charged relationships. Nightshade and wild mustard come to mind. I can pick out either of these from seedling size on up, can predict the size and spread of the roots, may be able to find one in the dark by its smell or feel, and even know the sickening sound of a root snapping in escape.

Seedlings Bigger Trouble Than You Think

In the category of well-known weeds is one subgroup you might not expect—seedlings. *Every* seedling in a perennial bed is a weed unless the space it occupies is assigned to a biennial or self-sowing annual. In those spots, a very limited number of seedlings of the desired species can stay to replace the previous year's performers.

People tell me this is harsh, but to me it's just common sense. This is an established bed, and any ground that looks bare now is actually already assigned. The

---

Be Ruthless

As usual, the worst seedlings in this bed were the ones snugged right up to the crowns of the rightful residents. Every day those seedlings stayed, the crowns of the host plants would be more distorted as leaf buds in the shade of the weed fell behind buds in the sun. Although a seedling may not cast much of a shadow, it has a big effect in spring when plants are growing so quickly. The shaded plant will redirect all its stored energy to any bud that's receiving even a bit more sun. In a matter of days the desirable plant can become very lopsided.

All the while, the hosts' and weeds' roots will become more entangled. Every extra twist will mean more stress to the host plants when I finally wrench out the parasites. I rate seedlings next to the crowns "urgent" and pull them all out pronto.

---

plants that truly belong will soon be puffing and stretching out, above and below ground. Every opportunist in one of those "bare" spaces will compete for light, water, and nutrients with a plant already promised the spotlight.

If I'm curious about what species a particular seedling is, I might leave it for a few weeks to let it develop more telltale foliage or habit. Even this requires that you have room to spare in the bed.

Take No Prisoners

In all those spaces between and within the crowns of the plants, I waged a thorough campaign against every visible known weed. Pursuing those I could see led me to some not-yet-sprouted varmints, too. A wise gardener learns the look of a weed's roots as well as its top. He or she is able to recognize and remove them at times like this.

I worked from the edge in toward the center, clearing out everything in a 3- or 4-foot-wide strip. Then I moved over 5 or 6 feet and cleared out the next 3-foot strip from edge to center. Every little while, I stretched and raked up the debris I was pitching out onto the lawn.

Weeding took a little more than an hour, or fifteen minutes per 100 square feet that hadn't been touched in the edging process. A weedier bed of this size would take a total of fifteen to thirty minutes longer.

The same procedure is required to keep up an already clean bed as to clean up a badly infested one. Aside from the slightly higher initial investment of time, a year's maintenance will total the same for both, as long as you start in early spring. More vigilance is required throughout the year after reclaiming a weedy bed, however. You can't relax and let weeding take a backseat to other priorities as you might otherwise, or you'll see some backsliding.

There is such a thing as a hopelessly weedy bed. Most often this comes after two or more years of no weeding. I'll tell you in the fall how to work on those situations.

Question-Mark Weeds

The second type of weed is the question-mark weed. In this bed, there were four such characters. It was possible that they'd invited themselves in, as opposed to being placed, but they seemed to be occupying unclaimed space. Many times such weeds turn out to be desirable plants, but they're question marks as long as I can't be sure.

Question marks must be sizable plants — remember that all seedlings fall into my "well-known" category. They also have to possess some regularity of position or size that smacks of human intervention. By virtue of their size and use of space, they get priority treatment. Leave them, but identify them as soon as possible. No sense giving any extra growing time to something that will later prove to be a pest.

I found two question-mark weeds on my first visit to the garden in early spring and two latecomers two weeks later. The first of these weeds was almost certainly a rightful occupant — there were seven plants, evenly spaced. Still, I couldn't match it to any species on my mental diagram of the bed. I weeded around them and looked at the paper diagram on my next stretch break. Reading the names of the surrounding plants stirred a memory of what I had seen in the garden when I'd walked through the previous season.

Hadn't there been cardinal flower somewhere around here? Is that what cardinal flower's basal leaves look like? This was clearly a plant to note on the diagram, even as a question mark. It could be checked out later against known plants.

The second weed also seemed to belong, but an animal had chewed all three almost to nonexistence. I guessed they might be red leaf loosestrife (*Lysimachia ciliata* 'Purpurea').

Reasons to Wait

To some people, puzzles like these seem silly. "Who cares?" they ask. "If it looks as if it belongs, just leave it." That is a valid question and a practical plan.

The reason I don't follow that tack is that if I don't know what the plant is from the start and don't make plans to find out, the mystery might continue until the plant blooms. Yet if I can identify it before it blooms I can make informed decisions about its care — what insects and diseases to watch for, whether to stake it, and so on. I prefer to enter a new relationship with my eyes open rather than suddenly finding out that I've nurtured a common goldenrod or spotted knapweed.

There is another perspective on the question-mark dilemma: "Unbelievable. Plants do not lose their identity from one season to the next in any garden and certainly not in a botanical garden."

Anyone who holds this point of view must be of that rare breed that never forgets a plant or planting. Such gardeners are cherished where they occur, perhaps especially in botanical gardens, where there are always so many new plants.

Each new plant in a botanical garden is inventoried and marked on master plans and so can always be identified through records. But out in the field, plants do get "lost" or forgotten. Even professional gardeners suffer lapses of memory. Also, even the best labeling systems have high attrition rates. For instance, at least seven markers were missing from Bed Three.

I've pulled up many an innocent creature that I myself introduced to a site. New, single plants are at greatest risk. I've probably pitched some as weeds without even questioning their identity. Others I retrieved and replanted when bare crumbs of potting soil at the roots reminded me of their deliberate placement.

Faced with my question marks, I decided it wouldn't do to lean on the garden's official horticulturist. Care of this one bed had been given over to me with a promise of noninterference. In return, I swore to keep it in award-winning condition. The only gain for the botanical garden staff was a little time saved. I wasn't about to negate that by dogging the horticulturist for plant names.

In this experiment I did everything as a home gardener or a professional tending an isolated bed would. Neither of these gardeners would have a consulting horticulturist on call, so I wouldn't either.

Aren't Puzzles Fun?

The third question-mark weed emerged near the blue fescue. It came as a pair, both with pale yellow shoots and leaves that only faintly rang a bell. The sprouts were large enough to indicate a two- or three-year-old root system, so I worked around them and thought about them for a while. I kept an eye out for anything nearby with a similar leaf — perhaps they were stray sprouts off a running-root perennial.

That day, working at the far end of the bed, I noticed a monkshood leaf and realized that the question-marks were its relatives — delphiniums. *Struggling* delphiniums. I decided right away to remove them. (I will explain more on that a little later.)

The final question mark also came in a pair. Two closely-furled, slightly fuzzy, maroon shoots had just emerged between the 'Golden Showers' coreopsis and the coralbells. I was knocking down seedling weeds with my hand weeder when I noticed them and barely avoided slicing off their tips.

Their size and something about the leaves said, "Young plant, maybe even a hardy self-sown annual." It had been a mild winter, so they might even have been marginally hardy perennials that had survived in part. The spacing suggested that the two might have been a trio the previous season. If the foliage stayed maroon, it was going to look so good in contrast with neighboring plants that a designer may have planned it. So they stayed, turning out to be Arkwright's campion (*Lychnis* x *arkwrightii* 'Vesuvius'), a very attractive part of the bed.

I noted each of these question marks on my garden diagram the day I found them, along with my guess as to their identity and any follow-up work I could think of

Nice Plants Gone Bad

In the final and lowest-priority weed category — nice plants gone bad — *Coreopsis* 'Golden Showers', *Artemisia* 'Silver King', and Carolina lupine all contributed to the weed problem in this bed.

The coreopsis was already showing this tendency in early spring. It was only one-half inch tall but coming up like a lacy red-brown thicket that actually touched its neighbors on all sides.

Plants like this that are going to be 18 inches tall in bloom shouldn't be breathing down the necks of dwarf daisies and blackberry lilies. Those 18-inch stalks will lean out at least a trifle and cast considerable shade. It's also notable that their roots will stretch ever wider all season, depriving adjacent plants of their due.

I reduced the spread of the coreopsis while I was weeding out the grass at its feet. The other two species also were asking to be reined in. Once the first two weed categories were addressed, that's what it seemed I should do.

At this point, I noticed my cue word — *should* — and stopped. Once I start saying "should" to myself, I know I've strayed away from priority jobs. These weeds were good plants. I wasn't going to lose the farm if they got a little too cozy with each other or somewhat scrambled along their boundaries. I knew this on a gut level and so assigned the job "should-do" status.

How to Weed

The way to weed a perennial garden is to loosen the soil, grasp a weed, and then extract it and all its roots. Mulch keeps soil loose. Watering before weeding loosens the earth. A spading fork inserted under a weed or weed colony is all the extra incentive a weed usually needs. It will then allow itself to be coaxed out into the gardener's hand.

The real secret to success is to know, before you pull, what kind of root the weed has. If I anticipate an extensive, spreading root, I loosen a large section of the bed. Weeds with taproots don't merit that much effort, just a deep pry. If I'm not familiar with the weed and can't guess at the root system, I dig up a section and take a look.

If any roots break off in the process of removing a running-root plant, I track them down and remove them in turn. If a significant pest plant has mixed itself in or under one of the perennials in a bed, my surest cure is to lift the entire perennial or the infested portion

Cut or Smother Small Fry

Small weeds — seedlings with only a few leaves — don't have much energy in reserve. They're likely to die if their leaves are removed or covered. Even if they're perennials, I just cut their stems at the base with my hand weeder. If they're short enough to be covered or will lie flat if knocked down, I can forego the hoe and fork. It's easy to smother either of these under the mulch that's on deck.

of it out of the ground. I loosen its rootball, remove the weed roots, and then replant the perennial. If this shake-up is done in early spring, a quick, complete recovery for the perennial is 99 percent guaranteed.

Sizing Up the Culprits

A well-tended bed like this one will have mostly young weeds, but I always expect some long-term residents, too. In this garden, I found a mixture of weeds diverse in both type and age.

Grass had crept thickly into the penstemon, lamb's ears, and silvermound artemisia. I lifted those sufferers, removed the grass that was in their crowns, and replanted them. Ferny, dark green marguerites peeled easily off the surface of the bed. A healthy colony of mustard had gotten started all around the rue and I pulled them.

This mustard is a winter annual. It germinates in late fall or winter and is ready to flower by mid-spring. Normally, annual weeds don't concern me in spring as much as the perennials do. Most annual seedlings are candidates for smothering or hoeing, but these plants were big and liable to flower and set seed within a few weeks. I hunted them all down. This reduced the chance that they would self-sow around an even wider area for next season.

Coreopsis 'Golden Showers' was infested with grass. Lifting it to get out the grass rhizomes was more work than cleaning the penstemon because of this coreopsis species' dense, matlike root system. It had knit itself together to form one continuous crown more than a yard square. There was no real hope of lifting that in one piece, so I went to what appeared to be the center of the grass infestation and sliced the coreopsis-grass into squares like sod. I lifted each one, knocked the soil off the matted roots, and inverted it to see what I was up against.

Faced with a sizable colony of anything that must be removed, I always start from the center or near the center, slice down, and trace the invader outward in all directions from there. If I start from what looks like the outer edge of a colony, I'm almost sure to underestimate its sprawl. The first cut will sever many of the farthest-reaching roots. Since these roots don't have shoots above ground yet, they're very hard to track down one at a time — provided I even notice that I've cut them off from the main body.

The intruder this time was established bluegrass. It had probably been there since the previous summer, although the shade cast by that jungle of coreopsis had kept it thin and widespread. The grass runners were easy to see — white against the bright yellow of the coreopsis roots. With some plucking and additional sectioning of the coreopsis, they came loose. Wherever I saw that the grass roots had been severed at the edge of a section, I lifted the next section as well and cleaned it out.

This did not take long. The alternative was to pluck at running weeds from above, which works only if done and redone to starve the plant out. That approach can take much more gardening time over a season than if you lift the plant and clean it just once in early spring. I reserve it for special circumstances.

Post a Watch Against the Worst

The quack grass that came to light while I was trimming back *Artemisia* 'Lambrook Silver' turned into a special circumstance. When I came to those tall, wide grass blades, I loosened the whole area right up to and under the artemisia. I grasped the quack grass blade and jiggled, traced, loosened, pulled, and eventually teased it all out — except for a rhizome that snapped off where it dove deep under the artemisia.

Considering the amount of weed root that probably remained, the likelihood of its thriving at the base of a plant soon to fill out and cast considerable shade, and the amount of work involved in lifting the artemisia, I decided to let sleeping dogs lie. At the end of the day, I marked my garden diagram and notes for future visits to put a "watch" on that artemisia for quack grass emergence.

I borrowed this "watch" procedure from my dentist. He is forever marking one or another tooth on my chart to be rechecked for waywardness or whatever problems a tooth can be suspected of developing. It works for my dentist and in my gardens, too. If there's a watch marked on my notes, I remember to look for a problem on a regular basis. Even the most persistent weed can't stand up to consistent beheading. The root runs out of stored energy if it's denied the chance to mature a leaf and start photosynthesizing again.

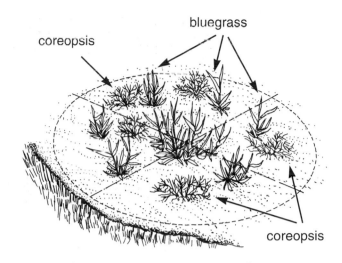

coreopsis   bluegrass

coreopsis

Bluegrass had established itself within the coreopsis. I went to the center of the visible colony, sliced down, loosened the soil, and traced the undesirable roots out from the center. Dotted lines indicate where I sliced down, starting from the center, to sever the invader's roots, and lifted whole sections to remove the weed colony.

One Priority Leads to the Next

Fine crops of chickweed and oxalis had germinated in many places. I plucked those that were in or right around the perennials' crowns and hoed the rest, slicing their stems at ground level. If I had intended to mulch right after weeding, I wouldn't even have hoed, just covered the varmints with 2 inches of mulch. Most would have been killed, and any survivors would have been easy to pull out of a moist mulch.

Mulching is a priority in early spring, but I had a full day's work to do on other chores first. It didn't trouble me that mulching would have to wait until my next visit. Given a normal, cool spring, a well-weeded bed, and my assured return in seventeen days, there was no urgency. Moisture was abundant. Any new weeds that appeared before my next visit would be small enough to smother under the mulch.

Two other thoughts figured in the decision to wait. First, some of the needed dividing would be better done later in the month. Second, I'd seen some things while cutting that caused me to plan a few moves and new plants. Better to wait to mulch *after* all these soil-disturbing chores were done.

Chemical Weed Control

What about some chemical weed control to reduce the drudgery?

In a university-level horticulture program, in a weed class one learns the main types of pest plants — annual, biennial, perennial, herbaceous, woody, with stay-put roots, with running roots. Knowing which weed is which one can decide which type of herbicide to use and when.

Then, in a weedy lawn, main weeds can be identified. If crabgrass is the enemy, it pays to understand that it's an annual, that its seeds germinate shortly after the forsythia blooms, and that some preemergent herbicides are especially good for killing its seeds as they sprout. This data helps you decide which product to buy and when to apply it. "When" is in early spring for crabgrass prevention.

In a bed of low junipers infested with grass, herbicide can be considered to clean up the mess. Weed text books may list that species of grass, plus herbicides and application methods to kill it without injuring the juniper.

That weed science works okay in agriculture, lawn care, and large monoculture groundcover beds. Yet it's limited because herbicides aren't practical tools for perennial beds.

Preemergent Herbicides

The following thoughts apply to how preemergent herbicides might work in a perennial area. They relate to both "chemical" products and "organic" inhibitors such as corn-processing by-products.

Preemergents kill seeds as they sprout. They don't kill weeds old enough to produce their own food by photosynthesis — anything with a leaf or two. So the time to use a preemergent is after established weeds are hoed down, pulled, or rooted out.

At just that point in perennial maintenance, however, when the bed has been weeded, our next step would be to blanket all the bare soil with a mulch. This blanket conserves moisture, provides organic matter and nutrients to the soil, and prevents weed seeds from getting the sun or warmth they need to grow. Why spend money on a preemergent, then cover it up with a mulch that does the same job plus?

Mulch doesn't stop all seeds from germinating, especially right around the crown of the plant where the mulch comes to an end. Weeds can get started there. But preemergents aren't 100 percent effective in killing seedlings, either. Some plants will survive — 5 to 20 percent or more, depending on the species. In a bed treated with such an herbicide, young greens will appear here and there, demanding attention throughout the bed. In a mulched bed, we can focus on fewer hot spots — those spaces around the crown of each plant.

It is noteworthy that in all the botanical gardens I've visited to interview the gardeners, when I ask about preemergents they've all said "We don't use them."

Questions without Answers

There's also doubt about the effects of preemergents on established perennials. By definition herbicides are toxic to plants. As a class of product, they're used in doses low enough to spare established plants. At least, species in agrochemical companies' test plots don't suffer. Most often, those test plots grow food plants and lawn grasses, crops that account for the biggest chunk of herbicide use.

Gardeners I respect, with long experience growing particular groups of perennials, say they see negative effects on some perennial species from contact with these chemicals. They suspect that preemergents also build up in certain soils. It's tough to prove or disprove these suspicions.

It's expensive to test short-term and long-term effects of a chemical. Separate tests have to be done for each chemical on various species or families of plants. Our trial garden contains thirty-three perennial species representing at least ten different families. In the perennial display area of which this bed is a part, there are more than five hundred species. Have all of those been checked for sensitivity to either preemergent or postemergent herbicides? No, and it's not likely that they will be. That would be an unjustified expense where a market for the product doesn't exist.

Postemergent Herbicides

The typical postemergent herbicide must be applied when foliage is present, since the active ingredient is absorbed primarily through the leaves. The gardener must allow time for absorption and death. This may be from four to fourteen days, depending on the product used. Don't cut treated plants off earlier, or the roots may not exhaust themselves completely and the plant may recover. Some weed species may require repeated applications before they die.

In perennial beds, this kind of weed killer has to be applied on the weeds but not on desirable plants. This entails identifying and touching the weed, plus shielding perennials nearby. Then you have to watch the weed die for a week or two until *maybe* it's gone for good.

Perennial gardens are ornamental in nature. Dying weeds are not. Time spent to find and touch weeds with a chemical is better spent pulling the weeds and foregoing the long death scene.

A postemergent can be justified for use on individual deep-rooted weeds that have resisted all other efforts at eradication. A bindweed whose root extends several feet into the ground may survive bed preparation and pop up at the base of a perennial or shrub. Unable to get at the root by digging, the horticulturist may choose to starve it out by weekly removal of any green it produces.

Field bindweed may have a huge storage root, able to fuel two seasons of comeback. If repeated hand-plucking indicates an extensive root and very long campaign, a postemergent is applied. Even if numerous applications are required, it may shorten the war.

First Visit Wrap-up

After edging and weeding the perennial bed, I compiled my notes and decided whether anything else needed doing that day. I used my diagram as a memory jogger, writing down what I had done for the bed in general and plans for next time. Then I went through the list of species, making notes about each.

From my notes and considering available time, I decided to start on an upcoming job — dividing. One blue fescue had a dead center, so I split it and reset the pieces to rejuvenate it. That took only fifteen minutes, so I also divided the purple-leaf sedum (*Sedum* 'Atropurpureum') to make more of this attractive but skimpy member of the garden. Then the day was done.

Dividing and Mulching

SPRING IS undeniable, now. For me, this second visit to the perennial bed takes place in late April. Forsythia and star magnolia are just past peak bloom. Early daffodils and *fosteriana* tulips are in full bloom. Daylily foliage is 6 to 8 inches high.

Greeting a remote-location garden for the second time in spring is delightful. Although I love seeing the daily changes in a perennial garden, this trial bed reminded me that distance has a benefit. I can claim to be a major contributor to its growth yet have all the fun of surprised rediscovery — "My, how you've grown!"

The Grass Is Always Greener

Some beds in this botanical garden hadn't gotten their first grooming yet, even though the staff was working at top speed. The visual contrast was dramatic. The trial bed seemed lusher than the rest, if only because its proportion of green to tan was much greater.

There's a common misconception that horticulturists and other workers in a botanical garden have it better than any other gardener. For those of us who know the truth about how pressed they are for time, it's that much more educational to note how these worthies cope. Unable to eke more hours out of each day in spring when demands are heaviest, they make choices about what needs to be done and what can wait. They pay for any poor planning with their own sweat or disappointment.

At times, their satisfaction with gardening is probably much less than a hobbyist's. Faced with set budgets for plants and other supplies, they often have more concrete reasons for feeling that a particular garden or project is not measuring up. Many home gardeners avoid a budget by deliberately failing to track the cost of their hobby. I know that I'm guilty of that evasion when working at home.

What Does It Cost to Maintain Perennials?

In my clients' gardens, as in this trial bed, I'm forced to look at costs. The season's plants and supplies for this bed came out of my garage or wallet, and I kept that record for those who need to know.

BEWARE: If you prefer to think of your own gardens as priceless, skip ahead to the next section.

Perennial garden maintenance has two components — labor and materials. Let's use as a basis a seven-month season and my estimate that it's possible to maintain a garden in an average time of one hour per month per hundred square feet. Hiring help all year will cost the going hourly labor rate multiplied by seven for every hundred square feet of garden. Materials may cost about one dollar per square foot of garden.

This year, necessary supplies for the trial bed included new and replacement plants, fertilizer, mulch, stakes, string, and pesticides, but no replacement tools. I was fortunate in not losing or breaking any tools in this garden. Check the chart in Chapter 13 to see the list of maintenance necessities.

Nature Sets Priorities

I intended to get my one "must" done that day — mulching — plus every "should" and "might" that I could think of. A few of the "should-divide's" were almost urgent enough to be "must's."

A nasty bank of clouds complicated the plan. There was occasional sun, but the clouds were persistent and threatened a thunderstorm. Light rain is of no concern, but a downpour or a thunderstorm is another matter. My gardening day looked as if it might end suddenly.

Mulching was the only unarguable "must" on the list, but for efficiency's sake it had to be done after all the day's dividing and planting were completed. I decided that if it began to rain, I could probably eke out a final hour before the rain got heavy or between storms. That's how long it would take to spread the two yards of mulch the garden needed.

So I sorted even my "should's" and "might's" into priority order and resolved to accept whatever I got done as enough.

Dividing

The bulk of my time would be spent making little plants out of big ones. If perennial gardeners could sell all excess divisions in April and October, the income would probably offset every new plant and material cost. Aggressive species really do carry on. In the seventeen days since my first visit, those I had tagged as bullies had taken even more of the bed hostage than I'd expected. A number of others weren't so pushy but stood to gain a lot if divided.

Profit By Division

There are several reasons to divide perennials. Most bloom better, grow most vigorously, and resist disease best in their youth. Although youth is a relative term — a single year for bee balm, ten years for a peony — any perennial is as young as its most recent division.

Some species also tend to build up a personal cache of pests. Splitting them and discarding old sections reduces attendant insect, fungus, or bacterial spore populations.

Keeping invasive species such as 'Silver King' artemisia and Carolina lupine in check is another motive for dividing, but not so important as the two main reasons: plant health and pest control. I turned my back on those rampaging bullies. There are ways to make them presentable even after they reach the flailing, red-faced, screaming stage. I started on those that would be unhealthy if not divided.

Divide First for Health, Second for Looks

By my reckoning, the coralbells, daisies, and golden marguerite would be dead or aesthetic failures this year if not divided right away. All three age quickly and die out at the center of the clump — marguerite in a year, daisies after two, and coralbells in their fourth year. Even this dead-center state doesn't put them in the "must-do" category because they probably won't die. They'll just look ungainly, as if they were running away in all directions from their own middles.

The daisies hadn't yet run far from center. They just resembled balding heads with a shaggy fringe all around. However, the coralbells were suffering from more than senescence. On my first visit, I'd inadvertently caught the rake's tines on the edge of a clump of coralbells and flipped it over like so much chaff. That caught my attention. I'd already remarked that these plants looked worn-out and in need of division, but this was more serious trouble. A client's message from a previous year came to mind.

You Can't Fix It
Until You Know What's Broken

"Janet," my client asked, "can you come look at the coralbells along the front walk? The man was here to put fertilizer and crabgrass preventer on the lawn. When he dragged his hose across the garden, the coralbells just rolled right out of the ground."

On that occasion, I'd taken a hard look at the roly-poly coralbells. A basic tenet of pest control — human pests, plant pests, or any other — is to recognize what a healthy individual looks like before you judge the symptoms of any other. So I compared the client's plant with a plant from my own garden. I picked one of my plants that was just as old as my client's plants but hadn't shown any yearning to roll loose and go traveling.

The leaves were far fewer, smaller, and drier on my client's plant. But many problems may be manifested in the leaves. On their own, dying leaves tell us only that the plant's not healthy. A close inspection of these leaves and stems showed no insects, signs of insects, or indication of rot or bacterial decay.

Examining the foliage is important, but overlooking the roots would be like finding a rash on a child's chest and not looking into his throat and taking his temperature. So I had to dig up my own plant to complete the sick plant–healthy plant comparison.

Getting to the Root of the Problem

The roots were like night and day. My plant had a hefty clump, from thick and knobby to delicate root ends. The client's plants had stubs. An insect, fungus, or bacterium must have destroyed them.

The roots weren't mushy or discolored — so fungal or bacterial decay wasn't indicated. The spot where they had been growing was a fairly good site with well-drained soil. So it didn't seem likely that they had rotted from damp conditions. That led me to check reference books for any note about insects that affect coralbells roots.

I looked up the coralbells' genus, *Heuchera*, in *Diseases and Pests of Ornamental Plants* for starters. (See the Appendix, "References and Tools.") There I found mention of root weevils, which sent me right back to the client's garden. I checked the soil beneath the coralbells for these small white grubs that spend the fall and early spring eating coralbells and other plant roots.

Weighing Alternatives
and Making a Plan

I remembered that whole episode in a flash when a coralbells plant rolled up under my rake on my first visit. All the conditions seemed the same. It took just a minute to lean down, examine the plant more closely, scoop up some soil, and find the same problem — weevil grubs. I knew the pest's name and could see it was bad enough to demand attention. I added a note to my diagram to recheck my library and consider options for controlling root weevils.

In the time since that first visit, I'd decided to do three things with the coralbells, starting with cleaning the grubs out of the plants when I divided them. Manual control like squashing is more effective on these grubs in spring than any pesticide, as they're resistant to most chemicals. Also, applying a pesticide to kill grubs means poisoning the soil. To kill one hundred grubs, I might harm billions of other organisms in the same ground, most of which were beneficial.

I had also planned to move the coralbells as far as possible within the bed. Adult weevils don't fly, and the grubs hardly even crawl, so an infestation can be pretty localized. Replanting the coralbells in clean soil could spare them the additional stress of losing leaves to the adult weevils' summer feeding.

It wasn't realistic to think that I could eliminate all the weevils from the current coralbells area. Some grubs were bound to elude me when I lifted the plants. It wasn't that they'd run away; they can only squirm. Nor would I have to search hard or far for them; they reside primarily on the roots at this time of year, are as big as a small pea, and their stark ivory skin stands out against soil and roots. Yet I knew that some would fall off into the loose soil and become the proverbial needle in a haystack.

Finally, I would mark my notes to watch for adults emerging in June and starting to munch on the

Ridding Coralbells of Grubs

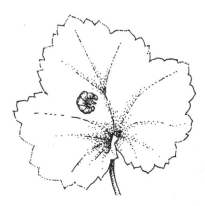

If you think coralbells are failing due to weevil grubs, dig up a suspect plant in early spring. Black vine weevil grubs are easily seen — ivory-colored against the dark soil of the root ball. This one is shown with a coralbells leaf, to illustrate its size.

Destroy all grubs in the root ball. Divide the plants, looking for more grubs hidden in the crown. Every division with leaves or leaf buds, stem, and root can now be moved to a new location.

foliage. If I was on the ball, I could kill them before they laid more eggs throughout the bed.

Isn't This Pest Control?

I told you we'd start with dividing, and instead I've led you into pest control. It happens that way all season. With weeding and watering, pest control is on the never-neglect list. Yet even these three items get the spotlight in this book only at critical stages. Those are the times when there's extra gain in focusing on one or the other. For instance, weeding is critical in early spring because it eliminates so much work throughout the year.

Pest control is critical in June and July because it is a chance to learn what's going on. That's when many things come clear — what various afflictions look like, how bad a particular one might get, and when prevention is best begun. By the next year, you've learned to add a moment of painless prevention to some other chore associated with that plant.

My current story might have started in June one year when I noticed the coralbells weren't blooming in my own garden. It turned out they were dead, a good excuse for not blooming. That was the beginning of learning.

I saluted those plants, accepted the loss, tried to remove any chance of poor growing conditions, and replanted. The next time I found formerly healthy coralbells inexplicably dead in June, a pattern suggested itself and challenged me to predict its next occurrence. I was then aware that there was something to diagnose and began to watch for coralbells in less advanced stages of trouble. That's what sent me running to my client's house and what indirectly saved the coralbells in this trial garden.

So in Chapter 7, I'll give you a basic diagnostic procedure and suggest some reference books. For now I'll get back to an example that will help you remember the process — dividing the coralbells and taking care of a known pest in one swipe.

Squashing the Pests

I dug the coralbells one at a time, cleaned off the roots over my wheelbarrow, and squashed about thirty grubs. I also rinsed off the nearly bare roots in my five-gallon bucket, which netted me a few grubs that had been nestled tight in the crown of the plant. A few grubs became pets. You'll hear about them in Chapter 7.

Dividing consisted of slicing the plant's crown into sections, each with a thick, vertical root, some hair roots, and a few leaves. I would have preferred divisions with three thick, vertical roots, so that the new plants would be respectable in size. Unfortunately, once I removed the central, oldest sections and tossed out pieces that had lost virtually all their roots to grub grazing, only small pieces were left.

Such close work brought another problem to light. Within the tight cluster of stems and leaves that made up the crown, there were slug eggs — translucent orbs the size of small peppercorns. I should have expected them, since slugs are a fact of life in gardens. They also seem to know that eggs are best left in places like tightly clustered and evergreen crowns, where they'll be protected all winter. I squashed them, too, and felt good about setting the slug population back by dozens of families.

I put the coralbells divisions to soak in my bucket while I made them a new home.

Deal with Slugs Early

Early spring is the time to address slug and snail populations, as many are still eggs or dormant. These creatures are perfectly in tune with their world — timed to come out in early spring when the succulent young foliage they love to eat is first abundant. However, eggs and overwintered adults have few places to hide in a clean spring bed. If I think there is a slug problem I set traps in early spring, close to their favorite plants' crowns. An early attack really sets them back for the year.

Transplanting and the Domino Effect

Finding a place to replant the coralbells was the toughest part of the process. Where to move something in a bed that's already full? What to put in their place?

If I dug up something to make way for the coralbells, that something also would require disposition.

Every move called for thought as to resulting combinations of height, texture, foliage color, and flower. It's a rare garden change where one plant can simply be swapped for another. More often, four or five species get relocated in the process.

This mental exercise can be the most wearing of all garden tasks. I call it "transplant dominoes" and see it happen in every redesign from a single plant move to a whole-bed remake. This time it demanded especially careful thought, since I'd agreed to keep this bed picture-perfect.

I found a fairly simple answer. I could make a space for the coralbells by reducing the golden marguerite's area. The remaining golden marguerite would still be a significant mass of color. I thinned it to leave only five small starts. Excess plants could have been transplanted to the university's holding garden or composted. I chose the compost. Species as prolific as this one are not in great demand at a botanical garden.

In thinning the golden marguerite I was handicapped because I didn't know whether the variety 'Kelway' would come true from seed. I tried to leave only golden marguerites that were obvious offsets of the previous year's plants, because there was the possibility of plant-to-plant variation if the variety originally planted was being replaced by its own seedlings. Since even the husky plants I'd left in place might have been well-grown seedlings, I added a note to my diagram to look for any differences in height or flower color between the plants.

Filling in Holes

The next question was what to put in place of the coralbells. I'd answered it on my first visit when the problem had initially surfaced. I started with the objective of finding another low, spring-blooming evergreen species to preserve the existing balance of heights and seasonal interest. The replacement also had to bloom in a hot color or white, to fit the bed's color scheme. Finally, and perhaps most important, it had to be distasteful to weevils.

Coming up with the right flower color, size, and leaf was simpler than making weevils turn up their noses. Those insects eat hundreds of species — and maybe far more not yet recorded. I looked up each of my possibilities in a plant pest book to determine if it or any of its close relatives were already known to be weevil-prone, and picked one without an existing "record." Red-orange, June-blooming, evergreen rock rose (*Helianthemum nummularium* 'Fire Dragon') was the lucky winner. On my way to the garden, I'd purchased five of them.

Helping New Additions Settle In

I leveled the old coralbells area, set out the still-potted rock rose to consider spacing, and then depotted and sank them into the bed to the same depth at which they'd been growing in their pots. Although the soil was moist enough, both the rock rose and the coralbells benefitted from water's settling qualities. Poured around a new plant and allowed to seep in, water persuades soil to fill any air pockets gently. This eliminates those dry air pockets that can prevent root growth.

The biggest chunk of work connected to planting the rock roses was getting them watered in. The irrigation system was still not turned on in the garden, so I had to carry buckets of water to the bed from the greenhouses. Each 800-foot round-trip was equal to walking four times the length of a good-size suburban lot. I considered relying on rain to do the watering for me but decided against it. You've heard that washing and waxing your car is a sure way to bring on rain? I propose the transplanter's retort — the way to make rain pass by is to depend on it for watering.

When I finished watering, it still wasn't raining. I moved on to dividing the daisies.

Pushing Up Daisies

Some plants are tough to divide. An astilbe's woody crown demands a sharp knife. Siberian iris crowns may be so dense and large that it takes a long pry bar and two people to lever them up and an ax to split them. Some ornamental grasses may be best left for seven years and then dynamited. Even as I plotted my daisy work, I could hear the sound of an ax-and-mallet technique elsewhere in the gardens. A gardener was lifting old grass clumps, sinking an ax into the top of a root-

ball, and then pounding the ax head through with a mallet.

Daisies are much easier to divide. They practically fall apart, separating at the bases of last year's stems and trailing long roots like shoestrings.

The most efficient way to divide plants and keep a bed level and fresh is to clear the whole area, relevel that part of the bed, and then replant. So I slid my fork under each clump of daisies, popped it loose, and transferred it, whole, to my wheelbarrow.

New white roots were evident everywhere, confirming the notion that early spring is a good time for dividing because plants are actively growing roots with which to settle into a fresh spot. I selected the most vigorous clumps, loosened the soil, and let the plant break into several sections.

Since they split through the clump's weak point — the dead center — each piece had a bit of dead stalk and decrepit root that I snapped off. From the lively green sections that remained, I chose seven divisions to replace the original plants. Each replacement had about five sprouts.

Although several original clumps had more dead stems than live ones, division still produced many leftover daisies. Some of the extras went into a holding garden, but most went into the compost. It's best to avoid crowding replanted pieces; they grow better if they're not in close competition.

Correcting Soil Problems

My selected plants soaked in my bucket while I fixed a soil problem. While weeding and edging, I'd seen that the soil in the daisy area was not as loose as it should be. Perhaps someone had developed a habit of stepping into the bed at this location. Compacted soil is not as good as loose soil for plant growth, and it tends to drain more slowly. The compaction, or perhaps soil lost in earlier daisy divisions, had made this section of the bed a little lower than the areas around it. None of these conditions would help my daisies make a comeback.

In early spring, in anticipation of this common side effect of division, composted cow manure went onto my list of materials needed "next time." Renovating the soil while dividing plants is one way to avoid having to

Daisy Division

1. A daisy division, showing old stems still attached.

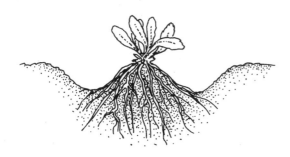

2. Build up a mound of soil within the planting hole and spread the division's roots wide and down the slope of the mound.

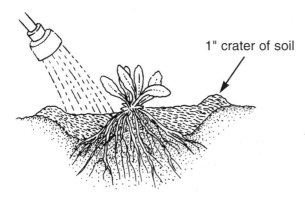

1" crater of soil

3. Cover the roots with soil. Then build a 1" crater around the plant and water it in. When the water settles, more soil may be needed to cover the roots exposed when the water washed soil down to fill air pockets.

rejuvenate the whole perennial bed every six or seven years. Things like double digging don't bother me, but I'd rather do them in small chunks than in whole-bed assignments.

Imagine that the daisy area of the bed was a three-layer cake. Each layer was about 9 inches thick — the depth of a spade's blade. I took the whole top layer off the cake and set it aside — it was enough to fill a wheelbarrow plus make a temporary mound next to and even on the coreopsis 'Golden Showers' and 'Silver King' artemisia. Then I used my spading fork to loosen the middle layer. No need to turn it over, just insert the fork and pop the soil loose throughout the area.

The compost went in on top of the crumbled middle layer, like frosting between it and the top layer. Finally, I shoveled the top layer back in place and leveled it.

Drainage Is Critical

Before double digging the area, I'd taken a few minutes to get acquainted with the bottom layer of the cake. That's the soil below 18 inches. Knowing how the bed drains and how deep the roots can go is the key to watering and maintaining the overall health of a bed.

To do this, I dug a 24-inch-deep pit in the daisy area. I was not surprised to find an abrupt change in soil color and density as I got into the bottom layer of the "cake." I'd heard that this site had been badly compacted before it became a garden. As the staging area for materials and heavy equipment used in a nearby construction project, it had become so hard packed that it might have been mistaken for pavement. Bed areas had been scooped out and the ruined soil discarded. Drain tiles had been installed under the beds and loam brought in to replace the original soil. What I saw now in the bottom layer was the site's original subsoil — hard-packed clay, light brown, in contrast to the dark loam above.

Looking at the sides of my pit, I could see white daisy roots had penetrated to surprising depths. Simple daisies — known for a rather shallow root system — had filled the soil with roots to a depth of at least 15 inches. Although I've seen this many times, it's still thought provoking. Imagine the total width and depth of a bleeding heart's rootball — I'd once severed roots on one I'd transplanted that were still as thick as my thumb at a 24-inch depth.

This mental image always makes me smile when a well-meaning gardener advises me to "be careful not to disturb the roots when you transplant." I've learned that even the biggest rootball I dig is a significant reduction for the plant. I've successfully moved perennials, shrubs, and trees with as little as 15 percent of their former root mass.

These daisy roots told a second story. The black loam was well-filled with white daisy roots, but not all the way down to the compacted clay. The lowest 3 inches of black loam were root-free. The implication was that water sits in the bottom 3 inches of this bed while waiting to drain away. Further, it must happen often enough to discourage root growth.

So this bed holds water. Like a potted plant sitting in a water-filled cachepot, its plants can drink from below. I decided to keep that in mind throughout the season when deciding whether to water.

Replant without Crowding, Water without Wasting

Spacing divisions is like setting a table, where the small plants are plates. I set the plants down, spread their roots, and checked that they would each have their own space, plus a little elbowroom. Then I replanted.

For each plant, I scooped out a hole as wide as the spread roots. I set each division on a mound of soil in the center of a hole so that its crown would be at ground level but its roots could spread down the slopes of the mound. Then I filled the hole, covering the spread roots with soil and ladling in water to settle the soil.

I scraped extra soil into a crater about an inch high around each transplant, just as I do for a newly planted potted plant. This crater was just a bit wider than the plant's roots had spread. It would accept and hold water, preventing it from running away, so that it could seep in over the root zone. Even later, when the bed was mulched, the crater would still be there. It would continue to ensure that the daisies got their full share of water. You can see this process in pictures and follow the daisies' progress through the year on page 15.

Replacing Plants

Replacing weak rue plants was next on my list. It was a surprise to see that one suspect was in much better shape than its remaining branches and buds had indicated. Too bad I had to dig it up to recognize that it had significantly more root than the true weaklings. All the plants' rootballs were equally wide, but this one was dense and pliant compared to the straggly, brittle nature of the others. A close look at its stubby branches showed another difference — many growth buds had appeared since the plant was cut back on my first visit.

I apologized to this rue for having too little faith, then lined it up for replanting with the new plants. The new plants also looked bad in comparison to this survivor.

Rue is not always easy to find at garden centers. I'd been glad to hear that my grower had some available in two quart pots, big enough to have a visual impact here in their first year. However, they'd been in their pots a full year when I bought them. The grower would have repotted them for sale as one gallon perennials. I could revive the root systems when I planted and so persuaded the grower to sell them to me "as is."

These pot-bound sufferers had sorry rootballs — rigid cylinders 6 inches in diameter. They would be drawing water from a much smaller area than the rue that was going to be replanted. Its rootball was more than 12 inches in diameter. The original plant's roots would cover much more than twice the surface area of these 6-inchers. It would have 113 square inches versus a little over 28 square inches for the new potted plants.

I was glad the bigger plant could grow alongside the newer ones. This would give me a chance to see how much difference that extra 85 square inches could make. Since the new plants were not the same variety as the old 'Blue Mound', I also might be able to evaluate differences between the types.

To give the pot-bound plants a fighting chance, I slit the roots with my knife — three times vertically and once across the bottom of each cylinder. I pulled the two sides of the cut mass open at the bottom to spread the lowest roots wide.

Some Contrast Near the 'Silver King'

After bucketing water to settle in the rue, I took another look at the sky and decided to go ahead with reducing the spread of the bullies — 'Silver King' artemisia, 'Golden Showers' coreopsis, and Carolina lupine. This is a simple process. I just drew a line beyond which the target plant should not spread this year. I made sure to leave enough space between the

---

Confining Artemisia

'Silver King' artemisia and 'Golden Showers' coreopsis were threatening to overrun their neighbors. The dotted lines indicate where I sliced down and removed all the roots and shoots that had roamed too far.

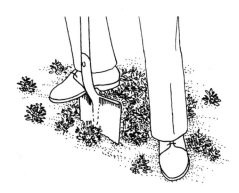

As when removing an established weed colony, work from the center of the plant out toward the perimeter. Here I am standing on the 'Silver King', within the circle of plant that will be retained. I am slicing down with my spade and loosening the soil to make root removal easy.

bully and its neighbors so that the stems of the two plants would not interfere with each other. I call this a no-man's-land between plants, and love to see it in spring. It means the plants have room to grow.

Once I determined where to draw the line, I used my spade to slice down through it, pop loose the soil around the plant, and lift out all the roots beyond. I worked as if the plant I was reducing was the lawn and I was defining its edge all around. I stood on the central mass of the offending plant while I worked, just as I stand on the lawn while edging.

While doing this reduction on the 'Silver King', my gardener's eye was at work, assessing plants to the south. The potentilla was a puny loner. Probably it had been losing ground and mates to the artemisia's annual spread and shady summer sprawl. I wasn't familiar with that species and had trouble visualizing how it would look if it was anywhere else in the bed. I decided to move it closer to the edge and let it recuperate while I got to know it better.

A single plant in a bed of masses can be a liability, so I rearranged the neighboring blood grass to create a niche where the potentilla would not look awkward. Then I went back to removing stray 'Silver King' roots.

Another Round of Transplant Dominoes

I couldn't stop thinking about the area that had been potentilla. A case of transplant dominoes was shaping up, but I found a way to keep it from getting out of hand.

I cut the 'Silver King' back even farther, beating its south edge almost 24 inches north. This left only the center of the old clump. 'Silver King' tends to die out as it ages, so I cut out and discarded the oldest part. Then I added compost to renew that soil, and filled the center with several young pieces of 'Silver King' salvaged from the outer edge.

Satisfied with the 'Silver King', I brought five 'War Bonnet' dianthus to the spot and arranged them for planting. I'd picked these up at the garden center on an impulse after I saw that one 'Fire Dragon' rock rose was tagged "Mixed Colors." My selections had been the only five rock roses in stock. That deviant pot tag put the coralbells replacement plan in jeopardy. Still, I had had my heart set on rock rose. I hedged my bets with the dianthus, giving myself the option to decide on-site whether to chance an off-color rock rose or use the dianthus instead. The loser was supposed to have ended up in my own garden.

The dianthus's blue foliage was a good contrast to the 'Silver King'. If the flowers were as red as the catalog's claim, I'd be happy with this serendipitous change.

Rescuing the Cardinal Flower

Reducing the spread of the 'Golden Showers' coreopsis was a snap. It came out like sod and didn't need its center replaced — all vigorous growth there.

Making the Carolina lupine area smaller was more work. It entailed lifting and replacing cardinal flower clumps and crocosmia rhizomes to extricate Carolina lupine runners (shown on page 22). Whereas most of the excess coreopsis and 'Silver King' were on their way to the compost, Carolina lupine is a bit more precious, so I saved several pieces for use somewhere else.

During the cardinal flower rescue operation, the question mark plants I had tagged *Lysimachia* earlier in the month kept calling to me. Now I recognized them as tall phlox (*Phlox paniculata*). Whatever animal it was that had eaten them before my first notice was still grazing here, more heavily on two than the third — those two were grazed almost to extinction.

Those sorry specimens would neither match each other nor make much of a show this year. That was sad, because they were located at a central point in the bed for viewers approaching from the north. I decided to replace them on my next trip with the variety 'Orange Perfection'. Its color would be well suited to this bed and it was rated resistant to mildew — always a plus.

A barrier would have to go around the new plants to prevent any more grazing. Normally I don't like the looks of cages, but I doubted that anything else would work. I'd once remarked to the staff on the proliferation of rabbit guards, made from rabbit caging, throughout these gardens and gotten a rueful laugh in response. They'd tried it all and were resigned to gardening in what they had dubbed "penitentiary style." I made a note to buy the new phlox and cages to protect it.

Ready to Mulch

My close inspection of the phlox drew my attention to its neighbor, 'Early Sunrise' coreopsis. I decided it needed even more room than I'd given it by expanding the edge on my first visit. I moved the plant most likely to be lying in the lawn by midsummer, setting it deeper into the bed. Then I called an end to almost three hours of dividing and moving. The sky was looking black again.

There were a few weeds in the bed. It took less than fifteen minutes to remove the ones that couldn't be smothered by mulch. Raking up the debris from dividing and weeding, then hauling it away to the compost bins, took another half hour.

Then began the tedium of wheeling back and forth between a pile of mulch and the garden. During this process, I reflected on gardens and delivery trucks. There are always significant time savings if bulky materials can be delivered to a spot very near the garden. When materials are reasonably close by, a cubic yard of mulch can be applied in thirty minutes or less. My pile was not close. I was glad the rain had held off because the extra distance would add almost thirty minutes to the hour I'd anticipated.

To gardeners accustomed to dumping whole wheelbarrows of mulch between shrubs or at the base of trees, even an hour to spread two cubic yards may sound excessive. After all, a cubic yard fills only about six deep wheelbarrows.

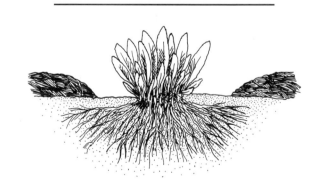

Mulch should not be allowed to touch the crowns of the perennials. Leave a shallow trough around each plant. Until the plants add more leaf and height, each will look as if it is in a bowl.

The difference is that mulch has to be put on a perennial garden by hand or bucket. It can't be thrown or dumped. Even in spring, when mulching is simplest because the plants haven't begun to spread up and overhang their no-man's-land, there just isn't room between them for dumping.

Throwing mulch is the other favorite application method for shrub and tree areas. Around perennials, it is seldom applicable. Doing so will cause mulch to stack up against the crowns of plants, unless there's a very large bare space and the thrower has great aim. If mulch is stacked against plant stems and crowns, it is an invitation to moisture accumulation and disease. Avoid this at all costs.

How Much of Which Mulch?

A cubic yard of mulch will cover 200 to 300 square feet of established perennial garden 2 to 3 inches deep. The amount varies with the density of the planting — less space between crowns means less ground to cover. Also, a 2-inch depth of wood mulch is plenty, while airier mulches can be 3 inches deep.

Some mulches are not purchased in cubic yards but by the bag, with the number of cubic feet commonly listed on the label. In that case, the amount needed is the same, but it helps to know that a cubic yard is 27 cubic feet. You can use the label information to estimate how many bags will be needed to yield 1 cubic yard. The cocoa hulls I used on Bed Three, for instance, were in large bags that contained 2.5 cubic feet of material. Between ten and eleven such bags will equal 1 cubic yard. The same amount can come from eighteen bags of shredded bark if each bag holds 1.5 cubic feet.

I decided to use several kinds of mulch so that I could check for differences in growth between plants of the same species surrounded by different materials. I put down fall leaves — saved dry in bags from the previous fall — cocoa hulls, finely shredded bark, and shredded hardwood.

Every geographical area has one or more materials available in such abundance that they're used for mulch. Hardwood bark is ubiquitous in my area, but elsewhere I've admired mulches of pine needles, seaweed, pecan hulls, ground corncobs, spent hops, and other substances. If I can get it in bulk, I'm game to try it for mulch.

I'm not in favor of landscape fabric and sheets of black plastic as mulch. I realize that it seems a good idea to put each plant in its place and leave it for years and years. However, fabrics and plastic are a barrier to soil renewal, redesign, and normal perennial spread. After accompanying me through the annual routine of digging, weeding with a fork, dividing, and replanting, I'm sure you agree that fabric and plastic blankets have no place in a perennial garden.

Choosing Not to Mulch

Giving each perennial its own blanket of mulch requires a lot of deep-knee bending. That's one reason many gardens do go without mulch. You might plant close and keep weeding each spring just until the plants themselves cover all the bare ground. Another option is regular, shallow cultivation between plants — the classic dust mulch.

I've tried both methods for extended periods and still recommend the mulch. Once mulch is down over a clean bed in early or mid-spring, weeding takes about three minutes per hundred square feet, and weeds are confined mostly to the edge and next to the crowns. Without a mulch, I spend fifteen minutes weeding each hundred square feet. I have to do this at least three times before summer while waiting for the plants to fill in. It also necessitates more reaching and crawling deep in the bed. Those are a strain on the back and a step toward soil compaction.

Further, going without a mulch in a region like the Midwest, where soil gets extremely hot in summer, can reduce the overall vigor of the bed. The plants' water requirements and heat stress increase in hot, uninsulated soil.

Finally, soil renewal is continuous when a mulch is used year-round. The soil in gardens I've kept without mulches has tended to get worn out. Mulch is replacement organic material for the perennials and weeds always being cut from a garden.

Early Season Slug Control

One reason to hold off on mulch is to help reduce a slug problem. In this case, mulching isn't eliminated, just postponed until late spring, after the slugs complete their early- and midspring wake-up-and-breed season. Raking away the old mulch removes some of the slugs and their eggs. Without a mulch to protect them, the remaining slugs are more likely to fall into the various traps we set for them. In-ground swimming pools of beer, upside-down half-rinds of grapefruit, inverted pots, or moistened sections of the daily newspaper can all be set near troubled plants in early morning and are likely to attract dozens of slugs by noon on a sunny spring day. Empty the traps every day until the catch decreases, and slugs may be rare well into summer.

So it's not to warm the soil but to wipe out slugs that I peel leftover mulch off a bed in the spring and cart it away to hot compost. There's a big difference between English and Midwest summer temperatures. I don't feel the English gardener's need to help the soil warm up in the spring because it'll do so soon enough on its own. Although a number of professional Canadian gardeners I've interviewed adhere to this technique, I find U.S. botanical gardeners leaving mulch in place year-round, topping it off in the spring and as needed through the summer.

Packing It Up for the Day

After making my notes on my garden diagram, I loaded my tools and empty pots into the wheelbarrow. Then I took one last look at the bed. Frost-burnt tips on the daylilies' foliage caught my eye.

There's no help for this kind of thing. Even if all of last year's debris had been in place when the frost came, that 3- or 4-inch matted layer wouldn't have protected the tips of these 6-to-8-inch mounds. I wondered if removing the tips would make any difference later in the season, so I clipped the tips of two plants. On the first, I snipped each leaf end individually — ninety cuts in all. The other took just two cuts: I grasped and

An Easy Slug Trap

A section of the newspaper makes a good slug trap in early spring. Roll the section and soak it in a bucket of water until it is thoroughly moist.

In the evening or early morning, lay a wet newspaper section near the crown of a plant. Pick up the section at noon. Scrape off the slugs that have gathered there or peel off one layer of paper to remove them from the trap. Destroy the slugs. Set the trap every morning until the catch falls off.

---

sheared a whole handful of tips at once, half the plant in one swoop.

It turned out that unshorn, shorn, and clipped plants were indistinguishable from one another within three weeks. Some people might say that these final few minutes of work were a waste, but experiments are fun and always worth a minute of my time.

The look of the mixed-mulch quilt also gave me pause. It looked less uniform than people might be accustomed to seeing in this garden. While I was weighing the possibility of hiding the oddball areas by applying a thin veneer of shredded bark, it finally started to rain. Wet mulches all look alike, so I called it a day.

Watering, Fertilizing, Planting, and Staking

THE MIDDLE OF SPRING is a wonderful time to be a gardener! Serviceberry *(Amelanchier canadensis)* is in full, fragrant bloom to cue you to action. The bed at its feet is full of late daffodils and grape hyacinth *(Muscari armeniacum)* at peak color. Even the myrtle *(Vinca minor)* puts on a show now. A spectacular display of spring species will continue for a month, with crabapple blossoms as the finale.

My schedule called for two visits during this period of unbridled growth — that's May, for me. My priorities on the first visit were to be sure the plants had enough water and to fertilize if I saw the need. Toward the end of the month, I'd see to any water needs again and patrol for developing pest problems. That was it for the "must-do's."

Planting, staking, and even weeding were only "should-do's" or "might-do's." This bed must always be made up for company, so even these secondary jobs would get done sometime this month. In any other garden, however, I wouldn't feel pressed to do them. I like to think that if a warm breeze sends a new butterfly my way in May, it's okay to drop my tools and chase after it.

Taking an Overview

A pattern that would continue all summer started on the first of my two mid-spring visits. Before doing anything else, I took a stroll around the perimeter of the bed to acquaint myself with the general conditions and give each species a nod. The horticulturist at a major theme park — a botanical display of no small accomplishment — gave me one piece of advice to make the most of my time and plants: reconnoiter the whole area before focusing on any one task. Often there's an urgent problem or golden opportunity just to the left or right of the busy gardener's bowed head.

I checked off my list as I walked around. A single blade of quack grass is showing at the base of the 'Lambrook Silver' artemisia. I won't miss that when I weed.

How about that front-row bare space between the 'Golden Showers' coreopsis and the rock rose? I had brought some bare-root myrtle euphorbia *(Euphorbia myrsinites)* to add there if needed. While thinning a patch of this plant in my own garden, it had occurred to me that its blue foliage and yellow-green flowers might be suitable to fill any hole along the edge of Bed Three. However, the Arkwright's campion (*Lychnis* 'Vesuvius') that had first made my list as an unknown was filling the gap well.

A volunteer oxeye (*Bupthalmum salicifolium*) that had snapped off within the crown of the Carolina lupine back in April was visible again. A quick pinch would remove the new shoot. I would mark my diagram for the next visit to keep an eye peeled for it in case it still had enough energy to try again.

A label claimed that Missouri primrose (*Oenethera missouriensis*) was occupying a spot on the northwest edge of the bed, but all that had sprouted there so far was a single weak shoot. It still looked sad. Perhaps it was the first casualty of the increasing shade from the oak, although competing for water with a growing oak's roots may have been even harder on the primrose than shade. It was likely this plant wouldn't put on any show in summer, so I decided to cache my myrtle euphorbia nearby as a possible replacement. The primrose was informed it had better come around by June.

Around the back, the monkshood beckoned and informed me that it would need help. I also saw that the 'Silver King' artemisia had gracefully accepted its new station. A spot near the moor grass was demanding a bit of color. The coralbells were chugging happily toward recovery. I completed my circuit in less than three minutes.

Water Where Necessary

Several quick stoops satisfied me that my main job for the day had been taken care of by Mother Nature. To see whether the bed needed water, I moved the mulch aside and inserted a bare finger. The soil several inches deep still felt cool and moist. Coolness is the telltale sign for both conditions, so it seemed the bed might have no need for water.

On my first visit during this period, both ends of the bed and the spaces within most of the new planting craters were perfectly cool and moist. The rue and dianthus areas, however, were warm and dry. I watered with a shower-type spray attachment, soaking the

ground around those thirsty individuals. Two weeks later, the whole bed was moist enough to pass muster, even though it looked very dry on the surface of the mulch. The newcomers were again a bit drier than the old-timers, so they got another drink.

My goal in watering is to get an inch of water into the ground. That's enough to soak the top 3 to 4 inches of soil within minutes. It also coaxes deep roots to grow over the following few days as the water sinks even lower.

An inch of water may come from a shower that lasts long enough to fill that inch-high crater built wide around new plants and divisions. It also may come from an overhead sprinkler left running until it fills an inch-high can set near the edge of the sprinkler's throw. Soaker hoses that drip directly onto the soil can be turned off when the bed at the far end of the line is damp 3 inches down. That can take a few minutes or hours depending on the area being covered, the delivery system, the water pressure, and how much evaporation is occurring.

Watering less thoroughly does little good and may do some harm. When the only moisture is at the surface, shallow roots grow while deeper ones wait. If the

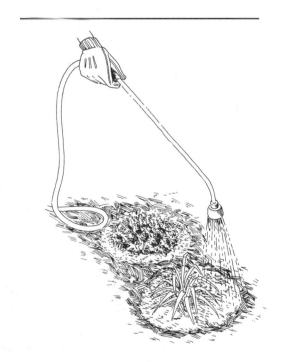

A shower-type, hose-end wand is ideal for spot watering.

surface ever dries out — as when the gardener goes on vacation — so do those roots that have become the plant's main support. I'm more attentive to this chore in spring than in summer, since spring moisture sets the stage for the rest of the season. It beefs up the plants' tops as well as their bottoms.

Perennial Reality —
Two or Three Soakings Per Year

Supplemental water is rarely needed in this area in early May, as spring rains are generally reliable. My hoses stay coiled unless a bed is excessively well-drained (dries out quickly) or unless it's planted with annuals that require steady moisture all the way to a mulch-free surface. Sprinklers may be needed in June or July, but it's unusual for established perennial beds such as this one to need more than two or three supplemental soakings per year.

Established is the key word. People often ask me which drought-tolerant species they might plant in a spot that never gets water. "Silk flowers," is my usual response, "though even they can benefit from a rinsing now and then to keep the dust down." Even the most self-reliant species takes time to develop a root system extensive enough to see it through a truly dry year. The plant's top may grow slowly, if at all, while its roots probe steadily down and out. It may take five to ten years for such a plant to get going on its own in a visibly big way. Yet one or two years of assistance are all any perennial needs to take hold in a reasonably good bed. That's a total of ten to twelve minutes spent checking its water needs and perhaps half a dozen actual bouts with a hose or watering can.

Annuals and Lawns
Need More Frequent Water

Lawns and annual beds planted with flowers or vegetables are another matter. Turf is often planted on soil so compacted that it can't get roots down where they can become self-sufficient. Also, we like grass to be green even in the dog days of July. At that time, it would like to escape into dormancy. Water keeps it awake. So lawns grow best when they get one-quarter to one-half-inch of water every couple of days.

Annuals, planted at the tail end of the spring rains, need encouragement early to spread out beyond their cubic-inch rootballs. At the beginning of the season, they too need water more frequently than perennials.

For lawns and annuals, daily timing is also important. It's better to water them in the early morning so that their foliage can dry out before sunset. This avoids courting those fungi that grow so well during moist nights.

Perennials - (including shrubs and trees) - shouldn't be watered on the same schedule as annuals and grass. Where separate schedules are impossible, daily timing becomes even more important. Many fungal and bacterial problems may occur in perennial beds and shrub borders. The majority of these problems are linked to improper watering.

If you follow an "as needed" schedule, you may water the bed at any time of day you like. If you notice that a bed is dry when you arrive home one evening, go ahead and water right away. Don't wait and take the chance that it won't get done.

You will probably find that you water once a month or less. Under this regime, the plants' leaves may be wet one night, but not every other night or twice a week. Spontaneous watering once a month is comparable to an occasional evening thunderstorm. Even the most careful horticulturist doesn't worry about a nighttime rain.

Pampering Individuals
with Extra Water

Most watering in a perennial bed is aimed at individuals — species that use up their reserves more quickly, junior members with confined roots, or thirsty souls that share their space with a tree. Use a can or a shower-type hose attachment to concentrate the water where it's most needed — on the soil at the base of the plant, drenching the rootball, plus an inch or two farther out. Avoid watering the space between the plant and its neighbors. That's weed territory, not a place to splash any encouragement.

When it's necessary to carry water to a bed, as I did in my earlier visit, a five-gallon bucket and a modified one-gallon plastic jug are my delivery system. With a bucket in either hand or two in a wheelbarrow, partially filled so they don't slop, I can carry enough water in one trip for twenty-four transplants or newcomers. That's an inch of water in each of two dozen 10-inch craters, scooped and poured from the cut-down jug. You can see this jug on page 15. Maybe that seems stingy, but seen another way, it's coddling. We all know how well plants respond to special attention!

For a special case or a struggling specimen, I might even install a temporary water supply on-site. All that takes is a large, long-necked bottle or an expendable bucket or plastic jug. Fill the bottle, hold your finger over the opening while you invert it next to the plant, and press its neck deep into the soil beside the rootball. Water will seep slowly from this source for several days or a week. A bucket or plastic jug, filled and capped, can be punched several times with a nail on its bottom and then pressed firmly onto the soil. Experiment with the number and size of holes to keep the leak going for several days or a week.

I had no intention of littering Bed Three with candidates for the recycling bin. Yet as I meted out water to the thirsty new rue, I recalled one June in my own veg-

Long-term water source for an individual plant: a long-necked bottle filled with water and then plunged neck down into the soil. Water seeps slowly out of the soil-plugged opening.

etable garden. Business had come up that would keep me away for two weeks shortly after planting. Then, my neighbor had asked me whether I intended to grow grapes out there from all those upended wine bottles. Now, it made me smile to think what visitor reaction would be to such a sight in a public garden. Perhaps some techniques only apply in a backyard.

Fertilizing Based on Soil Test

Some people use fertilizer unnecessarily, broadcasting formulations of dubious merit, liming, or acidifying based entirely on hunches. A test would help them spend their time and money more effectively.

Testing Your Soil

Soil testing through the Cooperative Extension Service is inexpensive and accurate. Also, the results often come back to you with a fertilizer prescription based on the bed's current nutrient levels and soil composition.

I buy a soil-testing package from the local Extension office for each bed to be tested. I gather soil from several spots in the bed, mix the samples, and use the prepaid package to mail a composite to the soil-testing laboratory of the state's agricultural university. A form that accompanies the soil sample tells the lab what "crop" I'm planning to grow and where to send the results.

In about three weeks, I receive an analysis of available potassium, phosphorus, and calcium; soil pH; and soil texture (sandy loam, clay loam, and so on). Also included is a measure of the soil's fertility, plus a prescription for what kind of fertilizer and how much to use.

Usually I order tests every other year for the gardens I maintain. The botanical garden's horticulturist submits samples several times each season. The current test results for Bed Three took fertilizing off my "to do" list, at least for the time being. Nutrient levels were good, and pH was acceptable. No supplements, acidifiers, or lime were needed.

Contact your local Extension office about soil testing. A standard test is probably available to give you the information listed above. Special tests may be available for organic matter content and other features that your local Extension agent may advise for your area or situation.

Raw Materials, Not Energy

The nutrients in fertilizer are used by plants in making new cells, but they don't cause cell growth. They're the support, not the starter. So the best time to apply granular and other water-soluble products is in spring as plants begin their period of rapid growth.

In early spring, I had spread and worked fertilizer in around all the plants that were emerging. I'd reserved the other half of the bed's annual dose for this month. Now I knew the soil here offered everything the plants needed in abundance.

That's the case more often than not. Many times, the only nutrient apparently needed is nitrogen. It's constantly in demand as plants grow. It's also continually being released from decomposing organic matter and being fixed from the atmosphere by lightning storms. In this second form, it falls with rain. Plants really are greener after a thunderstorm — they've just been given a nitrogen-rich solution and packed all of it they could into new, green chlorophyll.

Easy Does It
with Quick-Release Nitrogen

Take it easy on perennials when it comes to quick-release nitrogen. Too much nitrogen often stimulates leafy growth and makes foliage tastier to herbivorous insects and mammals. Perennials that overindulge in nitrogen often bloom less well, host more insects, and have weaker stems than you might like.

To figure how much fertilizer you need if you don't have a soil test, start with a general-purpose mix. Do some math to find out how much nitrogen it contains. Think about one with 5-10-5 on the label. It doesn't matter whether it's granular, powdered, in stakes, or in cartridges. The numbers will all be the same to your plants.

The first number tells you the bag contains 5 percent nitrogen by weight. The middle number is the percentage of phosphorus, and the last is the percentage of potassium. Therefore, a 10-pound bag rated 5-10-5 has one-half pound of actual nitrogen:

$$\text{pounds of fertilizer} \times \text{percent nitrogen} = \text{pounds of actual nitrogen}$$

$$10 \times 5\% = 0.5$$

One other fact you need to calculate fertilizer required is the amount of nitrogen the "crop" will need for the season. These nutrient rates are most often figured as yearly doses for 1,000 square feet of a particular species or group of plants.

Annuals and lawns are greedy nitrogen users, requiring two to five pounds of nitrogen per 1,000 square feet per year. Perennials like it "lean" — one to two pounds of nitrogen per 1,000 square feet per year is enough.

Now you can compute how much fertilizer you need. Compare the size of your bed to the standard 1,000 feet. Then adjust the annual nitrogen rate as given for 1,000 square feet by the same figure. In the following equation, N is nitrogen:

$$(\text{square feet in bed} \div 1{,}000) \times \text{annual } N \text{ rate} = \text{pounds of } N \text{ needed}$$

$$(250 \div 1{,}000) \times 2 \text{ pounds} = 0.5$$

So, for a perennial bed of 250 square feet, one 10-pound bag of 5-10-5 is enough nitrogen for the whole year. I used these formulas to calculate how much of other fertilizers might be used to give a 250-square-foot perennial bed a dose equivalent to 2 pounds of nitrogen per 1,000 square feet.

Slow-release products don't dissolve all at once, so they can be added at the beginning of the season with long-term effect. Most organic fertilizers release nitrogen slowly. Those listed in the second half of the chart are all slow-release products. Most granular and powder fertilizers are quick release. Read the package label to learn whether a particular granular fertilizer has been treated to release nitrogen slowly.

Organic vs. Slow-Release Granular Fertilizers

Compost can be considered a slow-release fertilizer. You can make it in your own compost pile from yard waste or buy it as composted sewage sludge or composted cow manure, for example. Sludge and manure are often more nitrogen rich than compost from yard waste.

Figure how much of the purchased form to use just as if it were a granular, salt-based formula. Use the equations given on page 84, substituting the first number from the trio of nutrient percentages on the package label.

It's often necessary to use more compost than a granular product because compost generally has a

Annual Amount of Fertilizer Needed

for a 250-square-foot Perennial Bed

Fertilizer	Amount (pounds)
5-10-10 granular (quick-release)	10.0
10-10-10 granular (quick-release)	5.0
14-14-14 granular (slow-release)	3.5
20-20-20 powder (quick-release)	2.5
23-15-18 powder (quick-release)	2.0
4-3-2 poultry or cricket manure	12.5
5-3-2 fish emulsion	10.0
6-8-2 bat guano	8.0
6-2-2 cottonseed meal	8.0
6-2-0 Milorganite	8.0
9-1-0 blood meal	5.5

I usually use complete, balanced fertilizers such as 10-10-10, 12-12-12, or 14-14-14. I apply the whole season's fertilizer at the beginning of the season if it's a slow-release formulation. Other types I mete out from April to early July.

lower nitrogen content. For instance, compost may have been tested and packaged as 2-1-3. A 10-pound bag of this contains just two-tenths of a pound of actual nitrogen. That's enough for 100 square feet of perennials for a season, or less than half the coverage obtained from an equal amount of 5-10-5.

If I had opted to use a 2-1-3 compost as fertilizer on Bed Three, I could have spread 50 pounds through the bed as if it were a very thin layer of mulch. Instead, I sprinkled the granular product more sparsely, like salt.

Compost has advantages over granular and powdered forms to compensate for the inconvenience of lugging around the extra weight. Compost and other organic slow-release fertilizers don't cause leaves or roots to burn from salt dehydration. They also provide organic matter, which increases the soil's humus content, microbial life, and ability to store water and nutrients. That's a recipe for healthy soil and vigorous plants.

Compost is the only fertilizer I use regularly on my own gardens. I use finished compost from my pile or buy it in packages. In many of my clients' yards, I opt for slow-release granular fertilizer in spring and a fall layer of compost-in-the-making. It's a personal and complex choice for each gardener. You'll hear more of the reasoning behind my choice as we move along in this book.

Time Spent Weeding

There were very few weeds in Bed Three after the first month of maintenance, but they were worth pursuing. A few were late-emerging perennials missed in earlier passes, such as yellow nut sedge. Inserting the fork, loosening the soil, and extracting each plant took just a moment.

Most of the other weeds were seedlings that had sprouted in the shallows between the mulch and the desirable plants' crowns, or where the mulch trailed off at the edge of the bed. These were dispensed with the sharp edge of my hand hoe or tweaked out by hand. My combined weeding time for the two visits during the second month of maintenance was under thirty minutes.

A long-handled hoe isn't the best tool for me, even in the vegetable garden. My nearsightedness may be to blame, but I wonder. Have you ever hoed off a desirable plant with such a tool? Or nicked its stem? It may be that some fine work will always be required.

A friend who recently launched a business growing field-grown perennials asked me about weed control. Cultivating between plants and maintaining a layer of mulch-covered newspaper were keeping weed growth at bay between rows. Wasn't there some way to avoid hand-weeding around the stems of the crop? Sympathy was the only thing I could offer, plus the thought that the task diminishes greatly by summer, when perennials start shading their own bases.

Hand-weeding also ensures the continuing benefits that come from a close association with plants.

A Slice of Insurance

A head gardener at a large English estate talked to me about edging one March day. He leaned on his half-moon edger while his three assistants worked to clean up the long line he'd just finished cutting.

"In the States, people are always after me about why I don't use more power tools," I said. "So it makes me feel good to see what you're doing. But this place is so huge, I have to ask you the same question. Isn't it an awful lot of edging to be doing with a hand tool?"

"It is a lot. We figure we have five miles of edge here," he replied. We talked about the disadvantages of using power tools next to gravel paths that run arrow-straight, nearly to the horizon. I could see that one drawback would be the need for a new "ruler" for the work, as the edge then being cut was outlined with a low string guide likely to interfere with a power tool.

That obviously wasn't his first thought, however. The chance that a power tool might hit a rock, buck, and ruin the lawn edge was what made him grimace. "With a sharp tool, it's probably as quick this way as any," he advised.

"How often do you do this?"

"Along the paths and drive, twice a year. Around the beds, once a fortnight." Those beds, I might add, looked as if they'd been outlined with the proverbial hot knife through butter. That's the tool my clients keep asking me to use.

Severing Roots

Thinking of him, I walked around Bed Three in May and sliced straight down with my spade all along the lawn. During this, the prime turf season, I wanted to sever any roots that might be growing into the bed below the trench. I didn't pop the spade to loosen the soil or reach down and lift out any roots. Given the short period of time since I'd created the edge and the barrier that air presents to grass roots, I knew there would be only tentative new roots crossing that line. Cut off from the mother plants, they would be unlikely to have enough energy to grow on up through the mulch.

New Plantings

Next I planted *Phlox paniculata* 'Orange Perfection' to replace the old phlox, and myrtle euphorbia as insurance against loss of the Missouri primrose. The phlox plants were in four-inch pots. The euphorbias were one-year-old transplants. I'd hoped to acquire larger, well established phlox, and would have been satisfied with young euphorbia, but was unable to find them at this point in the season.

The phlox occupied a position of importance. Large clumps would have made a respectable splash. Unfortunately, I hadn't anticipated this need in February, when the whole country's perennial production was at my fingertips through catalogs. It was something I'd added to the wish list in April. I had purchased it locally so that it could be in the bed before hot weather set in. Thus the Murphy's Law of Horticulture applied: any plant for which you develop a crying and sudden need will be unavailable or pitifully small.

The only sizable phlox I'd been able to locate through my inquiries were pink or disease-prone varieties. That made them even less desirable than the ravaged specimens already in the bed.

So I grouped six small plants in two 10-inch circles to take the old phloxes' place. I gave each plant an inch or two of breathing room around its roots. Once that space was filled, I hoped they would join forces to simulate two large plants.

Allow Enough Elbow Room

It's always difficult to plug replacements into an established garden. There is no substitute for time and the grace it gives to plants that must share space above and below ground. Better to accept the fact that change must occur and get on with it than to try to crowd plants.

Look around the next time you're in a public garden. New additions will be obvious. Even if they were grown to good size in another bed before being moved into place, they can still be distinguished from their new bedfellows for a season or two.

Ideally, new herbaceous plants are introduced in early fall. Then foliage can be cut back, roots are given six months to find their space, and growth that comes the following spring will arrange itself to conform to the allotted air space.

In a professionally tended garden, late additions are given elbow room, even if doing so makes that portion of the bed seem a bit bare. Inexperienced gardeners often tuck their latest acquisitions into unreasonably small spaces and wonder why they fail to thrive. Often this happens early in the season when false openings appear, only to vanish along with the unfortunate new-

comer when established residents surge up to claim what's rightfully theirs. Professionals learn to give their new prizes a fighting chance by reducing the spread of flanking plants' stems and roots or rearranging the bed.

Caging the New Phlox

As a final touch around each cluster of three phlox plants, I added a hoop of rabbit caging nearly 18 inches tall. It dwarfed the tiny creatures and called even more attention to their puniness. I imagined them peering through the bars of this prison to ask what they had done wrong.

This caging is used to make rabbit hutches, with sturdy wire crisscrossed to make rectangles less than an inch square. The horticulturist who designed, planted, and nurtured this perennial display area through its first years had learned quickly that local rabbits are a major problem. She'd bequeathed to her successor an impressive collection of plant cages and urged her to use them.

Trapping or killing is no answer when the countryside all around is populated with critters eager to line up at the salad bar. Just as at this botanical garden, it often applies to residential neighborhoods as well. Repellents don't work when animals are really hungry.

Plant Gently in Tight Spaces

Even when there's ample room, digging and setting plants into an established bed is a juggling act. It's an especially delicate act when the bed's just been neatly mulched.

First, rake the mulch to one side or scoop it into a bucket or wheelbarrow. Clear an area at least twice the size of the rootball or pot you'll plant.

You may need to install temporary restraints to hold neighboring plants out of the way. That's a nod to the fact that even if there's leeway for the plants you're adding, there's often not enough room for your big feet. I use bamboo stakes connected by a string to do this. Push one stake into the ground, gather the offending foliage and stems gently up and back, pull the string around the bundle of foliage, and anchor it by jabbing the other stake into the ground.

Bring a five-gallon bucket into the bed with you to hold the soil you must displace. There are two reasons to avoid spreading it on top of the mulch. First, it's full of weed seeds just waiting for a chance to sprout. Don't delude yourself on this point. Many species have short-lived seed, but crabgrass seed is just one that can wait twenty years for its chance to germinate.

Second, mulch that's not thoroughly rotted will cause more of a nitrogen drain if it's mixed into the bed than if it's just sitting on top. By keeping mulch and excavated soil separate, you reduce the chances that the mulch will be inadvertently buried.

Once the newcomers are settled in, use the soil from your bucket to build a watering crater around each, then remulch the area. Untie the surrounding plants and dust off your hands

---

"I've watched them. Even right after I spray, they just hold their noses and chew," one frustrated gardener told me. "The only real solution is to fence the rabbits out." This refrain is echoed all around the world in reference to a variety of warm-blooded herbivores.

"A penitentiary garden," the horticulturist called it one June day when the beds seemed to bristle with cages. Each tempting rabbit treat was clearly marked with metal. Later in the season, the plants would grow over the tops of the cages and fluff out the sides. They also would become less tasty as they aged, so the projecting foliage would go unchewed. So the effect of the cages would be diminished if not eliminated.

A Stake in the Future

Stakes are to me what cages are to others — anathema. In my reckoning, any garden plant that can't stand up on its own deserves to be shown the door. I have nothing against stake-dependent plants; it's not the plant's fault that it was bred for huge flowers on weak stems or that it flops like a rag doll when grown in over-rich soil or an under-sunny bed. I just dislike the whole idea of staking.

Even after building the most graceful supports to buoy my clients' plants, even in July when foliage cloaks the hardware, my handiwork is just too apparent to me. In my own garden, I grow sturdy soldiers; put swooning characters upwind of rock-solid species such as maiden grass (*Miscanthus sinensis*), where they can lean to their hearts' content, and send true weaklings to the compost.

The farthest I'll go toward staking my own plants is to put a hoop around a peony. Even that can gall me. In the last four or five years, I've been in my garden only once in early May at peony-hooping time. That time, blessed with five minutes, I did this service for a single, favorite peony. It turned out to be the only year in five when there was no peony-flattening thunderstorm during the week they were in bloom. Every one of my peonies, hooped or loose, stood tall that year.

On this date, I was sorely tempted to chase butterflies rather than tend to staking. It took self-deception to load the necessary bamboo stakes, string, wire for

hoops, and salvaged bits of shrubbery into my car. "I'll do this for science," I told myself. "Test and compare different staking arrangements. That's a worthwhile cause." Even so, I almost managed to put it off and plant annuals and new perennials instead. But I know it's better to see to the needs of current denizens before installing new ones.

More Than One Means of Support

All this effort would go to support golden marguerite, a species that would have been banished for sloppiness from my own garden years ago, except that it seeded itself into a spot next to some blue oat grass.

Staking with twigs is less expensive but more time-consuming than other methods.

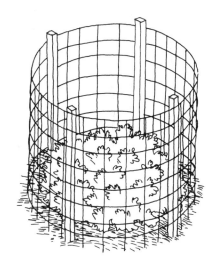

Stakes and hoops like this one of fencing wire usually are not long-term visual distractions. Plants soon grow over them.

Its butter-yellow daisy flowers and the blue-green grass foliage were attractive together, so I left it. The stalwart oats have accommodated the other's tipsy habit ever since.

One of five golden marguerites in Bed Three became my control — no supports. Of the others, two received hoops, one was surrounded by stakes webbed around and through with twine, and the other got a framework of twigs to lean on.

The twigs were 24-inch pieces of burning bush and spirea, saved from March pruning. I pushed five branches firmly into the soil around the outer edge of the marguerite, thick ends down. Then I bent the tips to meet in the center, 18 inches above the ground. These I laced together with twine. Side branches along the main supports would offer their crotches to keep the marguerite's stems off the ground. This was the least expensive staking arrangement of the three I used, based on material cost. It was the most expensive in terms of time spent and manual dexterity required.

I made the hoops by cutting 18-inch-tall fencing into 18-by-36-inch rectangles. The horizontal wires from one 18-inch side became hooks around the vertical wire at the opposite end of the rectangle. This held the hoops closed. Bamboo stakes inserted through the fence openings and into the soil anchored them over their respective marguerites.

These hoops looked like steadfast, overtall, cylindrical stockades. That's the secret — get the stakes in before they're needed. If there's anything less attractive than bare stakes, it's a plant that's been scooped up after collapsing under its flowers or a cloudburst and then strung up as for a crucifixion. There's no grace there, just mud and tangled stems.

Hoops of fencing aren't my favorite type of support. Although they're simple to construct, it's usually difficult to weed around the plants inside the wire. The grid extends all the way to the ground, gumming up the works if you need to reach into the crown to pluck a weed or clip out a dead branch. Also, although the sides of a hoop will stop the marguerite stems in their inevitable sideways sprawl, there's nothing to stop the central stems from leaning every which way and presenting an open center.

Stakes and String

My favored arrangement uses stakes and string. Five stakes inserted evenly around the crown can be connected to each other with string to form a pentagon, then the string can be run back and forth across the pentagon like a multilayer spiderweb. Look to the drawings on this page for clarification. One gardener told me that when given only verbal instructions, she used half a ball of string and a quarter of a day to stake a single plant.

Stakes-and-String Support

My favorite staking arrangement is stakes and string. Start with five stakes around the crown. Link them together around the perimeter, then across the top of the plant. Make the first loop at least a hand's breadth above the soil to allow weeding room.

As the plant grows, the string web provides support for the central stems, and the whole structure gradually is covered by foliage.

This string web breaks any sideways fall and gives the central stems some support. Placing the lowest level of string a hand's breadth above the soil leaves a gap for grooming the base of the plant. The stakes can be strung together up to their tips immediately, or if invisibility is important, string can be added a layer at a time as the plant grows up into the web.

This is relatively inexpensive and quick to put up. Component parts also store neatly over the winter. Bundled stakes take up far less room than the unruly stack of wire fence pieces and hoops that accumulate over time.

A Staking Kit

A prefabricated staking kit is available for many-stemmed, bushy creatures like crocosmia. It consists of a wire grid disk attached to three metal rods, rather like a three-legged stool with a woven wire seat. By pushing the legs into the soil around the crown, you can position the grid to intercept the plant stems as they grow. Hollow sockets at the upper end of the rods can accept and hold the legs of a second kit, so that you can add another level of wire grid for tall plants. A colleague swears by them, but I find the price a bit high. Suppliers are listed in the Appendix, "References and Tools."

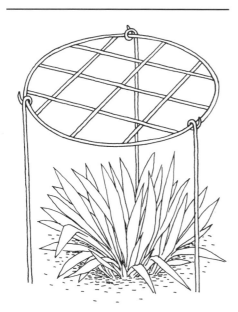

This prefabricated staking kit is easy to use. Stems will grow up into the wire grid, hiding it as they lean on it.

Adding Annuals to a Perennial Bed

Two weeks after my frost-free date the soil was quite warm and it was safe to put in a few snapdragons to buoy the show near the recovering coralbells. I also dropped three canna roots in around the perimeter of the oriental poppy to take over that space as the poppy checked into its summer dormancy.

Putting annuals into a perennial bed can add a lot to the summer show, but it also can detract if not done thoughtfully. To make the most of annuals, look past their flowers. Critique them as if they were perennial additions.

Canna's foliage — large and tinged with maroon — was what I wanted as a foil for the reedy green column of crocosmia at its back and the gray artemisia alongside. Any flowers would be a bonus.

Red snapdragons might jazz up the scene next to the daisylike golden marguerite, but they were selected more for their spiked inflorescence. That would offer contrast to round and trumpet blooms in the vicinity.

Annuals go into my perennial beds in clusters, just as if they were permanent residents. One look to avoid is an edging or one type of annual dotted throughout the bed. In dots or strung out along the edge, the unchanging aspect and whole-bed position of the annuals becomes a compelling focus. It overwhelms the more subtle relationships between perennials' foliage colors, textures, and shapes. As a consequence, worthy perennials can appear to be sluffing off when they're not in bloom.

Caution: Perennial on Trial

Three Grecian foxgloves (*Digitalis lanata*) also joined the company during this period. The space was there, where the delphiniums had checked out. The plants presented themselves to me one day at a garden center. I remembered that the botanical garden didn't have any of their kind and thought that they would add to the variety of display. My work on the bed was going smoothly, so it was likely that I would have time to make space for them.

As I planted the foxgloves, I reminded them that

they were on trial and had better behave. This is a reasonable request to make of foxglove, a genus of basically well-mannered species. Other species, especially those related to troublemakers I've known, do not get so much of my trust. I also treat warily anything with a deep running root and a catalog description that includes the words "aggressive spreader," "naturalizes readily," or "good groundcover." Still others I distrust on intuition or horror stories heard from other gardeners. All of these characters go into a safe holding plot for a year or two of evaluation, preferably separated by pavement or distance from established and orderly beds.

This is not a design tip so much as a maintenance warning. There are perennials in my own and my clients' beds that may never be fully evicted. This is a grudging tribute to their rapid spread and tenacious hold. Just a few of the species involved are Houttuynia (*Houttuynia cordata* 'Chameleon'), gooseneck loosestrife (*Lysimachia clethroides*), showy primrose (*Oenethera speciosa*), various dwarf bamboos, snow-on-the-mountain (*Aegopodium podagraria variegatum*), blue lyme grass (*Elymus arenarius*), plume poppy (*Macleaya cordata*), ostrich fern (*Matteucia struthiopteris*), creeping buttercup (*Ranunculus repens*), and groundcover strawberry (*Fragaria* varieties such as 'Pink Panda'). Each prefers to be the only plant in town. They are all valuable where masses are needed but cause long-term trouble in beds where variety is prized. You may be able to control them in some situations, such as where soil or light conditions dampen their enthusiasm, but don't bet your bed on it.

The Garden under a Microscope

During this period I spent a little longer with each species on my opening rounds. Some of the insects and diseases that can devastate a garden later in summer get started in late spring. I was looking for the early signs and found several.

The inspection process I use is very much like meeting an old friend on the street, so I've dubbed it "shaking hands with your plants." First, you give the friend an appraising once-over and decide whether he or she looks well, happy, older, younger, prosperous, or poor. Then you look him or her in the eye, shake hands or embrace, and exchange news. Approaching a plant, the same steps apply. Compare the foliage color, firmness of the leaves and stems, fullness, and height to what you know a healthy member of this species should present at this time of year.

If there are several of each species, decide whether they are all on equal footing. If not, look for variations in growing conditions that might account for the differences. Giving the daisies the once-over, I noticed that one was much taller than the rest, and I wondered whether an off variety had slipped in somehow. Taking a wider view of the situation, it seemed certain that the height difference was just a response to shade from the adjacent daylilies. The odd plant was the one being shaded most, and it was stretching out to be lean and tall.

My answer was to cut back the overhanging daylily foliage and provide stakes for the daisy. Then I marked my garden diagram to divide and reduce the daylilies in the fall. Prompted to view them critically, I saw clearly that far too much of the bed was occupied by these gregarious plunks.

When you suspect a problem but you can't pinpoint it in the big picture, "shake hands" by checking the underside of a leaf. Many leaf diseases and insects become established first in the relative safety of the leaf's darker side. Predators, including birds, may miss seeing insects that live on or duck under a leaf when disturbed. Rusts and bacteria are likewise more protected there from drying air currents and sun.

Keep a Saner Distance

Save this close inspection for times when you have real suspicions, just as you reserve probing questions about a friend's health for times of real concern. If you look closely at any leaf or interrogate someone in depth, you're bound to find something of note. Whether it's relative to any current business is another matter.

Very few leaves in Bed Three called for close inspection in early and mid-spring, but the monkshood nearly begged to be examined. On my first visit, it had been emerging with all the appearance of health. Seventeen days later, it had become a lush, dark green mound, but I had seen a faint discoloring of the foliage that made me suspect trouble. Two weeks more, at the beginning of this mid-spring chapter when I looked again, there were enough signs there for me to attempt a diagnosis and take some steps to correct the situation.

Seek a Positive Diagnosis

Also during this period of monitoring the monkshood, I identified two former unknowns in the bed as sickly delphiniums — one of which expired, the other I removed. Delphiniums are subject to numerous leaf diseases and insect problems. In the heat and humidity of midwestern summers, delphiniums and their relatives, including monkshood, seem particularly susceptible to fungi and bacteria.

One ailment I've seen at work is caused by the bacterium *Pseudomonas delphinii*. It overwinters as resting bodies in the soil around the plant and on old plant parts, attacking new foliage as it emerges in spring.

Signs of Black Leaf Spot

Infected leaves become discolored, first darkening and then developing shiny blackish spots on the top that are light brown and almost scabby on the underside. The lowest foliage, closest to the source of the bacteria and least disturbed by cleansing breezes, is usually involved first. Eventually, diseased leaves die, having passed the sickness on to the surrounding foliage.

The Bed Three delphiniums had shown the pale, distorted growth of virus-infected plants but also had blotches that might have been due to this bacterial problem. In light of my suspicion about the delphiniums, the monkshood's symptoms seemed even more ominous.

By the end of the month, the monkshood was in tough shape. Although I couldn't know for sure which bacteria or fungi were at work, I took some basic disease-control steps. The first was to get a positive identification of the disease. That would help me find out whether there were any techniques or pesticides that could help control it.

The second and most practical step was to keep the area clean of diseased foliage. This applies to both fungal and bacterial problems as a way to reduce the sources of infection. Clipping every discolored leaf, even those only barely showing trouble, I put them in a plastic bag and disposed of them with my non-compostable trash. A photograph of one of these leaves is shown on page 25.

I marked my diagrams to groom the monkshood at every visit, not because I might forget this obvious task but so that I would remember to record the progress of the disease and my control efforts. I asked my photographer to take pictures as an additional gauge and hoped for the best.

Disease Control Options

Between the end of May and my first June visit, I was able to send a suspicious monkshood leaf to a plant pathology lab for an answer. I was not exercising any special privilege of botanical gardeners. Anyone who has access to a Cooperative Extension Service can do the same. Check the listing of county offices in your phone book to see if it's listed. You can call to get instructions and the fee schedule for submitting a problem for diagnosis.

Permit me to jump ahead to the June lab report, which confirmed that the monkshood's leaf spot was bacterial in nature. It was not one of the many fungal ailments that can prey on it. That meant, in part, that what I had been doing was about all that could be done for the plants. The only good news was that there were no delphiniums or other susceptible species in this bed, so at least there would be no epidemic.

Bacteria are tough to control in people, worse in the garden. Few plant antibiotics exist. Those that may have some effect on this disease, such as streptomycin, are out of everyday reach in terms of price, availability, and practicality of use.

Removal or quarantine and increased cleanliness are the two options the home gardener can exercise against bacteria. I discussed the possibility of removing the monkshood with the horticulturist when I first suspected the disease and was urged to try everything else first. So I continued the only course of action open to me, which was to remove and destroy infected leaves to reduce the disease's spread.

Expect the Usual Problems

Another plant that asked for attention was the golden marguerite. The first of two problems was limited to one plant. It was lying on the ground when I arrived on May 23, and its hoop was nowhere to be seen. At first I thought someone had needed and taken the fencing. Closer inspection changed my mind. Probably a lawn mower had snagged the cage and pulled it away.

A replacement hoop might well meet the same fate. I wondered why it hadn't been apparent to me earlier that this one plant was too close to the edge of the bed. It took only a few minutes to clip back broken stems, eliminate branches too near the edge, and erect a new support of bamboo and string.

Looking at the whole group of golden marguerite, I saw a remarkable number of spittlebug sites. This bug is normally of little consequence — a few here and there, living within their protective foam bubbles and sucking nutrients from stems. This year there seemed to be a bumper crop of these insects in many gardens.

All my reference books relegate spittlebug to the "don't worry" department. I wasn't contemplating control strategies, just indulging my curiosity, when I noticed the rabbit. It was sitting at the base of the plant, *inside* the remaining golden marguerite hoop, frozen so still that I never would have seen it if the spittlebugs hadn't drawn me in close.

Confronted with a warm-blooded enemy with fur and big eyes, I'm hopeless. I tested and confirmed its resolve by touching its nose with a bit of bamboo, called the photographer to come see the brazen creature, but never considered trying to catch it and wring its neck.

After having its picture taken, the rabbit scooted off, and I continued down the line to see how much damage had been done.

A Pound of Cure . . .

The dianthus had been grazed to nubs and the 'Early Sunrise' coreopsis was chewed, especially the plant closest to the monkshood. That's standard — eat the one nearest a significant bit of cover for a skittish bunny. Why hadn't I thought of caging these species when I locked up the phlox? They'd certainly fallen prey before in other gardens of my acquaintance.

All my rabbit caging had gone to protect the phlox, and the garden staff didn't have any left either. The only fence on hand had the same size openings that had so comfortably housed the resident of the golden marguerite. In desperation, I doubled that fencing in such a way as to halve the size of the openings and used it to cage the vestiges of the dianthus and coreopsis.

Followed by an Ounce of Prevention?

Speaking of the caged phlox, a bit of leaf spot I'd seen in the eastern grouping when I'd planted it was advanced by my next visit two weeks later. 'Orange Perfection' is resistant to most of the phlox leaf diseases, but resistance isn't immunity. These young plants, each with only six to eight leaves, couldn't afford even a minor infection if they were going to amount to anything at all this summer.

Anticipating this problem from my May 9 notes, I had brought three antifungal products with me on my next visit. I intended to use a different one on each plant. The first was a systemic fungicide — meaning it's absorbed within the plant cells rather than being worn as a coating.

The others were a superfine horticultural oil called Sunspray and the antitranspirant Wiltpruf. The fungicide prevents infection by making each cell inhospitable to fungi. The oil and the antitranspirant both form physical barriers against a fungus's attachment to a leaf.

As if on cue, a day-ending rain started at this point. Not wanting to repeat the rabbit debacle in another form, I abandoned the idea of experimentation. I doused the eastern cluster with the one remedy that could be applied to the soil and absorbed through the roots — the systemic fungicide. The oil and antitranspirant both have to dry on foliage before it rains, or they're sure to be washed off. Then I ran for cover, and May was gone!

Controlling Pests, Watering, and More Planting

AT THE END OF SPRING and start of summer, it's time to exercise the eye. For me, it's June, but you'll know it's time when the first ornamental allium species are coming into their best season. Oriental poppy pops, the little blue fescue along Bed Three's border erupts with wiry-stemmed tassel flowers, and arrowwood viburnum *(Viburnum dentatum)* is splashed with white. In the low, wet areas, American elderberry *(Sambucus canadensis)* starts its long season of tempting butterflies. Between June 1 and July 1, at least one hundred species in the botanical garden come and go. Dozens more thrive in the surrounding shrub borders.

It became difficult to keep my photographer from wandering, especially since so much of the color was in other parts of the garden. Bed Three was promising a high-summer show while holding its cards close for now.

Keep Your Eyes Peeled

The watchword in June is just that: watch. Monitor the bed's water needs and pay attention to new pest and disease development. There was little else to do in Bed Three, as there were virtually no weeds. Very little grooming was required because most of the inhabitants hadn't flowered yet.

Pests and diseases are the big concern in June throughout zones 3 to 8, not because they occur only in this month but because the consequences of a late spring problem may affect the performance of the garden for all of summer. In areas that have definite winter and summer, late spring is when stores of water, pollen, and fresh foliage are coincidentally high. That spells food and drink, two of the three keys to life. Consequently, plant-dependent organisms are also at a peak.

From here on out, it's all downhill for these organisms. By late summer, more than half the perennial species in the area will have finished blooming; all will have foliage that's older, more bitter, and less palatable to salad lovers; and many coexistent life forms also will be finishing their seasons.

The coziness of an early summer garden is attractive to many guests. It's shelter, the third leg of that tripod that supports life. Branches stretch and mingle, offering uninterrupted passage for six-legged travelers and continuous cover for those that scuttle along the ground. Airflow is slow through this jungle. Drought-intolerant fungi and bacteria can breathe freely and multiply. As summer goes on, various plants will die back or trade their tall flower stalks for a basal rosette of foliage. Openings in the canopy will give air, light, and predators a better chance to penetrate.

A Complex System

Don't hide from this. It's a sideshow, laboratory, and religious experience all rolled into one. I'm convinced I will never be really old and worn-out as long as these complex relationships are around to observe and second-guess. Since there are thousands of insect species in every yard and unknowable numbers of microscopic players, it'll be a long time before the reruns outnumber the new dramas.

Nature's on the side of life, which means that the long-term outcomes are usually happy. For every "bad" bug, fungus, or bacterium out there at any given time, several beneficials are also hatching out or building for the attack. A gardener's part in all this is to referee, which means keeping track of what's going on and stepping in only if the natural contest threatens to get the best of the flowers, lawn, shrubs, or trees.

This means getting to know your plants — what they look like when they're healthy and what problems they're likely to develop. That's what early and mid-spring are for. Working close to the plants with short-handled tools and hand clippers makes this possible.

Dealing with Species' Weaknesses

Each plant species has its own shortcomings, just as every human family has its characteristic weaknesses. Some afflictions are big trouble, others just inconvenient. Each affliction is linked to certain times of the year or stages of life. Some may be stronger in one individual than others. For each, there's a distinct strategy for managing the problem. Because I grow only as many leafy species as I can keep straight, including their potential problems, gardening is even simpler than keeping my family healthy and happy.

Delphiniums come to mind for an example of effective management strategy that wouldn't work on people. The majority of delphiniums grown in areas with hot summers are plagued with fungal and bacterial leaf diseases. My usual response to deteriorating delphiniums is to destroy them and avoid growing the species in that vicinity for several years.

Compare that to managing a tough case of diabetes. Throwing the person out is unthinkable. Unless there is a magic, curative climate to which the afflicted person can be taken to heal, a strategy patterned on delphinium care won't work.

So in late spring I look for the things I suspect may go away. It's a happy irony that failing in my search now will mean less trouble during the growing season.

Plant-by-Plant Inspection

It's time now to start each visit with a plant-by-plant inspection. The dianthus and 'Early Sunrise' coreopsis were first on my rounds, as recovering patients. Either the cages were working or the rabbits had found tastier surroundings, because both had recovered well.

A moment's thought kept me from patting my own back. Short on fencing material in spring, I had protected only the worst-chewed coreopsis. Since even the unprotected coreopsis showed no signs of recent nibbling, the fickleness of bunnies was probably the reason for the reprieve.

The phlox I had treated with fungicide had become marginally bigger and cleaner of leaf than the untreated trio. I'd packed the fungicide again today and would use it before leaving.

A digression: By rights I should have dosed all the phlox, to keep up my end of the bargain about making this a picture-postcard bed. My scientific curiosity got the better of me. It seemed that disfigurement or loss of such tiny plants wouldn't make a difference in the bed's overall appearance. The odds were in my favor if this variety of phlox really could resist leaf disease.

Many of the lower leaves on the monkshood were discolored, spotted, or fading to dead yellow. Removing and destroying them was still only a holding action. I could do it without frustration only for the sake of seeing just how much control it would provide. As I worked, clipping off and bagging foliage, the notion grew that this was not a first-year infection but a recurring case. The soil all around the plants and even their crowns probably harbored years' worth of bacteria. My strategy, based on preventing the spread of the bacteria, would have been more likely to succeed in the early stages of the problem, but I was committed. So I kept them plucked clean of suspicious greenery, although that made them leggy and bare by month's end.

Forces Beyond Your Control

I was especially disappointed to find that a hint of yellow I'd noted earlier on the rock rose had been the first sign of a major injury. Rounding the west end of the bed, I was stopped cold by the sight of a shriveled rock rose. It had been doing fine. I had even dug two of the poor things up a few weeks after planting them to be sure they were putting on plenty of new roots. Now here was one apparently dead and another with several branches dying.

This not only called for a closer look and a handshake, but it also demanded that I prop up my suffering ward and ask, "Who did this? Tell me what I can do!" The leaves were distorted and dry, but not chewed or marred by fungus. The plant most affected was closest to the lawn.

On the far side of the bed, in my hurry to get to the rabbit-harried dianthus, I'd walked right past the rue. Now I recalled a brown branch among the blue and went to look again. There, too, a plant close to the lawn had shriveled, brown foliage, dead branches, and yellowing that showed more to come. It was the unfortunate veteran that I'd unearthed in error and replanted in early spring.

Mowers and Gardeners: An Uneasy Truce

Almost certainly, this damage was from an overspray of liquid lawn weed killer. That can happen easily. All it takes is a wider swing of the applicator's arm or a sudden breeze to scatter a few droplets beyond the lawn. This was my punishment for paying too little attention to lawn care. If I'd been in tune to lawn care in early spring, I would have been more aware that it was broad-leaved weed killer time when I was planting the rue and rock rose. I could have looked up the lawn crew and asked them to be extra careful around Bed Three.

The oxeye and Carolina lupine next to the dying rock rose also might have been contacted, but they were able to shrug it off. That can come from being older and better established or naturally resistant to the particular chemical. Both original rues were close to the edge. Both may have been touched, but only the one recently stressed by transplant had succumbed. All I could do was to prune off the dead and dying limbs and make a note to watch for further decline and any need for replacements.

Learn at Every Turn

The feeling of powerlessness that comes from seeing a garden damaged by forces beyond your control is tough to deal with. But we all have to come to grips with these problems. None of us is alone in the world. There will always be black Labrador retrievers that bumble ingenuously through a week's worth of planting, just to say hello to the gardener they love. Neighbors will continue to cut each other's shrubs and trees out of necessity, ignorance, or spite. Storms will happen the day before a garden party, and so on, for all our gardening lives.

Most things that happen in a garden are not major catastrophes, no matter how unexpected or disappointing they may be at the moment of discovery. At least once every year, I find myself pausing over an aggravation that ultimately proves too minor to warrant the attention. So I've learned to take advantage of the focused attention of the moment to look for hidden value. You can learn many lessons by looking at your garden from a new perspective, however uncomfortable.

Coreopsis in the Line of Fire

Such was the case a week after I discovered the herbicide damage. I arrived at the garden to find that the monkshood had been treated with a fungicide. The white coating on the leaves was distinctive, and its appearance understandable. I'd discussed the monkshood problem with the horticulturist. The disease had progressed despite sanitary measures. There had been no chance yet to report that the lab had identified it as a bacterial problem, one not likely to be controlled by a fungicide. Even if that report had been made, however, this outside chance would have been worth a shot.

Botanical gardens do not hire pesticide application technicians very often. Such a person had been called in to treat a fungal problem in another bed, and with fungicide left in the tank after completing that job, the technician had been directed to the monkshood. That is the best way to dispose of unused pesticides: apply them where they may do some good.

It wasn't the monkshood's condition that gave me pause. It was the effect the spray appeared to have had on the coreopsis at the monkshood's feet. The 'Early Sunrise' that had been most abused by the rabbit was now white-coated, too, but its foliage had been burned by the fungicide. Twice now it had had a hard time just because of its position near the monkshood.

Many chemicals that we use to cure ills have side effects, and some plant species are more sensitive than others. Every pesticide label lists the species on which the product is known to be safe if used as directed.

Fretting over this problem was a waste of time. The coreopsis would live, and by year's end it would endear itself to me as one of the longest-blooming, lowest-maintenance species in the bed. In retrospect, I see that it was only right that it had had this chance to prove itself one of the toughest as well.

Watch Newcomers Closely

Unexpected developments such as herbicide damage along the bed edge or the appearance of new leaf-chewing insects are the best and worst things about June pest school. What you haven't seen before is what you should scrutinize most carefully, because Mother Nature, in all her wisdom, will repeat the episode again later. If you know the cause of the problem, you should put it on your personal garden maintenance schedule so that you can head it off at the pass in future years.

The Grecian foxglove was my new species for the season, so even though it looked fine in passing, I bent down and gave it a thorough going-over. Was it growing? Yes. Were the stems strong and the foliage uniformly green? Yes ... make that no. One plant had two leaves with a few brown spots. None of the characteristic signs of a disease were present, such as powdery pustules on the underside or spots in several stages of development.

Hunkering down and using my handy eight-power loupe — the inexpensive kind you can buy at a camera store to inspect slides — I searched the leaves for insects, insect eggs, webbing, or shed skins. I didn't find a thing. All I could do then was to record the problem so that if it continued, I would have an approximate date of onset to enter on next year's schedule. That could become my preventive action date. Later, I'd check my pest-management library for any references to foxglove ailments that fit the ticket.

Get the Number of that Bug!

Some gardeners break out a fertilizer or combination insecticide-fungicide whenever they see anything off-color, bitten, or marred in a garden. "Better safe than sorry" is their creed. Oddly enough, that's my operating theme, too, but it makes me forestall action. Maybe it takes firsthand involvement in an episode such as I had with a magnolia to foster this attitude. Or maybe hearing it from me will be enough to put you on track with the cautious approaches taken in all twenty botanical gardens and parks where I did interviews for this book.

There were actually two magnolias involved in my experience. The first tree was practically a member of

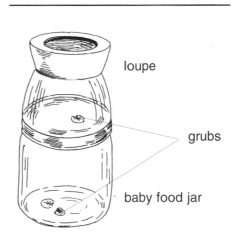

An eight-power (8X) loupe is perfect for close examination of damaged leaves and insects. The lid of a baby food jar makes a perfect cap for the loupe. Placed as shown, it keeps your specimen at the correct focal distance. The baby food jar is a handy carrier for specimens that need further inspection.

my client's family. Like many magnolias, it was host to scale insects. The infestation was severe when I first saw it. Several years of applying preventive horticultural oil in the spring to smother any adult scales that had overwintered, plus a follow-up with insecticidal soap late in the summer to kill any new young, finally brought the tree back to vigorous growth. This convinced me that the regimen was a sound one for magnolia scale.

The second tree was a magnolia I met one May as the foliage was emerging. In the habit of shaking hands with that other magnolia, I looked at this one, saw some slight signs of scale, and described to the owner what had kept the problem under control in the other yard. I went away satisfied with myself, having done some extra work in a yard where my primary purpose was to design a flower bed.

Later that year, while I was studying another topic, a photograph of ladybug larvae caught my eye. These youngsters are voracious predators of aphids, scales, and other plant-eating bugs, but they resemble their parents not a whit. Spiny, with long-oval bodies that appear to consist of overlapping segments like an armadillo's hide, they fascinated me.

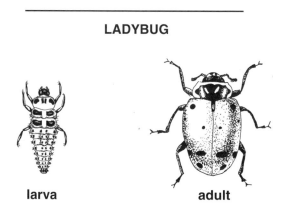

LADYBUG

larva   adult

Immature lady beetles bear little resemblance to their well-known parents, but they're even more effective in eating aphids and other harmful insects.

While I looked at the larvae, another picture came into my mind with great clarity. It was what I had seen on the second magnolia, which had not registered earlier. That second magnolia had been loaded with lady-

bug larvae, probably plenty to control the resident scale. I felt terrible and hoped the owner had not rushed out, bought an insecticide, sprayed the tree, and ruined that balance.

Now I wait to make sure an unfamiliar problem legitimately warrants interference. In the end, few problems do.

Using Reference Books

The reference books that help me identify a new problem, learn the prognosis, and find possible treatments are organized much like my home medical adviser. Problems in the medical adviser are listed under the body part or system involved. There's a complete description of the symptoms, mention of similar conditions, a blow-by-blow account of typical stages of the condition, and recommended remedies.

Diseases and Pests of Ornamental Plants by Pascal Pirone is one of several books listed in the Appendix, "References and Tools" that follow the same organization for plants. These books list plants genus by genus. Each genus name is followed by the diseases, insects, and other pests that are likely to occur.

Given these resources, I don't have to know the name of a disease or insect to get help deciding what to do. All I need is the name of the plant. That reduces the brain strain, since I can generally remember or look up a plant name. What I can't seem to do is memorize several insect and disease names for every plant or even pick them out of a lineup in an entomology or pathology text.

Some of the pest-control books I use prescribe treatments that are not to my liking, including one old text that still lists the banned substances DDT and chlordane. That doesn't stop me from using the books. My purpose is identification and understanding of the problem. There's no discord, to my mind, if a staunch organic gardener has the *Pesticide Applicator's Handbook* open on the desk or an up-to-date licensed applicator checks the listing for black vine weevil in my 1940s guide. There's information to be had there that a reasonable person can use to develop an acceptable strategy for handling a problem.

When Books Fall Short

Sometimes books fail me, but with good reason.

Every one of my books was open as I looked for suggestions for handling the 'Silver King' artemisia's problem. The foliage was wilted in some spots, and the associated stems were wasted away at ground level. Some kind of stem rot seemed to be at work. Maybe it was a fungus that affects both roots and stem. When I cut loose a few failing pieces, they came away with just little bits of unhealthy-looking root.

Most of the books were of little help, not even giving artemisia its own listing in the problem section. A few mentioned in passing that some growers had reported stem rot in artemisia, but the consensus was that the species is normally pest-free in a sunny, well-drained site. The difference between the growers' reports and the authors' majority opinion probably has its basis in culture — the way the plant is being grown.

Fingering the Culprit

Healthy, vigorous plants have remarkable resistance to infection and attack. From cell walls that are tough for fungi to penetrate to internal fluids that have subtle insecticidal compounds, artemisia is a super creature. But plants under stress are more susceptible to their usual pests and may develop atypical problems. Too little or too much light, a nutrient imbalance linked to soil pH or elemental deficiency, or even too much or too little movement in the wind can create differences so small that we can't detect them. However, plant predators sense the openings and move in.

Artemisia confined in a moist growing mix in a greenhouse with high humidity or reduced airflow may rot at the base. Bed Three wasn't too moist, but my inspection had turned up another stress that might have opened the door to the same problem.

Looking at the wilted stems, my first inclination was to curse myself for banking mulch up against the crown. That practice can trap moisture and incite rot and it looked as if that's what had happened. I looked at the mulch there and thought, *Why did I dump mulch 4 or 5 inches deep here?!* However, one poke at the mulch showed that it was just the right depth.

The Ants Go Marching In

It was the soil level that was high. Ants had moved in underground, and their excavations had raised the whole area. I've seen other cases where extensive ant colonies have dried out a bed and seriously weakened the plants in it. So in my research I looked for references to dry soil causing stem rot in artemisia.

Lacking anything conclusive, I decided to act as if the ants were the underlying problem. More than 80 percent of plant troubles are secondary, caused by poor culture and corrected not by medicines but by changes in watering, plant location, soil condition, and so on. Even if there was a fungicide that could safely control root rot in artemisia, it would be useless to apply it without attacking the primary cause.

My target on the next visit was the ants.

Establishing Your Own Level of Tolerance

Poison baits and crystalline insecticides can kill ants, but it seemed there was time to try some slower, less toxic strategies. If the artemisia had been in danger of dying or looked really terrible, stronger measures might have been warranted. Neither criterion applied. The portions of the plant not growing in ant-disturbed earth looked good. Most people walking by wouldn't even notice the few wilted stems in a naturally gray mass. It was fortunate that most of the ant tunneling was going on along the south side of the bed, while most of the human traffic strolled by on the north.

Focus on Intolerable Damage

This tenet of rational pest management is one I've heard over and over, at every botanical garden I've visited: set a level of damage that is tolerable, based on your perspective and the plant's continued well-being. Act only if that level is exceeded. Then use the tactics first that are least likely to have detrimental effects on the surroundings.

None of the professionals I interviewed followed a set routine in using pesticides. Every one practiced the technique of watching, evaluating the actual and potential damage, and intervening only if necessary. All felt that they had healthier, lower-maintenance gardens as a result. Several remarked that this policy also reduced their personal contact with substances whose long-term cumulative effects may not be known.

The Water Treatment

My first attempt on the ants would be with water. It's a trick I picked up from a farm boy turned gardener in retiree's overalls. A lifelong naturalist, he knew that ant colonies could be killed by flooding their egg chambers. Those portions of their tunnels, he pointed out as he dissected one for me, have domed roofs lined with a crusty, waterproof material so that the eggs stay dry.

I used a hose with a root-probe attachment to punch holes in the ants' work. I let the water run a second or two in each spot, until it bubbled back up at me through adjacent holes. I could feel the scrunch of the probe's tip when it got to the ant-plumbed depth. It was as if the probe were pushing into sugar cubes rather than soil.

Don't jump at a pest-control measure like this without thinking. If the bed had been wet already, the extra water could have caused as much trouble as the ants themselves. No pest-control measure, however benign it may be in comparison to other options, is without repercussions.

Two weeks later the ant activity had dropped off drastically in the spots I'd flooded. There was a problem, though. They appeared to have moved north and east along the edge of the bed, to an area more visible to the public. Soil was puffed up all around the fescue and was raised almost like a mole's surface tunnel at the west end of the lamb's ear.

Cosmetic vs. Life-Threatening Problems

If the insect or disease at work is marring the looks of a plant but is not likely to kill it, it's a cosmetic problem. Such was the case with this new ant work. It takes a lot to kill lamb's ear (*Stachys lanata*), and dry soil hardly fazes fescue. Yet while this went on, the carpet of gray lamb's ear was going to look very ragged. As it rotted at its base, it played the 'Silver King' artemisia's role all over again, at center stage.

I consulted the horticulturist at this point. I learned that ant activity was terrible all over the garden, a problem significant enough that the horticulturist had arranged for a licensed applicator to come in and prime the worst areas with an ant-specific pesticide. It wasn't clear exactly when this would happen, so I flooded and chased the ants one more time. There's no telling whether this had any effect, since the survivors were dispatched by the other means shortly thereafter.

The Return of the Root Weevils

The reemergence of the root weevils illustrates the other side of the cosmetic/life-threatening coin. The notches that adult weevils create as they eat foliage are a cosmetic problem. But the combined damage from juveniles eating roots and adults eating leaves, multiplied by the insect's capacity to dine on so many species, pushes this problem into the life-threatening category.

Yet even here, options are legion. Take the case of the coralbells-munching grubs you met back in Chapter 5. Standard treatment for an infestation is to drench the soil with an insecticide where the grubs are known to be. Insecticides are then applied to plants visited by the adults, at two-week intervals from June through September.

That's more than I wanted to do. It would require too much time, expense, and personal exposure to pesticides. In addition, I wasn't convinced of the program's effectiveness.

While cleaning the grubs from the coralbells area, I had tried soaking them in various insecticidal substances. All the guinea grubs had survived, and some had given me the distinct impression that they'd enjoyed the bath. This supported textbook reports that weevils are resistant to numerous poisons, at least in that final stage of grubdom.

The Power of Healthy Soil

Pondering the grubs in their little pools of test chemicals made me think. How much insecticide would have to be applied to drench the soil to the 9-inch depth that seemed to define the grubs' home? It was clear that at least some grubs would survive simply because the toxin wouldn't reach them. Another thought sprang from this one. Since the grub population was well below one per square inch of bed surface, any drench would contact more grub-free than grub-infested earth.

Tread Lightly: The Soil's Alive

A single teaspoon of healthy soil might have millions of bacteria, hundreds of beneficial nematodes, miles of beneficial fungal strands, and many other life forms. These "soil animals" decompose organic matter, thereby releasing nutrients to dissolve in water and be taken up by roots.

Some of the fungi also team up with roots in symbiotic fashion. Fungi increase the roots' ability to absorb nutrients and in exchange extract a bit of plant carbohydrate for fuel. Soil fungi-to-root relationships are only beginning to be discovered, and understanding them may be decades away. It's been estimated, though, that more than 90 percent of plant species can and do form some of these mycorrhizal associations.

Plant health depends on root health and the soil's ability to recycle nutrients. So, at the expense of sounding radical, I usually opt to avoid dabbling in soil chemistry unless there's no other way.

I warned you that you'd hear more about my reasons for using compost as fertilizer at home. This argument against unnecessary soil drenches applies to the salt-based elements in fertilizers, too.

Weevils Tripped Up by Informants

Let's go back to the specifics of dealing with weevils. My best option was to attack the grubs in early spring, then do what I could to rob the adults of a ready food source. I had tried to do the latter by replacing the coralbells with unpalatable plants. The strategy didn't end there, however. I saved the rest of the story for this chapter. In early spring, it was only a plan. It makes better sense in action.

Two of those early spring grubs went home with me. They moved onto my back porch, in the shade.

They were secure in a baby food jar half-filled with soil and closed with a bit of old panty hose and a rubber band. My books told me that they finish feeding for the year by mid-spring. This was confirmed, since in early spring when I found them they'd been *on the* roots and a little more than two weeks later they were just curled up in the soil *near* the plants. They were entering a resting state while their bodies transformed into something like small black beetles. They didn't need to be fed, just kept.

My kids were glad of that. Finding specific leaves to feed some of our guests is no great chore. Asking the kids to dig fresh roots every so often to feed a grub would be pushing my luck.

It Takes No Time If Your Timing Is Right

What was the incentive for keeping these odd pets? Timing. At least some grubs must have escaped Step One of the weevil war. When the test grubs hatched, I would know to start hunting adults in the trial bed. Books tell me only roughly when to do this. My own schedule wouldn't let me go to Bed Three every day to catch the first appearance of telltale weevil-notched leaves.

On June 13, a weevil made its opening bow in the baby food jar. Having served its purpose, it could have been killed right away. However, we kept it for two more days. We fed it coralbells leaves that it ate by night and hid under during the day. It was enlightening to see how much a black vine weevil can eat — each night a piece bigger than its own 3/16-inch body. The notches were classic. They always started from the edge of a leaf, never as a hole in the center, and every one had an arcing inner edge.

Seeking Organic Solutions

Hoping not to find anything, in late June I looked at the lowest leaves of every plant, starting with the rock rose. A minute later, the Carolina lupine yielded the first sign. One of the phloxes was notched as well. No other notches turned up anywhere else in the bed.

Now the question was how to kill as many of the adults as possible. If it had been my own garden, I might have been able to use a manual control method.

After dark, with a sheet spread under the affected plant, I could have shaken the branches to dislodge the weevils, picked up the sheet, and emptied it where we could see and squash the culprits. Here that tactic would probably get me an interview with the campus security officers, even if a nightly visit were practical from my distant base.

A second manual control method had to be passed up because it also required daily visits. Weevils hide at the base of the plant during daylight hours. Crumpled newspaper there often attracts them and can be gathered and destroyed, weevils and all.

The Bottom Line:
Least Environmental Impact

All this thinking took just a few minutes. I was still low on the pest-management ladder, which goes up from options that have a narrow range of toxicity to those that are toxic to many organisms and may be more persistent in the environment.

Introducing beneficial nematodes is a low-rung strategy. These tiny animals attack and parasitize weevil grubs. Tests at such prestigious institutions as Boskoop Garden in the Netherlands have shown that introducing nematodes to weevil-infested beds can significantly reduce the grub population between September and April.

A nematode may have been responsible for the death of my second test grub. That second weevil never appeared, so I went looking. I never found the corpse, but something caught the light as it moved, hair thin, in the last clod of soil I dissected in my vain pursuit.

Learned friends told me that I couldn't possibly have seen a nematode in that baby food jar. Nematodes are too small, they said. Yet something had killed that grub. Nematode, disease organism, or whatever, if some of these creatures were already inhabiting Bed Three and killing grubs, they were on my side. A nematode release would be a reinforcement, like releasing extra ladybugs, without the colorful display.

Beneficial nematodes can be purchased at garden centers and by mail (see Appendix, "References and Tools"). The trouble is, they kill weevil grubs only if that prey is present, which is not the case in June. I made a note on my early fall diagram to buy beneficial nematodes and let them loose in the bed then, when the weevil eggs were hatching.

Cannons against Flies?

Meanwhile, I still had weevils in the bed. Soon, if not already, they would be laying eggs. The feeding damage was minor, so there were probably few weevils at work. The damage also told me approximately where the adults were. That's useful information for reducing a pest population even further.

One tactic open to me was to spray an insecticide on the host plants. Yet breaking out a spray gun every other week struck me as ludicrous, since there were few

---

BLACK VINE WEEVIL DAMAGE

Black vine weevil grubs eat roots from early fall until early spring. They rest in the soil as pupae until late spring or early summer. Adults eat the foliage of dozens of species and lay eggs throughout the summer.

Black vine weevil damage is distinctive. The leaf margin is notched. Damage is often found on lower leaves, where the insects find more shelter. Notching on upper leaves often indicates a heavier infestation.

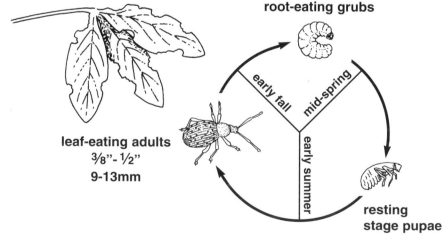

root-eating grubs

early fall

mid-spring

leaf-eating adults
3/8"- 1/2"
9-13mm

early summer

resting
stage pupae

weevils and many miles of leaf surface. To kill them with an aerial spray, I would have to coat an area that to a weevil must be the equivalent of the state of Montana. A weevil could escape the barrage, even if it were repeated often, as prescribed.

A systemic insecticide could work more effectively. That kind of pesticide is analogous to an antibiotic in the human body. The chemicals are taken up by a plant's roots and leaves. Insects that eat the treated plant ingest the poison.

I planned to water the Carolina lupine and phlox with a solution containing a weevil-killing systemic pesticide. That would deliver the chemicals to the affected plants' roots and allow the plants to distribute the pesticide throughout the foliage. The toughest part of the campaign was reading numerous pesticide labels to determine which pesticide listed black vine weevil.

Keeping Tiny Friends from Harm

A precaution was necessary. Throughout June, I was impressed by the variety and number of beneficial insects in the bed, from assassin bugs to lacewings and several types of lady beetles and spiders.

On one occasion, looking for the plant bug responsible for pockmarks I'd found on the oxeye, I was stumped. Rocking back on my haunches to think gave me a wider view of the plant, and the likely answer was sitting right there. Just above where I had been searching was a small jumping spider, tensed to spring. There's a good chance it or another predator had ambushed the guilty plant bug or bugs.

Systemic insecticides make all parts of a plant poisonous, including the pollen. Many beneficial insects eat pollen at some point in their lives, even if they also prey on other insects. To protect them, I deadheaded the Carolina lupine, which was in its last few days of bloom anyway.

Then I mixed the insecticide in a bucket according to the label directions and poured it slowly onto the soil throughout the area shaded by the Carolina lupine and phlox. As a way to gauge the results, I removed all the Carolina lupine leaves that had notches and made a note of how many notches were on the phlox; they were still too small to donate any leaves to science.

LACEWING

larva/nymph   adult

Lacewings also are predators. These and several other beneficial insects were present in Bed Three.

Caution: Systemics Are Not Vitamins

Some people hear about systemic insecticides and fungicides and ask, "Why not just douse everything regularly and skip all the watching and diagnosing?"

First, systemics kill beneficial as well as harmful insects. Second, they are foreign substances introduced into the plant for remedial purposes. They are not without side effects. We may never know how a rose feels with systemics in its sap, but we can guess from personal experience that there is a difference from the rose norm. Internal human medications such as antibiotics can adversely affect some people's digestive systems or cause rashes and other difficulties. It's recently become news that certain antibiotics are less effective than they were a decade ago. Surviving bacteria may have passed on a resistance to their descendants. Research into pest resistance indicates that this pattern of diminishing effect also applies to some pesticides.

Second, soil gets involved when systemics are applied, so all those life forms I mentioned earlier stand to feel the effects. Systemic fungicides will probably contact beneficial soil fungi. Soil fungi's role in plant health is only beginning to be understood, yet it's clearly important.

Using systemic pesticides can result in less total use of chemicals, since they can be targeted at the base of a single plant. This can reduce unplanned exposure that comes from aerial drift. Still, be as stingy in using them as you would be in using prescription medicine.

Now I could watch for new damage and reapply the pesticide when it was clearly needed, not "just in case."

Take Time to Smell the Flowers

While all this close inspection and battle to the death were going on in Bed Three, the scenery was gorgeous. People were walking by. Some didn't even notice a gardener crouched under the Carolina lupine or plucking at the monkshood. Their comments drifted back to me and made it plain that no one else was concerned with these insects, fungi, consequences of chemical use, and so on. Some asked me the name of a plant in bloom, remarked how beautiful the gardens were, or reminded me how lucky I was to have this job.

The troubles described here are potential problems — the garden seen under a microscope. Of the thirty-three species in the bed, only six were of any concern to me in late spring, and only two showed much outward sign of that. Yet gardeners can get wrapped up in problems. They look up one day and realize it's fall. Be sure to take breaks like this once in a while. Step back and enjoy the big picture you've been painting.

Uninvited Guests

In the center of the bed, the blackberry lily *(Belamcanda chinensis)* had long, thin gashes in its foliage.

The *Crocosmia* 'Lucifer' 6 feet away had some similar interveinal scars. It was interesting to see this problem surface at this point, however, as it's usually apparent earlier in the year. It was probably the work of slugs, a ubiquitous pest. When people say they've never seen one or had a problem with them, it's likely they just don't know what to look for. Every bed has slugs, but not every bed has slug problems.

No One Likes a Slug

These slimy, nonshelled snail relatives are a trial to horticulturists all over the world. Maybe people despise them for the damage they do, the way they sneak around in the dark, and even the queasiness that follows their slimy touch. Whatever the cause, the loathing is real.

It seems that slugs couldn't be more infuriating if they tried, or more uncouth. For instance, Bed Three's Missouri primrose beat the odds in its shady spot and produced a few leaves and two flowers. Slugs ate both blooms. Taking pleasure in beating them at their own game, I refused to rise to the bait.

All the energy spent looking for the magic recipe to eliminate slugs amazes me. The existence of so many tactics for trapping, drowning, burning, electrocuting, and repelling slugs ought to clue us in. If there were a best way to clean them out of a growing area, it would have been discovered by now, and probably patented.

Slug Damage

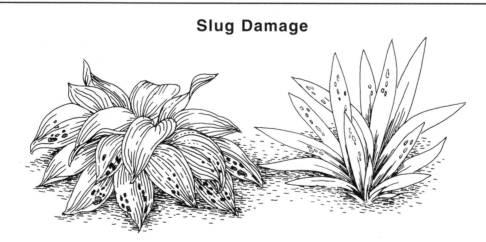

Slugs use rasplike mouths to scrape holes in foliage. These holes are almost always within the leaf margin rather than on an edge, and often the damage follows between leaf veins. This hosta (left) and this blackberry lily (right) have both played host to slugs.

Purely Cosmetic Damage

Holes in the blackberry lily, crocosmia, daylily, and foxglove were not a surprise or a worry. It was clearly normal slug shenanigans, not the kind of infestation that can take a ten-leaf balloon flower or phlox down to a leafless stalk overnight. It was within the tolerance levels I'd set, so it deserved nothing more than a notation.

In fact, by July the slug grazing appeared to have stopped. By then, the newest blackberry lily foliage had no holes at all. It got very hot in July, which can put the damper on slug antics, but the herd also might have been thinned by hungry shrews or birds. My watering practices may have helped send them into a dehydrated dormancy, too. The worst slugs I've ever seen have been in shady beds kept constantly wet. Bed Three got water just once in late spring, so it remained moist under the mulch but never wet. The surface of the mulch became quite dry — oh, so unpleasant to a slug.

Plant Bugs Make the Scene

Some problems are not linked to one plant species but to a date. I could set my calendar to the week based on the appearance of the four-lined plant bug. It's a small, piercing-sucking insect with catholic tastes, from America's favorite Shasta daisy to Japanese anemone, then back by way of every conceivable herb and numerous trees and shrubs. I watched for it as spring progressed and wasn't disappointed.

The marks it leaves behind are as distinctive in their way as weevils' edge notches and slugs' punch card holes right in the middle of the leaf. This bug inserts its mouthpiece into the leaf, takes a few sips of plant juice, leaves behind a toxin that ensures the death of cells at that feeding site, takes two steps, and repeats the process. It prefers tender new foliage. The result is a pattern of small dead spots, giving the appearance of pockmarks on a plant's upper leaves. If the feeding is very heavy, the pockmarks may coalesce, and the whole leaf will shrivel and die.

Four-lined plant bug adults are about ⅜ inch long and ⅛ inch wide, tennis-ball green with four dark stripes running lengthwise on their backs. They move quickly, darting to the underside of the leaf when they sense danger, dropping off the plant into the safety of its base, or flying away. Almost any kind of insecticide will kill them instantly. You just have to catch up to them first.

Nipping Them in the Bud

The four-lined plant bug is an insect I know well, dating back to a June perhaps nine years ago. The cosmetic problem caused by these bugs had been getting worse for several years, as results of insect infestations often do. I had been hoping there would be a crash season soon, one in which the bug's natural predators also occur in great numbers and bring the prey population tumbling down. It didn't look as if that were happening. In late June, halfway through the bug's season,

Four-lined Plant Bug Damage

The four-lined plant bug pierces the leaf and sucks out the plant's juices. Like many insects, it prefers tender young foliage so its damage is often worst on young, upper leaves. The resulting pockmarks are ugly but not life threatening.

numerous perennials in my beds even from a distance looked as if they had been singed. I decided to bring about a crash myself the following year.

I knew I'd need help from someone who could be in the garden more than I could. It would cost me a nickel a bug, but that would buy me the two best pest managers around: my son, Cory, and daughter, Sonja. Armed with the following intelligence report, they signed on about May 23: The enemy is red when it first hatches and can't fly. It feeds on top of the leaf but hides quickly under it. It is most often seen first on our perennial salvia and mint.

They agreed to meet with me each evening when I came home for a debriefing. They'd report the number of enemy caught and squished, where, and the date when the first adult was seen. That would be when I would bring in the big guns.

Insect Life Cycles:
What You Know Can Help You

Two days later, they met me as I pulled in the driveway and reported finding some of the nymphs. We went straight up onto the roof, looking at the whole yard as a map spread out below us.

"Where are they?" I asked, expecting to hear that they were in the herb garden near the old sandbox or along the lilac border. Nymphs can't fly, so they tend to be concentrated near hatch sites.

"On the south side of the plant," my lieutenants reported.

Funny what you find out when you don't have preconceived notions. Turns out the kids had agreed to "work" a suspect plant together, to confirm each other's counts. Keeping the other one honest was a concern with such big stakes. What they'd realized was that the picker on the south, whoever that was, netted twice as many bugs as the picker on the north. These two, who had been reading maps and calling compass directions since they were in preschool, now had another reason to keep north in mind.

Several days and hundreds of nymphs later, they were able to conclude that the bugs preferred to feed when it was sunny and warm. I learned this when both capitalists stayed inside one Sunday morning.

"Don't you want to be out there racking up nickels?" I asked.

"Nah. They won't be out until it's warmer. They're never out before we leave for school. They'll be there by lunchtime."

Experiment to Test Your Ammunition

Ten days after the war began, the first adult was sighted. It was likely that all the eggs were now hatched. Also, since the generation was coming of age and could fly, the kids couldn't count on nabbing dozens of nymphs from one plant. They'd have to cover the whole yard. So we escalated to chemical warfare.

A neighbor, interested in the project and schooled in scientific experimentation, offered to conduct the attack. We used plain water, water with one or two tablespoons of oil soap in each gallon, and insecticidal soap. We knew all three would kill the bugs, since we'd caught some bugs and dunked them in each solution. In the case of the water, they had to be drenched until they drowned, but it did work.

After a week, we knew that the one tablespoon of oil soap in a gallon of water worked best. The campaign had been a success. Plant bug damage was very light that year, and we had an arsenal of information to use in future seasons.

The last time it was necessary to employ the kids, they were aware of the fact that one good year of bug-catching meant years of low pay, so they asked a quarter per bug. Some people thought my husband and I were crazy, but we paid it. We considered it cheap for all the horticultural and character-building benefits it afforded.

The Most Efficient Choice

That's why, in early June, I looked for and found the first few marks of four-lined plant bug damage on the daisies. In less than two minutes there were a dozen red squash marks on the daisies — thumb and forefinger as pesticide.

Could I have sprayed the plants instead? Yes, and I did have insecticidal soap with me in case the numbers had warranted that. Yet that tactic would take just as much time. Given such a light population, a spray might not have killed even as many as I had pinched.

It's tough to spritz their hiding places under flat-to-the-ground daisy foliage.

One week later, there was a little more damage on the daisies, and ten more bugs bit the dust. Some bugs were working the 'Early Sunrise' coreopsis, too. The population was low, hardly a trace of what I knew to be a bad infestation.

After two more weeks, I found just a few adults. Damage was very light. Elsewhere in the botanical garden, handpicking also had been the weapon of choice. It's an option applicable to all pests, and an attractive one, since it never requires lugging around extra tools.

Watering

The soil throughout the bed was moist, though drier than it had been earlier. However, the newest plants were dry again, so I went after the hose. Perhaps my philosophy about infrequent watering developed in part from my lifelong struggle with hoses. There may be no other tool that is so cantankerous, so energetically devious, as a tangled hose pretending to be neatly coiled.

During the tedious process of straightening and connecting the rascal, I had time to think about watering — and an opportunity to get steamed. The weather forecast for the next week called for unseasonably hot days and no rain. That news or my overheated state after wrestling with the hose prompted me to water the whole bed.

This turned out to be a fortuitous decision. The following three weeks turned out to be a minidrought. All the inhabitants of the bed weathered it well. There was no wilting, although the new plants asked for a drink again a week into the drought. As it turned out, that would be the last watering any of these plants would need for six weeks.

Wired for Success

It was now time to give up on the oriental lilies that had once been in the bed. On my first visit in early spring, while cutting down the dead stalks of the moor grass, I'd noticed a tunnel. It may have been from a vole, also called a meadow mouse. It angled under the clump of grass and over toward the oriental lily marker.

Knowing rodents' love of lily bulbs, I'd prepared for the worst. When the lilies were still no-shows two months later, I started shopping for replacements and a way to protect them from voles.

I sat down under the east oak to construct baskets from hardware cloth — contraptions to be buried as underground armor for the replacement lilies. This technique had always intrigued me. I had read that rodent damage to bulbs could be prevented by lining the planting hole with hardware cloth.

Finding the "cloth" to be stiff wire fencing with tiny openings, I dropped the idea of digging a hole and draping the cloth into it. I'd imagined doing that, then adding soil, bulbs, and more soil before folding the

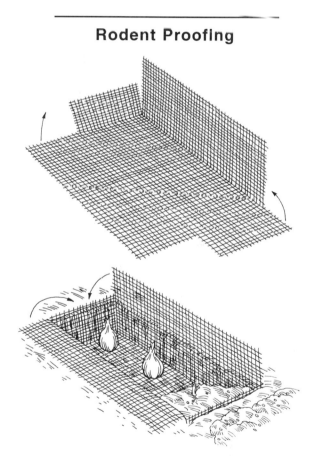

Rodent Proofing

When tunneling rodents are present, protect bulbs with a cage of hardware cloth. From a rectangular piece, cut out corners as shown above, then fold up sides to create a box. Place bulbs, fill "box" with soil, then close long ends over the top. Leave an opening for the plants to grow through.

edges of the cloth over the top. Instead, my tools for the day included tin shears and needle-nose pliers.

After thirty minutes of clipping, hooking wire ends together, and nursing pricked fingers, I had produced one wire box with an opening on top. Experience paid off immediately, and the second box took only twenty minutes to complete. I was grateful for the oak, which provided me with a cool place to do this miserable work.

Between the moor grass and the 'Silver King' artemisia, I scraped away the mulch and removed enough soil to fit the whole wire cube in the ground. Its top edges opened up like flaps on a cardboard box. Into this I put soil and then two potted *Lilium* 'Red Night' plants, added more soil, folded the wire lid down around the lilies' stems, gave them a drink, and wished them well. Recalling a garden in which all fifty lilies were stripped of foliage one July, and knowing a rabbit lived nearby, I made cages of the remaining hardware cloth and stood them around the lush foliage.

Nitrogen Snacks

The daisy foliage nearby was slightly paler than I thought it should be. This made me wonder about nitrogen depletion, alkaline soil, and the hot weather coming on. Any of these could exacerbate chlorosis — a deficiency of chlorophyll linked to low nitrogen, iron, and other elements.

Some perennials are naturally greedy when it comes to nitrogen, as compared to the average species. I took a look around the bed to see whether there were any other pale individuals on board. Perhaps the plants surrounded by a certain kind of mulch were feeling a strain.

A circuit of the bed didn't support that hypothesis, but it did turn up the notion that the daisies, phlox, coralbells, and annuals could stand a bit of fortification. I watered each with a powdered mix of 21-7-7 fertilizer. Any effect would be obvious by my next visit.

Wait to Make Design Changes

Not a year goes by without some species failing to live up to expectations, an old faithful beginning to fade, or an opportunity for change that I passed up returning to haunt me. Such feelings began to surface in early summer. Why hadn't I divided the Early Sunrise coreopsis and moved it all farther from its shading neighbors? How had it happened that other beds in the botanical garden had some spring color, while Bed Three was still holding out for high summer? The best answer to these design questions is a notebook. Early summer is not the time to make design changes.

Let Spring Work Bear Fruit

Transplants and recruits cannot take hold and make a significant difference now that the season of most rapid growth is past. In addition, disturbances now will affect the late-season bloomers, often for the worse. That can create a snowball effect ensuring that every remaining month will be disappointing. This is especially true in a garden that hasn't even had a full season's evaluation.

Make Allowances for Youth

New additions, even when made in spring, need more than a year to prove themselves. First, there is the issue of size. Even the very large new rues I'd found were significantly smaller than their established companions. They were full and bushy in bloom, but with only half the flowers and density I expect them to have next year.

At least the rues were blooming at the right time. They were container-grown but produced outdoors and still dormant when planted here. Thus their development was in synch with the existing inhabitants of Bed Three. Many garden-center purchases are started early in cold frames and greenhouses, to ensure the fullness and early bloom that will help them sell well in May. The Grecian foxglove was in bloom in June, but the grower might have started it early in a greenhouse. If so, it might bloom later next year, showing its colors in different company, and grown bigger as well.

That's why in late spring I curbed my desire to design. Better to make notes about which species flowered when and how well, whether colors that appeared together were pleasing or discordant, and what could be added or moved when the time was right.

Staking and Cutting

Notes can also help when it comes to amending or correcting maintenance work. I noted that Bed Three's oriental poppy was already "lodging" — stems falling outward — as it bloomed. So next spring, I would add a peony hoop or another support for the stems.

The golden marguerite finally came into bloom at the very end of spring, simultaneously thumbing its nose at two of the three staking arrangements. Growing and tangling at a rapid rate, it got way ahead of me during this period, requiring a return to the drawing board and leading to much grumbling on my part.

Saving a Spineless Wonder

The unstaked "control" marguerite had served its purpose by this time. It was already lodging before it flowered. This was not what I'd expected, having become accustomed to a fall after bloom. There's no accounting for differences in varieties beyond what the plant was bred for. In this case, *Anthemis tinctoria* 'Kelway' had been developed for large flower size and clear color. Taller stems with even more than the usual propensity to collapse might have been an unfortunate part of that genetic bargain.

I made a note for future reference: "For this variety, use 36-*inch* stakes and pinch it to keep it bushier." Then it was time to roll up my sleeves and fix the mess I'd created in underestimating these plants.

Picking up a fallen plant is laborious and, if not handled carefully, a waste of time. It has to be done while there's still hope for new stem and leaf growth and with respect for the stems to avoid bruising or worsening the tangles. Then, given a gentle touch, it can be roped into respectable limits and left to rearrange itself.

This rearrangement will take place quickly, within a week or two. The result will never be as graceful as if the stems had grown gradually up into or around well-placed supports, but the plant will pass muster.

After pounding a single stake firmly into the ground, outside the marguerite and toward the interior of the bed, I gathered a dozen of the nearest stems, coaxed them upright, and tied them securely but temporarily to that support. Next I gathered another dozen stems from farther away. I arranged them in an orderly sheaf (this meant clipping a few) and tied them up as well. Now I had two loops of string anchored to the bamboo cane, each holding ten to twelve bunched stems. I turned to the remaining tangle of branches to select the straightest. I bundled and tethered three more times, the last with long strings that let them belly away rather than snap from being pulled too tight.

I clipped away the rest of the low-level mess. Now I could build a webbed cylinder out of five bamboo canes and twine, as I described on page 89. This time, though, the stems were already grown, so my ball of twine had to weave in and out of the bundled marguerite. When the web was ready, I cut loose the restrained stems. They collapsed against the cords, seeming to gasp and reproach me.

It looked dreadful. Flower stems were bent like elbows at the top of the plant. Those right-angle turns had developed to lift buds up from prone branches that were now vertical. Still, the plant was upright, and it was young. It would find "up." I turned my back on it and looked to the others.

Beg Forgiveness and Cut

Two plants could be fixed with clippers and additional stakes. I removed the lowest and widest stems at ground level, coaxed a few to bend in and up rather than out, and added string to restrain others that wanted to make a break. The third and fourth plants were total losses. My twig stakes had not borne the weight. The stems had collapsed in a heap and taken a neighbor down with them. These two plants were wedged in between other marguerites and the 'Lambrook Silver' artemisia. In that spot, there was too little room to maneuver or hope that a respectable result could be achieved.

I tried anyway, for the camera and to figure out how long it would take. Then I put them and me out of our misery, as I would in my own garden. In short, I chopped them off a few inches above the ground and erected new supports for the growth that would come later.

Plants Are More Forgiving Than You Think

If you have never cut back hard in late spring or early summer, the idea is tough to accept and even more difficult to implement. "What if it dies?" is the most common stumbling block, but it may also be the key to making the most of this technique.

I learned to cut back hard because I faced instances in which it made no difference to me whether the plant lived or died. My first subject was a perennial bachelor's button (*Centaurea montana*), but later I operated the same way on columbine (*Aquilegia* hybrid), on golden marguerite, and on other species that tended to look terrible after they bloomed. In later years I was harsh with plants that hadn't bloomed yet but had been damaged in a storm or similar knock-down disaster. Balloon flower (*Platycodon grandiflorus*) and globe thistle (*Echinops ritro*) are examples. In each case, the plant was disgracing the garden, was not so rare that it couldn't be

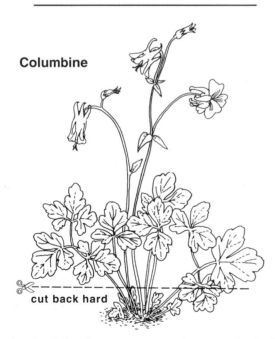

Columbine

cut back hard

Cutting back hard removes more than one-third of a plant's foliage. The dotted line indicates a hard cut on this columbine. For some problems, I cut hard to remove disfigured or pest-infested foliage. The garden is neater right away. If the cut is made before high summer, the plant has time to recover.

replaced, and caught my eye when I was in a hurry. I whacked it back to a foot tall or within a few inches of the ground — whichever worked best to improve the appearance.

There was no worry in my mind, just relief at the neater vista. Finding that the plant had grown back was a pleasant late summer discovery. In the case of spring-blooming species that make such a quick descent to shabbiness, there is a second surprise. Treated this way, they sometimes produce a second crop of flowers in late summer. These blooms are never as numerous or as large as the first crop, but they are welcome nonetheless.

Late bloomers cut back ahead of season sometimes act as if pinched. They bush out and bloom later than normal.

The dianthus in this bed is a good example of cut-back recovery. Although it had been cut to nubs in spring, within a month it began to bloom beautifully.

After years of whacking away at my plants, getting bolder all the time, I've developed a firm opinion: **If cut back before summer begins, most perennials have enough fine weather and time to produce and mature new foliage before fall.** Perhaps the plant isn't as big the following year as it would have been if left unpruned, but I haven't noticed that it makes a significant difference. Besides, those that most often need cutting back are rampant growers that call for restraint.

Sometimes You Don't Know a Plant Until You've Killed It

This is why, when the oriental poppy had finished blooming, before it had even turned yellow, I cut it off at ground level. This is contrary to all the advice about letting the foliage of species with summer dormancy die back naturally to finish replenishing their roots. After weighing the pros and cons and watching poppies for a while, I felt I could make my own choice about the best compromise between the poppy's needs and mine.

Look at an early summer poppy, making the usual post-bloom poppy mess. Imagine that it's surrounded by cannas just beginning to pack on some leaf. Isn't it high time the cannas got some space? As for the long-term effects on the poppy, I've noticed that one run-of-the-mill oriental poppy may store enough energy in its roots to be five times larger the next season. If, as in this bed, there is no room for a fivefold increase in poppies, some reduction in energy this summer can save time next spring. Then, there will be less need to reduce the plant's spread.

It's part of the "what can you lose" philosophy, which falls under the umbrella of "you don't know a plant until you've killed it." Once you see how far you can push a plant, you can predict its behavior better.

That's what growing, maintaining, and designing is all about — predicting plants. Whenever there's an opportunity, try pushing a species to the limit. See, for instance, how much shade or sun it can take and what it looks like under that condition. When you have some extra plants or divisions on hand, plant them in some "wrong" places or treat them in unconventional ways. All this will make you a more confident gardener and designer.

I'm amazed at the differences between plants grown in deep soil compared to the same species grown in compacted soil, the diseases that occur on a plant when it's too wet but never appear when it's drier, and so on. Sometimes a site that seems perfect turns out to be less than ideal for unexpected reasons. How will we ever know if we don't conduct a few trials? Just because balloon flower grows well for me in full sun doesn't necessarily mean it needs full sun. It may be that sharp drainage or rich soil is the critical element for success.

When people ask me whether they can grow a certain species in a given site, they have often already made up their minds to plant there. They may even ask me to plant or design for them. At times I have to contradict or sell a different species. My argument is more convincing if it's a testimonial to how the flower and leaf will look there as opposed to somewhere else. Facts pay off — any extra care it may need, whether it will bloom at the expected time, and so on.

Grooming the Prima Donnas

Late spring was a peaceful time overall. I pinned down problems and did what I could to alleviate symptoms. It was easy to keep up on the water and pull a bare half-

bucket of weeds. I made dozens of notes about what to do differently next time. Still, there was plenty of time to play the game I call "gardener in white gloves."

Many of us have seen paintings or movies in which the gardener, usually on a spacious estate, ambles down the lane, basket in one hand, clippers in the other. Spotless white gloves gesture here and there, pointing out to a comely companion all the delights of the garden. A few snips here, a graceful stretch or two, and the work is done.

That's what deadheading, pinching, and other grooming can be. Of course, it can also be done with a string trimmer and debris carried out by the cartload. I'll save production grooming methods for later this year, when it's time to talk about reducing maintenance. Now let me cover the conventional technique. That will prepare you to make your own choices later on.

Clipping a Billowy Edge

The artemisia and rue were threatening to tumble out onto the lawn — a romantic look but a nightmare to maintain — so I clipped both of them back. Say I had left that *Artemisia* 'Lambrook Silver' to billow over the edge, what would have happened next? The person mowing the lawn may have run it over or taken pity and swerved around it. Either way, I would lose

Unless the mower blades were extremely sharp, the artemisia would not only be clipped, but some of its stems would be yanked and torn as well. During this period, thunderstorms were rolling through this area frequently, and the lawn was growing like pasture. No doubt the mower blades were not especially sharp after laboring through the tall, wet lawn.

Then there was the chance that the mower would swerve. My softhearted husband used to do that, even though I begged him to mow down anything that had escaped my clippers. After the swerve, the lawn would become long and ragged under the branches of the perennial. Grass would quickly poke up through the perennial's foliage, and the edge would no longer be romantically billowing. It would be downright shaggy.

There was something worse: lawn roots are fueled by this extra leaf surface and made comfortable by the cool shade beneath the perennial. They would probe much farther into the bed than they would have otherwise.

I had another incentive to cut the rue. It's one of a number of species that produce oils within their foliage. The oils protect the plant against heat. The same oil increases sunburn potential for humans. If a bare-legged person brushes against the rue on a hot day and then stays in the sun for several hours, he or she might wake up the next morning with second-degree burns on that leg.

Crowding and Mavericks Fixed in a Slash

The Carolina lupine was becoming pushy by the end of June, leaning out over the oxeye, which in turn threatened to flop forward onto the lawn. Wondering why I hadn't noticed this earlier, I reached in and snipped off the guilty Carolina lupine branches right at their bases. This left complete, leafy stems rather than stubs. It also gave me a stack of five-foot branches to carry away rather than many smaller pieces. The stack on the lawn looked tremendous, but I'd removed only about 10 percent of the plant's leaf surface. That is hardly a serious reduction.

At the other end of the bed, the lamb's ear had to be saved from itself, much as the oxeye needed saving from the taller, more aggressive Carolina lupine. One stalk of lamb's ear began to extend skyward, a normal development in most lamb's ear but not welcome here. This lamb's ear is the variety 'Silver Carpet'. It was selected because it doesn't develop flower stalks. Although it doesn't bloom, it lacks the height and ragged postbloom look of its parent. It remains a low, gray carpet all summer.

The piece that was preparing to bloom was a maverick, a throwback to the species. Until then, it had masqueraded well as 'Silver Carpet', but as soon as it showed its true colors, I cut it loose from the crowd and removed it, root and all.

Many other perennials are known to revert: variegated forms of ajuga (*Ajuga repens*), hosta, or snow-on-the-mountain (*Aegopodium podagraria variegatum*) often revert to green; 'Red Baron' blood grass reverts to the taller, less colorful species; 'Moonbeam' coreopsis, with its pale yellow flowers, sometimes develops taller stems with brassy yellow blooms similar to 'Golden Showers'. All go under the knife in my gardens.

Pinching: A Crazy Way to Say Cut!

The closest I came to pinching anything in Bed Three was to wish I'd pinched the golden marguerite. That's the spring and early summer treatment given to mums, asters, and others to promote bushiness and delay flowering. Once, and still in some circles, it implied careful removal of the growing tip from each main stem, using small snips or thumb and forefinger. However, what I learned and see practiced in nursery fields is "Shear three times by the Fourth" (July 4). I use my hedge shears to cut mums back by one-third of their height. When I'm done, I laugh and say they're "pinched."

Now stand up straight and get that crick out of your back. About the only other thing of note I did in late spring was to take spent flowers off the potentilla. Since there's so much more of that routine coming in early summer, we might as well go there now to talk about deadheading.

Deadheading, Pinching, and Managing Problems

THE WORK THIS MONTH began the second week of July, a time when my calendar date and the floral date probably coincide across most of the country. Yucca (*Yucca filamentosa*) was at peak bloom, along with Shasta daisy (*Leucanthemum × superbum*) and perennial baby's breath (*Gypsophila paniculata*). These three and dozens of other species were trying very hard to look just like their catalog pictures on July 10.

July should have been a low-input, high-output time. For a little of my energy, there would be many flowers. Mother Nature kept her part of the bargain, but I couldn't seem to get a break. Although the schedule called for just one July visit, circumstances changed that.

On July 9, ten days before I had planned to visit Bed Three, a colossal storm rolled across the region, cutting straight through the botanical garden. Never one to wait for bad news, I made a dawn visit the next day to assess the damage. I was glad to see that the plants had weathered the storm virtually without harm. All there was for me to do was to pluck a few weeds and clip some spent flowers.

Then, during the scheduled visit on July 19, news came to me about an annual horticultural conference. On August 4, hundreds of extra people would converge here to attend lectures, take guided tours, and admire the garden. Putting myself in the horticulturist's place, I saw every good reason to want each bed touched up just before the big day. If my original schedule was kept, Bed Three's grooming would be nearly two weeks old at that time. So I added a special visit to fine-tune the picture for the celebration.

All things considered, these unscheduled visits were welcome. Bed Three put on its most spectacular makeup in July, and I was there to see it. Which is what most of us want from our gardens!

Neatness Makes a Good Garden Great

I've seen great gardens descend into shabbiness in the space of three or four weeks. It generally happens in July, right after the first hot, humid weekend of summer, when the spring flowers ripen their seed and lie down to rest. It so happens that muggy time also marks the beginning of a great green bloom of weeds.

The ragamuffin look seems to pop into place overnight, although it's a 10-to-14-day slide. Seeds germinate in the second half of June and stall a bit if there's hot, dry weather. Then, with the first thunderstorm, they get a glutton's dose of water and nitrogen, so they seem to explode. Out of curiosity, a few weeks earlier I had left a 3-inch-wide purslane where it was, hidden at the foot of the moor grass. In mid-July it was almost 8 inches wide and full, like a sheared rhododendron.

This change is most startling to gardeners who mopped their brows and celebrated their successful spring by taking a short July 4th vacation at the lake. What a shock to return to suddenly weedy beds, where every unmulched spot sports its rug of crabgrass, purslane, oxalis, and other heat-lovers. After a bit of weeding, a busy pair of hand pruners can easily revive a forlorn July bed. It just takes a gardener who is not afraid to cut away the tattered edges and excess.

Grass Shears Come in Handy

For me, a visit full of cutting started with the edge of the lawn. This had sprinted to full height and sprawl in several hard-to-mow spots, making a fringe along the perimeter.

Whenever I spend time on lawn before flowers, I recall a July interview I once had with a gardener. He had responsibility for perennials, shrubs, and lawn in one area of a well-loved public garden, where people commonly returned often and acquired great familiarity with particular spots. This can be a challenge to the caretakers, since even small inconsistencies may draw attention.

I asked about this gardener's maintenance priorities. He said that when pressed for time, he always cut the lawn first. That done, the perennial garden was less likely to attract any disappointed notice from his regular viewers. How true, and what an irony, that nothing makes a garden look better in passing than a neat lawn at its feet.

So I conducted my opening rounds with spade in hand, slicing the edge to neaten its shaggy profile as I made the circuit.

Lawn grass prefers to rest during the heat of summer, so edging is usually unnecessary in July and August, except to clip away at blades the mower missed. I wondered, though, whether any roots might have used their last bit of spring energy to run for cover under the bed's cool mulch. By setting the spade in deep and pushing the handle hard in toward the bed, I opened a window into the subterranean activity. Looking at the bed side of that open vee showed me there was no need to reach down and remove roots. What I was slicing off were rhizomes too small to carry on alone. Grass shears or a carefully handled weed whip could have served as well as my spade.

Hand Clippers: The Tool of Choice

On the subject of weed whips, also called string trimmers: it's not uncommon to see production-type gardeners on golf courses and large commercial properties use weed whips to deadhead (remove spent flowers). The pros and cons of that technique are addressed in Chapter 12, as a reduced maintenance option. For now, when you read "cut," imagine a hand with sharp pruning shears or scissors, because that's how it worked in Bed Three.

A Paltry Crew of Warm-Season Weeds

While checking the plants' health, I determined that the weeds were under control. Total pluckings barely filled the bottom of my bucket, and there were fewer than twenty weed plants in the whole bed two weeks later. All but one were warm-season seedlings readily identifiable as weeds: crabgrass, purslane, and oxalis. One, however, was a blackberry lily volunteer (a seedling related to one of the rightful residents of a bed). In early spring I had left it to grow in the hope that it would be short and yellow-flowered like the *Belamcanda* 'Halo Yellow' at its side. When it showed itself to be tall and then opened an orange flower, it had to be treated as what it was, a weed.

The soil moisture was taken care of by several storms and one hand-watering in late July. Most of the time, I was free to spend my time cutting.

Head Off Dead Flowers

Deadheading is done for one or a combination of these reasons.

- It makes the bed look neater, following the logic that if we can't have flower color, more green leaf is better than more brown seed pods.
- When developing seed pods are removed promptly, many perennials lose track of what they were up to and produce a second bloom. Although this second crop of blooms is never as big or as numerous as the first, it can be a welcome bit of color, coming as it does two to four weeks after a June or July cutting.
- Short-circuiting the seed crop can reduce subsequent weed problems. This applies to species that would otherwise drop seed all around. Left unchecked, such doting parents are often crowded out by their own unruly young.

No Sense Deadheading to Preserve Plant Energy

Sometimes I hear or read that deadheading saves seed production energy and lets a plant direct its resources toward building roots for the following year. Although this sounds logical, in the field it doesn't seem to make much difference. In general, seed-laden perennials in my own neglected gardens come back as strong the next spring as more carefully groomed celebrities in my clients' beds.

As for shrubs, lilac is probably the poster child for this cause. Yet if there has ever been a controlled test in which matched plants were deadheaded or not and flower production was rated in following years, it's well hidden. My own backyard hedge has defied that rule at least once, blooming to beat the band two years in a row without any attention from me.

Species known to be biennial to weakly perennial, such as Iceland poppy (*Papaver nudicaule*) and angelica (*Angelica archangelica*), may be exceptions but not worthy of special treatment on that account. At best, when growing Iceland poppy, deadheading will buy just one extra, weak year, whereas self-sown seedlings could have filled that next season with gusto. As for angelica, it will set an incredible amount of viable seed if you don't deadhead it. Gardeners learn to steal its developing seed pods to reduce the nuisance quotient, per reason three above. I don't use "preserving the plant's energy" as a practical reason to deadhead.

Three Ways to Flower, Three Ways to Deadhead

With apologies to my botany instructors, flowers can be classified from a caretaker's perspective. There are three types of flower arrangement, each deadheaded differently.

Category One: Individual Stems

The first deadheading technique applies when one or perhaps two flowers are borne on individual stems, that stalk being long enough to have hope for afterlife in a bud vase. Most often, the center flower opens and finishes first, followed by buds of side shoots that originate from low on the central flower's stalk.

In Bed Three, the mid-summer crop of this type of flower consisted of daisies, dianthus, and 'Early Sunrise' coreopsis. To clean up these plants and prod them toward continued production, I clipped off each faded flower's stalk just above a budded secondary stem. The daisies gave up half their flowers to the compost. The remaining heads looked brighter immediately. Three weeks later, all the remaining daisies were browning, so I cut them to the ground, leaving a scant few basal leaves behind.

Alternatively, I could have waited till that visit and shorn the lot to an inch tall. That wasn't acceptable, however, as it would have meant three weeks of shining white daisy ruined by an ever-increasing proportion of brown.

This daisy, *Leucanthemum* 'White Knight', didn't produce a second crop of flowers as some varieties do. 'Early Sunrise' coreopsis and 'War Bonnet' dianthus proved to be the dogged types that keep replacing cut color all summer. The bright red dianthus I had clipped were the second flush of the season.

DEADHEADING CATEGORY 1: INDIVIDUAL STEMS

Coreopsis lanceolata varieties such as 'Early Sunrise' belong to deadheading Category 1. This branch at left was never deadheaded, so you can see the pattern of flowering and deadheading. Ripe brown seed pods (1) mark stems that flowered first. The next flush of bloom came on stems where seed pods are now ripening (2). The third crop of flowers (3) is now fading and buds
(4) are ready. The stems holding buds will grow up as buds open into flowers. Bars mark where each stem would have been cut to remove a flower as it faded.

DEADHEADING CATEGORY 2: CLUSTERED ON A STEM

cutline

cutline

cutline

A

B

C

'Golden Showers' coreopsis (A), lychnis (B), and penstemons (C) are in deadheading Category 2. Shearing coreopsis along the arc shown by the cutting line removes spent flowers and developing seed pods and leaves flower buds lower on the stems to develop for second bloom. On lychnis, a stem is removed when all flowers on it have finished blooming. On penstemon, leaves grow only at the base of the shared stem. Bar indicates where deadheading cut is made.

Category Two: A Cluster of Pods Per Stem

The second deadheading arrangement is where flowers are clustered close on one stem, or on side stalks so short off a single stem that one bud can't be exhibited au naturel in a vase. Some species in this group have individual blossoms large enough to be plucked off one at a time as they fade, and the stem comes out with the last bloom. Most, however, are ushered out in a group by removing the whole stem when all the members have pooped out or are nearly done. The cut can be made just above the first sizable, good-looking set of leaves below the flower.

The rue and 'Lambrook Silver' artemisia were candidates for clipping. I sheared these two rather than clip a stem at a time, shaving several inches off their upper surfaces at a point where attractive foliage would remain and a minimum of stubs would show. Later in the summer, 'Golden Showers' coreopsis would receive the same treatment.

It surprised me that the rue kept opening new flowers all summer. They're attractive in a shy, yellow-green way. Rue had always been just a foliage plant in my mind, lumped in with the artemisias, whose inflorescences don't light up many eyes. But whereas artemisia pollen can stuff up allergic sinuses, rue flowers are essentially inoffensive and so were welcome.

Arkwright's campion (*Lychnis × arkwrightii* 'Vesuvius') is in this category. It almost kept pace with the dianthus and 'Early Sunrise' coreopsis for repeat flower production. Deadheaded in mid-July, it already had a new topknot of brilliant red-orange flowers by the end of the month. Several times during the season, I wished for a bigger patch of this cheery performer.

The oriental lilies (*Lilium* 'Tristar' and 'Red Night') and daylilies fit into deadheading Category Two. The lilies warned me on July 10 that they would open their last two flowers over the next week, and the daylilies offered some played-out stalks for plucking on July 31.

Oriental lilies have leaves all the way up the stem. Especially when new to the bed, as these were, they need every leaf to build a sizable bulb for the following year. So when the last flower shriveled, I snapped off the stem just above the top leaf. On older clumps in my own yard, I often cut long, budded stems of lilies for a

vase as early as July 1. That means many leaves come off way before they can do the next-generation bulb any good. However, in a five- or seven-stem clump, taking one whole shoot isn't as much of a setback as removing 6 inches of leafy stalk from a 20-inch tall, one-stem youngster.

Some daylily varieties will bloom again if deadheaded, but not 'Fire Cup'. Daylilies also refrain from throwing seed wildly, so there was no concern about losing the bed to a mob of daylily seedlings. When I slid my cutters down the spent scape and pinched it off within the concealing mound of foliage, I did so for neatness alone.

Bed Three's little penstemon (*Penstemon barbatus* 'Prairie Fire') is also in this deadheading category. It made its only demand of the season when it needed flower removal in mid-summer. Its flower stalks have no sizable leaves, so as each one finished showing off its bunch of scarlet tube flowers, I cut the stem at ground level.

Category Three: Spikes

Flowers lined up in a spike, or on very short stems in that elongated cluster called a raceme, usually have a peak that keeps on growing and setting more buds. Technically, this arrangement is called a *terminal inflorescence*. In this group, spent flowers are "left below" to develop into seed pods while the newest flowers are opening at the tip or "terminal." Not being shy of assigning human characteristics to plants, I view this as a sneaky plant tactic to keep us from deadheading. The foxglove stalk had been blooming for three weeks and become decidedly ugly on its nether end. But cutting it would eliminate all flower, wouldn't it?

Not true. Our Grecian foxglove behaved like most in this group. On July 10, I snipped a still-attractive spike off one of the three foxgloves. It obliged by extending side shoots from below the cut, forming several spikes where one had been. By the 19th, it already had seven blooming side shoots in action, and the stub of the original spike was hidden by this new growth.

Once the initial flower is clipped, dramatic spires become less so, as all second crops on perennials are reduced in size and show. Yet the color does continue longer if the cut is made. The gardener has to decide when the original spike has reached a point of diminishing return, when smaller but cleaner groups of flowers would be preferable. Consider my first-clipped foxglove, compared it to its untouched fellows.

Ten days after the cut, the clipped plant no longer terminated in a spire but in a cluster of smaller spikes. At that point, its untouched companions were more dramatic, if a bit seedy. Two weeks more, and the multitipped plant was still showing its stuff in neat fashion, but the two controls were single 12-inch spikes with three or four flowers at the tip and a host of knobby seed pods below. I called an end to the demonstration then and clipped the ungainly singles. My conclusion was that I could get a month of good color from the foxgloves and that the best time to head back the spikes would be midway through the show.

This conforms to my standard routine for terminal flower clusters: **When there is a greater length of seed pod on the spike than there is fresh flowering stem, cut it.** Put another way, when the seed pods outnumber the flowers, the majority has ruled itself out of the game. This seems to keep the first show going as long as possible without missing the period during which the plant has an inclination to fuel good secondary shoots. The control foxgloves, left to flower uncut until they had 80 percent seed pod to 20 percent bloom, produced only a few widely spaced side shoots in August. This was nothing like the dense gang of second shoots the first cut plant loosed in July.

Uncooperative Types

Some species don't form secondary spikes. Carolina lupine is one that I'd never experimented with before, always letting it bloom out. Deadheading it as I did even before the end of its run (see the systemic insecticide episode in Chapter 7), it occurred to me that here was a chance to see if it might produce a second show.

Side shoots came rapidly from below the cuts and for a month they kept me in suspense, waiting for flower buds. Nothing came of these laterals except leaves, however. That doesn't mean it couldn't happen, as many species that aren't expected to bloom again do

DEADHEADING CATEGORY 3: SPIKE-TYPE FLOWERS

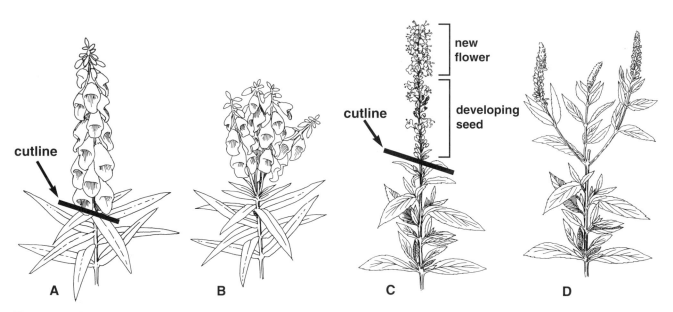

Foxgloves (A&B) and veronica (C&D) are in deadheading Category 3. The foxglove flower cluster has a more pronounced spike before any deadheading (A) than it will later in the summer (B). When veronica (C) has less new flower than developing seed, it is deadheaded as shown. In two weeks, secondary flowering shoots have developed (D). Drawings are based on actual photographs.

pull that trick out of their hat on occasion. The difference between these species and foxglove, Veronica (*Veronica* species), perennial sage (*Salvia* species), mullein (*Verbascum* hybrids), and others is that the latter are worth deadheading for the sake of prolonging the color show. Those that aren't reliable in repeat performance merit clipping just for neatness' sake or to prevent willful seeding. These can wait for "tonsure" until the last flower has fallen.

Deadheading with an Eye for Future Glory

On some species, I skip the clipping altogether because attractive seed pods will form in a month or so. Blackberry lily is one, opening capsules the size of fat pea pods to display the glossy black seeds that give it its common name. Some seedy types can even take the edge off a winter scene. Moor grass (*Molinia caerulea* 'Sky Racer') produces a shimmering fountain of tiny flowers in mid-July, but is most showy in winter when its wiry stems carry tan seed heads.

There are always some short-lived perennials in a bed that should be allowed to set a bit of seed, if the volunteers can continue the show when the parents check out. Foxglove, whether biennial or perennial, qualifies, and I planned to leave the last few flower stalks in Bed Three in place.

Some gardeners design and maintain with an eye toward providing food for birds and small mammals. It's common to see purple coneflower (*Echinacea purpurea*), blue globe thistle (*Echinops ritro*), and queen of the prairie (*Filipendula venusta*) indulged to the seed stage for the sake of attracting a goldfinch or chickadee. This is one point where a gardener's goals might conflict. It's nearly impossible to keep a garden both neat and attractive to birds.

This added dimension is not without cost. Blackberry lily stems often collapse under the weight of their developing seeds and are best staked against this possibility in any high-visibility garden. That's a laborious task. Each stem is tied to its own carefully placed stake so that the flaring lines of the clump aren't disturbed. Then the ripe seeds bounce and roll all over the bed, germinating quickly, so much so that the black-

berry lily rated a mention on my early spring list of weeds. In contrast, moor grass rarely causes problems as a volunteer. Thus each gardener has to make choices about the relative worth of a seed pod.

The perennial maintenance chart in Chapter 14 indicates species that can be considered attractive in seed. Since aesthetic value is subjective, it's always better to let an unfamiliar species do its thing for a full year in your garden while you make up your mind. After watching both flower and seed stage, you'll know which maintenance path to take.

A Few More Stakes

The crocosmia covered with brilliant red-orange, arching spikes, caught my eye as I made my initial rounds in mid-summer. The whole plant profile attracted my attention more than the flowers. The outer stems were spreading wide, maybe too wide for the good of the sedum at its side. If this sprawl continued, I thought, any chance that sedum had for putting on a good show in September would be over. Crocosmia leaves were hanging directly above the sedum, like sword blades. Those blades wouldn't slice off any sedum, just cause enough shade to distort the growth. You saw this all on page 23.

Leaning stems of crocosmia are staked singly. Insert a stake so that it is well anchored at the desired stem angle. Then gently draw one stem to the stake and tie it in.

Although I'm not a big fan of staking, I've come to realize that a gardener should never approach a flower garden in July and August without stakes and string. Thus a package of 6-foot bamboo canes and a ball of twine are part of my standard summer kit.

Staking plants like crocosmia so late in the season is tedious and expensive in terms of stakes. Select the stem that needs support, insert a stake next to it, push the stake in at the desired angle, and then tie it to one stem. There should be no bunching of stems, just an effort to support the naturally graceful lines.

While I worked, repeating those steps over and over, a mantra developed in my mind to accompany the motions. "Next year in May, five minutes' work, one peony hoop. Next year in May, five minutes' work . . ."

Pinching and Primping

Normally, my first July visit would have been my last chance to pinch fall-blooming species to keep them dense or stall off bloom. But Bed Three had no pinchable fall flowers. Instead it called for several other foliage-reducing passes for other reasons. This was one of those perennial beds with a few characters that coped with mid-summer heat by loosening their belts, ties, and manners.

Form a Police Line

First, the oxeye ungraciously set its elbows on the rock rose - the same rock rose that was struggling back from herbicide damage. Even if the rock rose wasn't at risk I would have lifted and clipped the oxeye, however, as it had shifted to tumble forward onto the lawn two weeks later.

I removed some of the oxeye's lower branches and checked the remainder with a "police line," my term for a fence of stakes and string along just one side. This line had to be installed while the bulk of the plant was being held even farther back than the intended final position. When the temporary restraints were released, the plant rushed forward to both lean on and hide the barricade.

Oxeye is normally well mannered. I blamed its wayward behavior on the sprawl of Carolina lupine

and my slow reaction. Rather than condemn the oxeye to the stake next spring, my notes recommend cutting the Carolina lupine roots back even farther in early spring and clipping any oxeye-shading stem sooner in late spring.

On the far side of the bed, the golden marguerite slipped its stays and tried to smother two of the coralbells. After all I'd done to rescue those coralbells from weevils, one might think I would have noticed the situation as it developed in June. Yet it wasn't until mid-July that I snipped off the offending stalks at the base.

Normally quite mannerly, the moor grass followed its neighbor's act by draping itself over the rue. For this offense, it forfeited some of its widest blades, also cut off at the base.

A Bow to Nature's Final Say

In the last chapter I advised, "Go ahead and cut it back hard. It's always worked for me." Now, I have to bow to Mother Nature's knack for putting a cocky, impatient gardener in her place.

July 1995 was the hottest on record for this region, with temperatures over 100°F by day and nights nearly as hot. In severe heat, leaves wilt even on drought-tolerant prairie species such as oxeye. This is a defensive move that prevents excessive water loss through the leaf pores (stomata). It's a fact of life that plants must have balanced amounts of sun, water, and carbon from the atmosphere to photosynthesize. Once the stomata close to prevent water loss, gas exchange through these pores falls off, too. The net effect is that when temperatures get too high, many plants stop growing. In this case, it dulled Bed Three's show.

I had cut back one of the golden marguerites and sheared the 'Lambrook Silver' artemisia just prior to the heat wave. They revived so slowly that they were aesthetic liabilities. I hope you'll still be brave enough, and cut back hard if neccessary.

In contrast, the poppy, growing from energy stored in the roots, reappeared just two weeks after I cut it hard in early summer. Throughout July's heat, thunderstorms came frequently. The *soil* in Bed Three was porous and accepting of such downpours, so it stayed cool enough to coax the poppy along. When those poppy sprouts got a taste of the hot *air*, growth ceased and didn't resume for a month.

You'll recall that the dianthus was damaged by rabbits in late spring. Though cut to the ground as if by a lawnmower, it enjoyed a period of clement weather in which to repair itself. Thus it was full again and blooming by early summer and putting on a second show in July.

I assured the elemental forces that their lesson wasn't lost on me, swearing that I wouldn't again cut back hard if I had any inkling that a heat wave was coming. Still, as if to reinforce her point, Mother Nature made sure that the uncut golden marguerite soon straightened its horizontally grown but vertically staked stems. Thus the ungainly appearance that had prompted the cutbacks was corrected naturally within two weeks.

Daylily Reflections

This kind of year is what makes some people switch to perennials. Prolonged bad weather or poor judgment may ruin an annual display for the season — no second chance for those plants. The same trouble can't stifle the perennial gardener's rallying cry, "Wait 'til next year!" Even though a perennial has an off year in terms of bloom or leaves disfigured by pests, as long as it's green at all, it's plotting its comeback.

The very unpredictability of the process keeps me coming back to learn a little more. The daylilies in Bed Three provided such a surprise lesson.

My early summer notes regarding the daylilies say that the plants promised to stage a good show, "25–30 buds per stem." In mid-summer, my reminder popped up from early spring: look for any long-term effects that might be linked to my removal of frost-damaged daylily tips. I checked the plants and wrote, "No difference, those cut back in April. All have same numbers, flowers, and leaves."

Deadheading the plants at the end of July, I also removed some deteriorating foliage. I made a note to use two plants that had cleaner foliage than the others when it came time to divide and replant that area.

Most daylilies beg for removal of unkempt leaves in late summer. That's why it's a noteworthy feature when a variety "exhibits clean foliage after bloom." It's also standard procedure to use the best individuals in a stand when propagating. Everything was proceeding normally, getting no special notice from me. Yet a gem of information was there waiting to be seen.

Delight in Discovery

During the thoughtful season, fall, I finally saw the possible connection between spring work and summer performance. I had expected and been looking primarily for some difference in the daylilies' finished height or flower production, since the leaf surface had been reduced early on. What may have occurred, unlooked for, is that the two cut plants developed fewer leaf diseases in late summer. A close look at my notes, bolstered by photographs, proved that the two plants I had singled out as cleaner of leaf were the same pair cut in early spring.

Every spring, there are new ideas to follow up. It may take years to find out whether the following explanation fits: Frost-damaged portions of foliage die. Opportunistic fungi, types too weak to invade healthy leaves, move in and devour the dead tissue. Later, as openings occur where snails chew or the gardener's movements bruise a stem, fungal spores are in place and waiting. Thus damaged foliage left on plants in spring may be a setup for the August uglies. Even though it's still a hunch, it has its parallels in other plant disease cycles. Now, I can weigh the disadvantages and possible advantages when the situation recurs. A minute's work per daylily in spring might reduce the leaf-removal chore in August.

Thinking Through Problems

On July 10, I sat drinking lemonade, admiring the bed and wondering about the monkshood and phlox. Both had better foliage now than two weeks before. Was that the effect of the fungicides? Perhaps it was too warm for those two pathogens to multiply? I removed fewer monkshood leaves than on any previous visit, gave the phlox a nod of encouragement, and made my notes for later consideration.

By July 19, whatever truce had been in effect

with the monkshood was over. Even its stems were dying now. By the time all the discolored leaves were off, the remaining stalks were 80 percent bare, with leafy tips but naked legs, called ugly ankles in some circles, though this was beyond the norm. On July 31, as I was clipping and setting aside more stems as contagious trash, it seemed to me that the plant wouldn't have enough energy left by fall to bloom. My notes reflect my dissatisfaction with all this work for only a scant chance of a show: "Definitely replace this next spring."

I'd seen no new weevil notching two weeks after the first occurrence but found some new damage after three weeks. I mixed another bucket of systemic insecticide and applied it under the phlox and Carolina lupine. At the same time, I made another note to remember the beneficial nematodes, to be introduced as preventive medicine in the fall.

The phlox got a second dose of quarter-strength fungicide solution. Up to this point, it had either helped or done no visible harm. It's rare to have a legitimate need for a pesticide in a well-drained, well-watered, well-pruned perennial bed. This year, the phlox got this little bit of help to set it on its feet. If it proved disease-prone the following year, the best answer might be to remove it and plant a different species altogether.

Some Insects Presumed Innocent

I hoped the fungicide and insecticide effects would be waning by the time the phlox came into full bloom at the end of the month. Otherwise, the moths, butterflies, bees, and hover flies that dropped in for the phlox nectar or pollen would be taking on poison, too.

There were so many insects in the bed! This unusual summer had already been dubbed an entomologist's and plant pathologist's dream. It wasn't the number but the variety of insects and diseases that was responsible for this excitment. And although some trees were laboring under record lecanium scale or plant bug infestations, for the most part a passerby wouldn't notice anything different.

Gardeners in the habit of sticking their faces into foliage were buzzing with new discoveries.

Some of what crawled or flew past me while I swigged lemonade were generally identifiable as leaf-sucking plant bugs or leaf-eating larvae. Beyond that, they were a mystery. They were neither common enough to be listed in my references nor numerous enough to make any control necessary. It was primarily a sideshow, and perhaps a bit of extra help. Probably a fair number of the strange insects in the bed were preying on other unknowns, plus eating a few of the regulars that were so nicely in check that July.

Those Elusive Voles

In early July, a darting, ground-level motion and then a rustle in the 'Lambrook Silver' artemisia caught my eye. It was a vole, a dark gray meadow rodent with smaller ears, a shorter tail, and a larger body than its mouse relatives. It eats plant roots, foliage, seeds, and bulbs. I had noted the presence of voles in early spring, when I'd spotted a tunnel beneath the moor grass. This had prompted my caging of the lilies.

Perhaps at some level I knew that it had been a mistake to assume that the vole presence would be minor. That's why I so readily caught and understood the movement in the bed. Indeed, voles may have been running around under my nose all summer, unnoticed until I slowed down. I once heard that if you see one vole, you can assume that there are thirty more you don't see. There's no telling whether this was true in Bed Three, but they certainly proved to be a problem that would make me regret my ignoring the matter in early spring.

By mid-July, the tunnels under the 'Lambrook Silver' were matched by tunnels and brazen entrance holes near the 'Silver King' artemisia, Carolina lupine, and monkshood. Still, it took a knock on the head in the form of vanishing lily and dianthus foliage to make me admit the depth of the problem.

By the end of the month, the oriental lilies had been plucked nearly clean. My notes blame this on rabbits, though with some wonder about how they could have reached so far between the wires of the cage. The dianthus, seemingly destined to be the fall guy among the newcomers, was again eaten back to nothing. Even while I was writing "rabbits!" in my notes, the voles were sitting in their dens, munching fresh-nipped lily and dianthus leaves.

In August, I watched a vole dart out and relieve a dianthus of another leaf, practically at my feet, and wondered, *How could I be so blind?* There was no answer, just a sigh over this new failing and a premonition that it wouldn't be the last.

On-site Pest Patrol

This was a sticky problem for a come-and-go gardener like me, since the practical options involved either traps or poisons. Traps would need daily tending to clear, bait, and reset. Voles prefer to feed under cover, so each trap would have to be set in a sunken, artificially covered vestibule adjacent to an entrance hole. If well placed, a trap can net more than one vole per day.

Poisoning meant the use of controlled substances that would have to be administered under the supervision of the horticulturist. Rodent poisons

---

Voles in the Artemisia

Voles eat plant roots, bulbs, foliage and seeds.

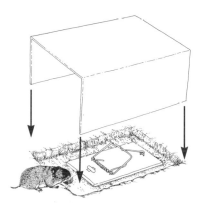

This mouse trap is placed in a depression at a vole's entrance tunnel and shaded with a box.

---

require great care in handling, especially in public places. Also, they're not nearly so effective when voles are numerous and surrounded by lush alternative foods. Thus traps were the initial choice, and all the work had to be done by someone who could make it part of a whole-garden, every-day vole hunt.

A Fall Alternative

The best time to act would have been early spring, baiting and trapping the voles when the population was low and very hungry. The next time to strike a really effective blow would be fall, by clearing away the mulch and other protective cover on the beds. With no foliage and less loose mulch to hide their activities, the voles would be highly visible to the resident red-tailed hawk. Perhaps some night-prowling cats and owls also would give us a hand.

Hear that perennial gardener's refrain? "Next year, I'll . . ."

Taking a Broader View

When things seem tough, it's important to look at what's going right. Overall, the bed looked good, now at its peak color.

Casual observers never noticed the voles. One visitor, an Australian, stopped to talk maintenance with me, and I remarked on the vole challenge. Surprised, he looked where I pointed and only then saw the signs so clear to me. He was so taken with this discovery, he waited around for quite some time. He was able to capture a vole on film and later sent a picture of it to me — my voles, internationally known!

The 'Silver King' artemisia, such a cause for concern in early summer because of the ants and side-effect aphids, was now looking great. The antworks under the lamb's ear were still keeping that area quite dry, but the plants showed much new growth by midsummer. There is nothing like a gray-leaved plant to bear up in the heat and drought.

The rescued coralbells were healthy and growing.

Two little girls asked for the flowers I'd taken off in deadheading and carried the bounty off as if each piece were made of gold.

When Water Becomes the Enemy

Another boon was that there had been plenty of natural irrigation this summer. Unfortunately, the gardening community at large wasn't as trusting as I was of soil moisture tests. In gardens all over my wide stomping grounds, I saw people responding to every day of heat-induced wilt by pouring on the water. Now, in beds that had received as much as 5 inches of irrigation water plus rainfall in just two weeks, the sad results were beginning to show.

Plants stressed by heat are not growing much leaf, as explained earlier. The roots are not growing, either. As excess irrigation water accumulates, displacing more and more air from the soil, roots are immersed in water, and they die from a lack of oxygen. Because no new root growth is occurring, lost roots aren't replaced. The plant becomes less able to provide enough water to its foliage during occasional breaks in the heat, and leaves begin to die.

Meanwhile, dead root tissue is open to colonization by root and stem rot fungi. In some gardens during that period of heat and overwatering, I saw even bog plants such as golden groundsel (*Ligularia stenocephala*) overwatered and flagging from root rot. These were tended to death, though they pled their cases eloquently by failing to come out of their wilt even during the cool hours after a storm.

Not Every Wilter Needs Water

In early summer, the lychnis in Bed Three resembled a puddle more closely than a plant. It was positively molten in the heat. My first inclination was to water, but instead I tested the soil around the plant. It was cool, capable of delivering water if the plant would only wake up. I set my wheelbarrow over it for an hour, and the minimally cooler bit of shade started bringing it out of its swoon. It would be fine, if only the heat would break!

Tough Love

The other thirty-two species in the bed were wondering what the trouble was with the fainter in the front row. Some species are so tough under adversity that we forget they're around. The moor grass, daylilies, coreopsis, yellow blackberry lily, purple-leaf sedum, artemisias, blood grass, and scarlet potentilla all went onto my list as real troopers that also knew how to dress up for company. Low-maintenance garden designs revolve around this caliber of plant.

Time Is Your Ally

On that 100°F day, even though my work in the bed had taken only thirty minutes, the notion of reduced maintenance was uppermost in my mind. While making notes about possible design changes, my inclination was to throw out every plant not in the "trooper" category. Stakes, overambitious creepers, vole delicacies, lackluster individuals, and sickly creatures all received the imaginary ax.

Yet that would have been premature, tossing out some plants that hadn't bloomed, forgetting the recent glory of some past their peak, and subverting the garden's primary objectives. It also would have been rash even to consider planting or transplanting in a heat wave. One of the reasons I chide myself about being an impatient gardener is because it's so clear that time is the designer's best ally. Wait a week or a month. Perceptions, plants, weather, and memory all will change.

Asked in spring or fall about when blood grass begins to color, my answer probably would have been "September, with the real show in October." Yet my notes show that it was beginning to color in mid-July. Those subtleties are worth designing for — a reward for putting off rash decisions. I held off on noting possible design changes and let the facts continue to accumulate.

It's always good to start with the positive characteristics of a garden. A summary of some of my July notes runs as follows: The bed peaks in July. We could use color in June to accompany the Carolina lupine. Probably there will be a fine show of foliage color in fall. The bed could use an adjustment to reduce the yellows and increase the red and oranges.

After ensuring that I'd recall the highlights, I could consider the problems, uncertainties, and possibilities more productively.

When Sun Becomes Shade

The far western end of the bed was in trouble in terms of showiness and meeting its objective to demonstrate the best use of various plants. To someone unfamiliar with the species involved or less demanding of plants in general, it would pass muster. Yet I recognized that plants there were beginning to thin out, lean more than they should, and flower below their potential. These are all subtle responses by sun-lovers to an increase in shade.

I had noticed several visitors during the season who had paused there to copy a species name from its label. Had they looked at the plant's location beneath the branches of a tree or seen them in that pool of afternoon shade and so recorded the names for their own shady gardens? Maybe, and that would be as unfortunate as allowing the plants to continue their fade.

So, Missouri primrose, purple-leaf sedum, and artemisia went on my list to be moved into the sun. My idea for using variegated cannas to accompany the poppies next year also came up for reconsideration, since the current cannas were not sporting any impressive number of buds per stem. A question about the floppiness of the crocosmia and Carolina lupine also nagged. Had these normally sturdy sun-lovers fallen away from vertical because they, too, had just a little more shade than they could handle? In the fall, when it was time to make changes, these thoughts would be added to all the others accumulated through the year and given their due.

Playing in the Garden

HIGH SUMMER — August in much of the country — starts with the white, fragrant blooms of *Hosta plantaginea* at their peak, waltzes through peegee hydrangea's show (*Hydrangea paniculata* 'Grandiflora') and the ripening of mountain ash fruit (*Sorbus aucuparia*), then exits to the scent of blue bush clematis (*Clematis heracleifolia*). It's the season of garden parties. They're thrown by gardeners with time on their hands, suddenly inactive people who realize the patio furniture purchased in spring has never been broken in.

Lightweight Gardening

Seriously, now, what's there to do in August? Nothing new, and very little in Bed Three. Weeds were few, there was no need to edge a heat-stalled lawn, the year's pests had already shown themselves and done their worst work, and rain once again took care of the watering. All that was left was grooming, a direct continuation of early summer's white-glove gardening.

Clippers in Your Pocket, Smile on Your Face

Spent flowers littered the lawn behind me as I worked and made for a colorful raking when it was time to clean up. The biggest variance from early summer's routine is that far more of the plants clipped now are getting their last trim for the season. When no more flowers can be expected to develop or production is limited to scant and tiny buds, it's time to stop looking at the plant as a flower producer. I scrutinized each shorn plant to judge whether it was handsome enough to pass on its own. Various additional cuts were called for, so that only clean foliage and a neat profile remained. I wanted no stalks left projecting, as these almost always turn straw brown and make the plant resemble a hastily stuffed scarecrow.

This is the time for gentle cuts and graceful exits, no cutting back hard (reducing a plant's leaf surface by more than one-third). Although some of my final deadheading approached that, it didn't go any farther than necessary to keep the subjects looking neat. My goal was that species no longer in bloom would contribute attractive foliage or form, or at least not detract from the shows in progress and yet to come.

If you cut a late-blooming species back hard in midsummer, the growth that follows may not have time to mature and set flower buds. For any species cut so hard in mid-summer, regardless of its bloom season, the strain of a comeback may affect the following year's performance. Should frosts come in early fall, the summer-grown foliage may not even have had time to repay roots for the energy drawn off since the cut.

You know all the terminology now and the history of this bed that allows you to read between the lines. So I'll let the diagram on page 128 tell you what was nipped and tucked.

Unstaking and Staking Again

After I removed its last flowers and neatened its foliage, the oxeye no longer needed a police line to keep its trim. I removed those stakes and tossed them onto the pile of bamboo reclaimed from the golden marguerite. The golden marguerite's final deadheading netted a pile of nearly leafless stems a foot or more in length. Once these were gone, the plants no longer needed support.

Those stakes went back in alongside a dozen main stems of the blackberry lily. This plant is not the late-blooming *Belamcanda flabellata* 'Halo Yellow', that cute half-pint with flowers in short-stalked, dense clusters, but *Belamcanda chinensis*, where the burden of ripening seed seemed about to topple the stems. Don't get me wrong. *Belamcanda chinensis* is a great plant. The fact that I repeated the tedium of single-stem staking already endured in July for the crocosmia should tell you how attractive this blackberry lily was. However, I couldn't chant any soothing mantra about preventive staking next spring. The plant's foliage and form are so clean until seed sets that any early supports would detract from it.

Speaking of the crocosmia, it finished blooming during this period. I clipped off each flower stalk at its leaf-sheathed base and stepped back to decide how the foliage looked on its own. I saw dramatic vertical lines for the most part — leaves worth keeping.

Some blades had fallen out of line, however. They not only presented a cluttered appearance but also were draping their tips and shade over oxeye and sedum once again. I'd staked these last month, but that was when the alternative — cutting out the offending stems — would have reduced the floral show. Now that there were no flowers to save, I cut to clear. This involved a much quicker series of actions: grasp a fallen stem, trace it to its base, and cut it out.

If you've ever planted crocosmia as a single tuber and nursed it through its first season as a skinny stem or

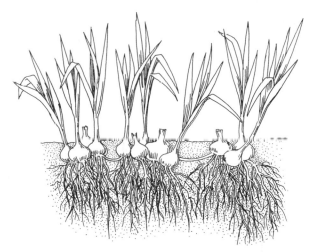

My late-summer prohibition against cutting off more than one-third of the leaf surface applies to whole plants. Up to 33 percent of whole stems has been removed from this crocosmia, possible because the colony has one common root system.

spare clump, it might be confusing to hear that I removed whole stems, right after hearing that you shouldn't cut back hard in mid-summer. The difference is that this crocosmia was one multi-stemmed entity, many tubers connected, whereas a young plant may have only one stem. Although my mid-summer work resulted in an impressive pile of crocosmia, consisting primarily of whole stems, the reduction of the overall colony was far less than 25 percent.

One staking assignment remained — the monkshood. In mid-summer, it not only produced flower buds but also offered a few new leaf buds, even at the bases of diseased leaves just removed. It wanted to provide a little color in fall. I wondered whether the spindly remaining stems were up to the task. The whole season of care might end as a tangled heap following a storm or freak wind. As insurance, I fenced it in with a rectangle of interlocking stakes.

Fertilizer: Not on the Menu

The golden marguerite cut so hard in late June was now blooming, but at a dwarfish 12 inches tall. You might think that July fertilization could have helped these plants to beef up or stretch farther, or that fertilization could still work that wonder in August. It's true that a water-soluble fertilizer *applied as new growth starts* can be helpful if soil nutrient levels are low. Remember, though, that heat stalled the growth of these plants and many others all through July. Air temperature was the inhibitor, not soil nutrient levels. At best, adding fertilizer would have been a waste; at worst, it would have contributed to excess soil salts.

From mid-summer through early fall, even though the weather may be gentle, fertilizer is superfluous. The plants' nutrient needs are much lower in high summer than in spring when they were building new leaf cells. They've set their full complement of leaves and flower buds by now. Some of those cells may still be expanding in late summer within unfurling cardinal flower, purple-leaf sedum, and the like, but they're already formed. Tossing fertilizer around is like giving vitamins to an adult with rickets-deformed legs. The vitamins won't change that condition, even though they might have prevented it years before.

Developing plant cells need energy. Energy comes from photosynthesis, not fertilizer.

Start of Prevention Strategies

Looking at the 'Silver King' artemisia in mid-summer made me think of harvesttime and overflowing cornu-copias. It also made me question my memory: was it really this year that this plant had had trouble with ants, aphids, and voles? Its bulk and distinctive foliage were among the bed's main attractions, even viewed from a distance.

It seemed a shame to harry this gray monarch, but it was leaning over the dianthus, shading them and denying them a full share of sun. If those poor vole-nipped dianthus were going to survive, they needed all the energy they could get, right away. Their red flowers and blue foliage had been an outstanding addition to the scene earlier in the summer. In hopes of keeping them, I removed the overhanging 'Silver King' stems with several ground-level snips.

Artemisia 'Lambrook Silver' probably would have been mirroring its cousin in any other year, but now it was only holding its own, still stressed by the vole tunneling. I removed a few dead branches and reinforced my notes about future antivole tactics.

At the end of the month, I introduced beneficial nematodes into the west end of the bed and near the coralbells. The product I used was Biosafe (see Appendix, "References and Tools"). I applied these weevil grub predators in a solution, sprinkling it on and then watering it in well.

Then I dusted off my barely dirty knees and packed up my tools for the month.

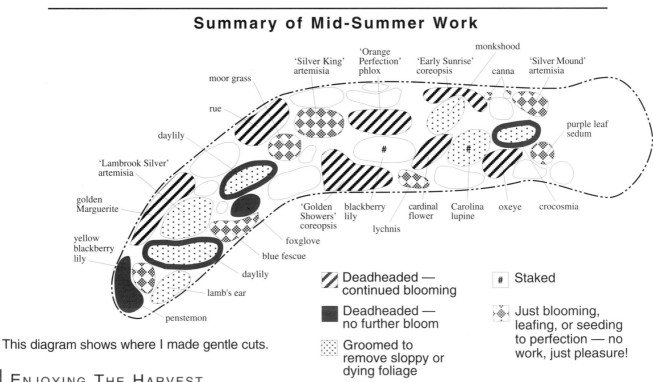

Summary of Mid-Summer Work

'Silver King' artemisia   'Orange Perfection' phlox   monkshood   'Early Sunrise' coreopsis   canna   'Silver Mound' artemisia

moor grass

rue

daylily

'Lambrook Silver' artemisia

golden Marguerite

yellow blackberry lily

purple leaf sedum

'Golden Showers' coreopsis   blackberry lily   cardinal flower   lychnis   Carolina lupine   oxeye   crocosmia

foxglove

blue fescue

daylily

lamb's ear

penstemon

This diagram shows where I made gentle cuts.

Deadheaded — continued blooming

Deadheaded — no further bloom

Groomed to remove sloppy or dying foliage

Staked

Just blooming, leafing, or seeding to perfection — no work, just pleasure!

Transplanting and Preliminaries to Closing

SUDDENLY, SUMMER IS GONE, and it's the last week of September. Japanese wax bell (*Kirengoshoma palmata*) and sweet autumn clematis (*Clematis maximowicziana*) are in full bloom. On the woods' edge, Virginia creeper vine (*Parthenocissus quinquefolia*) has begun to blaze, casting its distinctive ruby glow. In Bed Three, Japanese blood grass (*Imperata cylindrica* 'Red Baron') was warming up the first act of its fall show, half its green now gone to red and seeming to get brighter by the hour.

Most years, gardeners in my zone would begin watching for the first frost in a week or so. This year, that whisper of cold had its first conversation with the garden quite early just before I arrived. It rarely comes so early. The crocosmia foliage had gone a bit pale with the shock.

My priorities for this visit were cutting back and dividing. I knew that I might have to do some watering, weeding, and edging, but those tasks were all in the "should-do" and "might-do" categories. In late summer and early autumn, if there's time to spare after cutting back and dividing, I'm likely to let watering and weeding slide and opt for making moves and changes. Few things are as much fun as redesigning a garden on a fine fall day.

The Best Time for Moves

This is a great time of year for transplanting. With few exceptions, perennials, trees, shrubs, and even established spring bulbs are just beginning a period of strong root growth and can be moved without holding a grudge. Warm soil, cool air, and changing day length team up to keep leafy growth to a minimum, start energy flowing down into storage roots, coax all roots to stretch out for a wider hold, and warn woody stems to make ready for a long rest.

Plants moved at the leading edge of this groundswell have two months or more to settle in before winter, laying down anchor roots that will prevent their being heaved out of the soil by sudden freezes. Those plants also have at least two months' jump on April transplants, or three months' lead over typical spring additions. In short, moving and adding perennials and shrubs now is a good way to weather the edge of change so well that all the readjustment gripes are long forgotten by the next time the plant's prettier above-ground half comes up for review.

However large the root system is in spring, that's how large the canopy will be in summer. A 6-inch-diameter rootball relocated in fall may double in size by the next Memorial Day. A 6-inch potted perennial planted on Memorial Day will devote itself to top growth, an effort that will reflect the size of its roots at planting and no more.

Getting Grounded

According to tradition, all of the energy of the universe flows into the ground in early fall and rests there until spring. Perhaps you've noticed an invigorating charge that can drive gardeners to new heights of accomplishment in fall. Some people attribute it to the fact that we're in better shape after a season of working outdoors. Others say it comes from some primal instinct to finish our work and lay in stores before the cold weather comes. I think it comes from being out there when the energy begins to flow. We're in direct line for all the energy in the universe when we work in our gardens in fall.

Six Months to Settle In

Where do I come up with four or five months' growing time between an early fall move and spring? I'm not making it up, just pointing out what's going on behind the scenes in winter.

The uninitiated tend to think that plants stop growing when above-ground parts die back. The facade continues into the far end of winter, when we notice the first big show of leaf or flower and take it to be the starting gun for all plant development. Most northern gardeners learn the truth one bright February or March day when they're drawn outdoors. There they find that weed seeds have germinated and are growing in spaces known to have been cleared last Halloween. Buds are already swelling on some woody plants, and bulbs planted as late as last Thanksgiving have foliage that's already completed the 6-inch trip to the surface.

I did a lot of lifting and dividing in Bed Three back in early spring, so you know that early fall isn't the only time to move a plant. It just may be the best time.

When I came into the garden in early fall, I didn't even make the rounds. For weeks, since I'd made the last evaluative notes and written possibilities onto the summer diagrams, I'd been ready to make some moves, so that's where I started.

Making the First Move

Dividing, reducing, and replanting the daylilies was first on my list. Considering all the possibilities, I'd chosen this move because it would create some free space — that first opening in transplant dominoes. Also, the daylilies were neither contributing greatly to the fall display nor acting in a key supporting role to any of those that were currently starring.

As another illustration of how this works, cutting down and moving the Carolina lupine was out of the question. Even though that shaggy green hulk wasn't currently adding to the floral display, it was providing a great backdrop for the cardinal flower that still shone brightly. It also was helping the cannas to give the lower four-fifths of the monkshood some substance. If I had taken out the Carolina lupine, the most interesting acts in the early fall show would have been ruined.

I lifted the daylilies out of the ground, extracting rootballs that filled the wheelbarrow four times. I marked and set aside the two plants that I'd use to populate the new, reduced daylily area. One golden marguerite came out as well, the plant that had been so close to the edge that its first supporting ring had been pulled off by a mower.

After reworking the vacated sections and mixing in four wheelbarrows of compensatory compost, I split the two choice daylily clumps into five. Each had three or more *fans* (the foliage that rises from one growing point on a daylily crown). I laid these out in what had been the western of two daylily areas.

The foliage was still on these clumps, and I used it to judge how closely they might be planted to each other or neighboring species. When the divisions were set upright on the surface, the leaves still rose up and arced down at the tips as they had before. The foliage would spread that wide or wider next year, so I placed neighboring plants so that the leaf tips would just touch.

Planting these divisions was a repeat of the daisy episode in early spring (see page 74). Once each was in its place and ringed with a watering crater, I soaked them well and turned to the spot where the eastern cluster of daylilies had been.

Fitting Other Players into the Lineup

It was fun just to look at the eastern area. Not only had I been able to renew the soil there, but in the process I had reduced the spread of the 'Lambrook Silver' artemisia just enough so that I could dig safely into and scramble most of the vole habitat there.

Gardeners have always struck me as a gentle bunch. Yet I've seen in some the same Jekyll-to-Hyde transformation that I felt in dealing a blow to the voles. My Ms. Hyde was rubbing her hands together with glee.

Contemplating the effect of moving the purple-leaf sedum into this spot, my calculating Dr. Jekyll also was pleased. Here in the sun, near the blue-green leaves of 'Halo Yellow' blackberry lily, the glow of 'Elijah Blue' fescue, and the soft gray foliage of 'Lambrook Silver', the sedum could strut its stuff in style. Bringing it out of the shade took only a minute. The plants practically leaped out of the ground and onto my fork, as if they knew all about their glowing prospects.

There had been two clumps of sedum, and I'd split them in early spring. So in early fall, there were five clumps to work with, each larger than either of the original pair had been. Distributed across their new space, with leaf tips just touching on adjacent plants, four plants fit nicely.

Before settling on their final positions and planting them, I thought about the coming year, when this new foliage combination would sparkle all summer, with July flashes to the east and west when the penstemon and daylily bloomed red-orange. Everything about the picture seemed good, except the lamb's ear.

Recalling the threadbare appearance of that 'Silver Carpet' lamb's ear at midsummer, I decided to make an additional move. Even if that plant hadn't been beset by ants tunneling under its roots, there was a good chance it would have succumbed to a fungus-based meltdown during the hottest, most humid part of summer. The species is prone to this, perhaps because its furry gray leaves are best suited to dry heat.

Lamb's ear so affected almost always bounces back by summer's end. Yet the thought of such a visual distraction in mid-summer made me think of the scarlet potentilla (*Potentilla atrosanguinea*) on the north side of the bed. It had carried on in elegant form all summer. It had gray foliage and early, startling red flowers that could extend the color show in this revamped area. So the lamb's ear would drop out of the limelight in favor of the potentilla.

Dividing Just in Time

You first met the potentilla when I did, in early spring. It was a struggling loner and an unfamiliar species, so I'd set it into an appropriate spot to get to know it better. When I dug it in early fall, I was glad to see that its roots had increased dramatically. It would yield four or five pieces as large as the one I had moved in early spring.

The roots flared out and down from a central point. Near the center of a crown so tight it would have to be split with a knife, one longer, thicker root had formed and headed straight down. Some herbaceous potentillas and other perennials tend to form this taproot, which seems to become more important to the whole

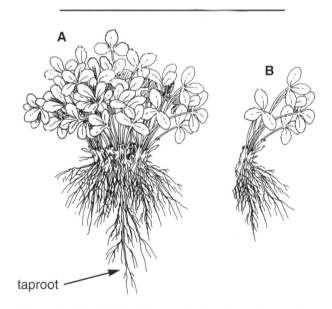

taproot

The potentilla (A) had begun to develop a taproot. Older plants with taproots tend to sulk when they are moved so it was good to divide this plant before the taproot developed any further. Using a knife it is easy to split the clump into divisions (B). The division with the taproot is best discarded.

clump as time goes by. In their old age, such species produce divisions that seem to sulk for an unreasonable amount of time after the split. They wilt and cry "Poor me!" if you so much as look at them cross-eyed.

The point is that although all plants tend to grow more vigorously when young, this factor is especially important to remember in relation to plants that develop a taproot. They fare better if divided more frequently.

To avoid working blind on that tight-knit bunch of roots, I shook and rinsed most of the soil off before proceeding. Then, using my folding knife, I sliced five times into the crown where the roots converged. I cut as if the horizontal plane of the crown were a pie and I was carving five fat wedges centered on that taproot.

Each wedge came away with its own roots and leaves, ready to make it on its own. I discarded the oldest root and cut the smaller divisions again to give damaged roots and ragged chunks of crown more clean-cut edges. Then they all went into a bucket of water to soak while I moved the lamb's ear out of the way.

With the lamb's ear settled in around the blood grass and its former area enriched and smoothed, I could lay out the potentilla. That involved some shifting of the sedum, which was waiting patiently above ground while all the other dominoes fell into place.

Staking After a Move

I was watering in the sedum and potentilla when I saw the wobble. The stems of the sedum, top-heavy with flowers and unbalanced after leaving some of their roots behind, were unsteady. Those branches were just inches from the lawn on both sides of the sedum's new space, exposed to feet and mowers. Given their relatively shallow roots, even a heavy rain might upend them if it came within the next month while the plants were settling in.

Cutting the stems back would reduce the chances of such an accident occurring, but I had intended to leave the transplants' foliage intact until later in the fall. As long as those leaves were attached and the plants could be kept from wilting, photosynthesis and fall's gradual transfer of energy to the roots would continue. Half that equation was in the bag, since heat, drought, and wilt were probably gone for the season. I decided to

As insurance against wind, rain, or stray traffic uprooting the transplanted sedum, I stabilized the outermost stems with bamboo crutches.

stake the stems for security. Short pieces of bamboo made fine crutches when stuck firmly into the soil and tied loosely to the main stems.

No Restrictions on Fall Cuts

This fussing with stakes was not essential. In similar instances, pressed for time or short on stakes, I have solved the problem with scissors or pruning shears. The plants wouldn't have died even if I had cut them clear to the ground.

By this time in early fall, perennials have been growing and storing energy for more than five months and have gotten their first cues from nature to get on with the process. New leafy growth slows or ceases. Root growth takes precedence in most species. Some years, plants enjoy a slow dissolve into middle and late fall. Other years, plants are reduced suddenly and early to the low foliage that survives frost by virtue of its proximity to a gentle radiator, the earth.

Gardeners can wait for the frost or take its place. The schedule called for leaving Bed Three essentially intact through October. Yet in this year, as in each of the past twelve, other beds under my jurisdiction would be closed for the winter as early as October 1, including all the drastic cutting you'll hear described in Chapter 12. I've had no regrets about any of these early closures, in subsequent springs. So if I had cut the tops of the sedum to protect the roots from upheaval, I knew the plants would not have held it against me.

Having observed the resilience of perennials after early frosts or cutting, I even had hope for the dianthus here. Although animals had cut them to evergreen nubs a month earlier, the roots would chug along under cover of the soil for two months or more while the leaves waited until spring to try again.

Great Expectations

Fall changes often please us more in the long run than do their vernal counterparts. All the extra time plants have to settle in before their next performance probably accounts for the greater dividends. There's also the added joy that comes from their appearance, as when an item long forgotten is suddenly rediscovered. Yet maybe there's something more to our pleasure than that.

When we plant or transplant in spring, visions of coming glory may impel us to inspect the garden for developments nearly every day. In fall, we're more patient, willing to let the plants go about their business. If plants can read and react to our emotional energy, as some research indicates, our continual attention in spring must be as wearying to them as daily telephone calls can be to expectant parents. Perhaps plants enjoy, and repay us for, the fall atmosphere of laissez-faire.

I applied this attitude to the oriental lilies. Animals had devoured all the foliage on two plants and most of the leaves on the third. I had little hope that they had made enough bulb to attain blooming size next year, but a pleasant spring surprise was possible. Rather than fret over this, I would just wait and see.

Other developments were more certain in their promise for spring. After removing and discarding the ill-fated rue that had been dug and replaced in spring only to be touched by chemical plant killers, I could shift the coralbells west. There they would have room to multiply and make a significant splash once again. When I saw their husky root systems, I responded a bit as a doting grandparent-to-be would, cooing over their progress and patting them indulgently into the new places.

At the far side of the bed, the myrtle euphorbia and rock rose bore some of the same promise. The euphorbia was finally showing significant new growth, and the rock rose had traded late summer's notable pallor for a healthier green. By spring, these plants and the coralbells could be particularly pleasant surprises, thanks to their evergreen foliage. The leaves would remain and keep working throughout the fall and even in the milder days of winter.

Renovating and Reclaiming

Early fall is the time to tackle beds or portions of beds if they were rated "hopelessly weedy" as discussed in Chapter 4. I rate an area hopelessly weedy when perennial roots have colonized there in a way that would make me happy if they were attached to plants that belonged in the bed.

This also happens when perennials that belong get out of hand and act the same way. A few days after finishing the work described in this chapter, I tackled a client's garden that I had rated hopelessly weedy. I had to reclaim it from a 'Silver Queen' artemisia that had spread around, under, and through rootballs of perennials for 5 feet in all directions.

Older perennial beds may not be hopelessly weedy but require extensive dividing, related amending and leveling of soil, and redesign. For such whole-bed and large-area renovations, I cut back the foliage and often reduce individual plant size. Be prepared for a shock. This work leaves the bed ready for and looking like winter more than a month earlier than other beds.

Step One: Lift and Hold Existing Plants

The first thing when renovating a bed is to lift all the desirable plants and stow them for a while. Pop up each plant with a respectable rootball and set it in a shaded spot out of the wind. It's now on hold for the better part of the renovation.

The holding period might last for hours, days, or even months depending on the state of the bed and your schedule. How you handle plants during the hold depends on the expected duration.

For renovation that can be finished within a few days, simply line plants up next to a hedge or on the north side of a building. Butt the rootballs up against each other to minimize the drying effect of the wind. If

---

Be Kind — Make Moves in the Fall

If you feel deprived by the early descent into wintery appearance that comes from early fall renovation, just remember it gives the plants the longest possible settling-in period. Often it's better for the gardener, too. Plants move well in early spring, but the season as a whole is already hectic without adding any extra work. Spring also brings such an onrush of plant top growth that you won't have any leeway for delays. Stall even a bit and you'll be far behind the plants.

Summer moves also have their disadvantages. Even if care is taken to keep the plants cool and well watered after the move, in that season they can't regain the grace they had before being disturbed.

I recall feeling sorry for about a dozen peonies we picked out of the ground and cleaned of scouring rush one July. That midsummer reclamation made sense in several ways. The owner had just moved in and had no attachment to the plants but did have a dread of scouring rush based on previous experience. There were many bearded irises in the bed, a species that responds well and even benefits from a July clean-up when borer grubs can be so easily dispatched. The neighbors had informed us that the bed also contained many tulips. Since tulips are dormant in midsummer, any that had to be disturbed would suffer the least possible trauma at that time. Finally, the weather was cool and promised to be overcast and damp for a few days following the work.

Still, the upset had the considerable drawback of robbing the peonies of grace. Although they recovered very well and bloomed the next spring, I will never forget the sight of their stems leaning at odd angles for the rest of the summer, as if rattled by an earthquake.

the hold drags on a few days and the weather is warm and dry, check the plants and add water as needed. To decide whether or not to water, feel the soil in the rootballs just as you would in a bed.

If any rootballs crumble in lifting or moving, line them up with the others and bank them around with loose soil or fallen leaves. Covering the rootball with plastic is another option.

It's not unusual for plants on hold in my garden to wait several weeks for final disposition. If you know the work will take a week or two, water any rootballs that come out feeling dry. Let any excess moisture drain away and then put them into large pots or plastic bags.

This also applies to plants with an uncertain future. The daylilies and other plants that would not be going back into Bed Three went into plastic garbage bags with a touch of water to prevent their exposed roots from drying out while the horticulturist decided their fate. Knowing that I would have to carry them away, I lightened the load by removing as much soil as possible from the roots.

Very long holds, even over the winter, sometimes are necessary. Consider digging a shallow trench somewhere nearby and "heeling" the plants into it. Set them in and cover their roots with loose soil or a combination of leaves and soil. It's okay to space the plants very closely, even with roots touching, so that many perennials can fit into a short trench. An alternative is to line the transients up in protected shade as for a short wait and mound soil over all the roots. Or rake leaves to make a 6-inch-deep blanket over and next to the rootballs and keep this blanket in place with weighted fabric, fencing, crisscrossed twigs, or a thin layer of soil.

Step Two: Give Weeds the Boot

While the bed is bare, loosen and replenish the soil. Remove all perennial weed roots. You can do this all at once, at the rate of about forty-five minutes per hundred square feet of bed. Or do it by smothering, if the resident perennials can be kept on hold for most of a season - this requires the least physical exertion.

I do all-at-once reclamation with a spade, cutting the bed into strips and then chunks as if the whole thing were an ear of corn. Every kernel is lifted and cleaned. Standing on still-weedy soil, I lift each chunk, tip it on its side onto already-cleared bed, bend down, and remove the weed roots, tossing them out onto the lawn for later raking. "Weed" here means all unwanted perennials with running or deep-seated roots, from the universally condemned quack grass to the often invited and later despised Canada anemone (*Anemone canadensis*) and hollyhock mallow (*Malva alcea*). Once you see them attached to their tops, you'll recognize them even as detached pieces. Until then, take out *all* roots.

I'm often asked about the effect this work has on bulbs already in place. The bulbs usually turn up during weeding and can simply be replaced once their site is cleared. Most bulbs that turn up in fall are just beginning to develop roots. They go back in with a minimum of fuss. A few get sliced, but that's a small price to pay for a weed-free bed.

Step Three: Divide, Clean, and Replant

Each perennial taken out of a hopelessly weedy bed has to be stripped down and cleaned of weed roots. I've learned that there *will* be pieces of undesirable root hidden within the perennials' rootballs. If you go through the process of reclamation once, only to have to redo it a year or two later, you'll understand what may at first sound like harsh treatment.

Loosen each rootball by dropping it or splitting the clump with two forks placed back-to-back and pried apart. Weed roots usually stand out in contrast to their perennial host's, but look closely and be as persistent as they are, even if it means reducing the precious perennial to bare-root divisions. Divisions are a good idea, anyway. Young bits will grow more vigorously and flower more freely than older, tighter clumps. They also may be healthier.

I have a stand of bee balm (*Monarda didyma*) in my own garden. Started from seed-grown plants more than fifteen years ago and given my customary neglect, it has nevertheless persisted and put on a show every year. Two years ago, I removed an adjacent quince and, faced with the bare spot, decided to extend the bee balm's spread. I took one division of the monarda, set it into the recently vacated and renewed soil, and forgot the whole matter. This past year, I noticed a startling difference between the old and new parts of the stand. Though both were genetically identical, the transplanted bit was a foot taller, still blooming when the original colony had finished, and still in possession of its foliage while the mother clump was sadly disfigured by mildew. Such benefits are my incentive to divide.

For an all-at-once reclamation, I clean weeds out of rootballs when it's time to replant, as opposed to baring

---

Smother Rather than Dig

If the bed is infested with roots that can regenerate from small pieces left behind and such pieces easily escape notice or snap because of brittleness and depth, I opt for smothering. Goutweed (*Aegopodium podagraria*) and Canada thistle infestations might prompt me to lift and put on "long hold" all desirable perennials. Then I trench around the bed to isolate it from surrounding roots. Without any other weeding, I then mulch the bed very heavily and leave it fallow. A mulch 8 inches deep, or a newspaper layer topped with 5 or more inches of mulch is usually enough to smother and starve vegetation.

Smothering is better than all-at-once digging when a bed is occupied by the roots of a desirable tree. These roots should not be cut up, both to avoid stressing the tree and to reduce the number of cut ends that will quickly branch to fill the bed even more thoroughly than before.

While the bed sits bare, I make bi-weekly or monthly visits to extract any bit of green that has made its way up through the smothering mulch. I use a fork to do this, but a systemic herbicide could be used. Either way, it usually takes the bits of weed root that escaped notice a few active growing months to exhaust themselves. Then the bed can be replanted. It's important to keep the bed edged to an appropriate depth and the surrounding lawn mowed close during this fallow period, so that remnants of the weed colony that have taken hold under the turf don't reinvade the bed.

---

the roots at the time of lifting and holding them in that condition. For longer holds, I clean the rootballs as I plant them in their holding bed or trench. Once the integrity of the rootball is broken, I prefer to get the perennial back into the soil without unnecessary delay, water it in, and tuck a blanket of mulch around it.

I've read of species that "resent disturbance" or that we should "leave undisturbed once established." Often such references catch my eye only after I've divided and moved the plant. In those cases, I've apologized, then kept an eye on the plants. So far, I haven't seen any big difference in results between a species heralded for reticence and one supposedly more amenable to transplant. Maybe the apology is the key.

Step Four: Throw Things Away

Just as in spring, fall division will result in an excess of plants. Compost them, donate them to a plant swap, or line them out in the vegetable garden for later disposition. Don't put them back into the bed, where they will crowd and deform each other and ruin your design.

Some species might even be shown the door during renovation. My own bent is toward composting those that have turned out to be more trouble than they're worth. Some gardeners can't do this. You can see the results where a single variety of hosta rings an entire house foundation, one type of daylily holds sway over the majority of a border, or every third plant in a bed is *Achillea* 'The Pearl'.

Occasionally, I've faced considerable criticism for dividing and reducing when I renovate. Once I had to direct a client to his own compost pile so that he could see that prized daylilies had not been spirited away. Expect this. Prepare yourself and others for a season of recovery, during which the bed may look sparser, albeit clean. It's a sad fact of life that the year a perennial grouping is most spectacular is probably the year it also begins to decline from crowding and wearing out its own bed. By the sixth or seventh year, most perennials need separate vacations or a soil pick-me-up. Do something before the spectacle actually becomes a worn-out memory of itself.

New Plants on Hold

Getting back to the work at hand in Bed Three, moving the sedum left room to introduce a new species. Reducing the spread of neighboring plants might provide space for two or three additions. I had my notions about what these could be, but no plants on hand. My goal in early fall was to get the existing plants tended and rearranged as completely as possible. I let the grower keep those new plants until it was time to install them.

Surprise and Opportunity

The daisies were a case in point. When I arrived to do this early fall work, I found that a commemorative plaque had been set up in the middle of the daisies in Bed Three. It reminded me of the evening I'd returned home to find a portion of my garden converted into a par-three golf course. On both occasions, it was instantly clear that the best route was to accept the unexpected change, but for two very different reasons. At my home, I could only applaud my son's industry and ingenuity, then enjoy watching the muddy group of boys practice chipping over the pond and putting across the back of the rock garden. It was their yard, too. This time, all I could do was blink and think how to incorporate the plaque gracefully.

This botanical garden, like many public gardens, is the result of donations and community support. Scores of paving bricks, along with engraved plates on benches and in individual gardens, recall grateful alumni and other patrons. These are visual reminders of all the hard work and the hosts of individual supporters needed to design, plant, and maintain the beds.

In this case, the wife and family of a young AIDS victim wanted to preserve his memory on the campus where he had been homecoming king. The formal dedication was going to take place the following day, and some of the family came to the bed while I was working there. They told me how much this young man had loved the calm, meditative feeling of this garden.

My family also has felt the tragedy of young lives lost to AIDS. I've dedicated this book to that young man because it seemed more than simple coincidence that put me in that spot on that day to meet the family. May he live on in other gardens and perhaps inspire other people to support a botanical garden, too.

The plaque itself was low and small, but the installation of a concrete footing to support it had taken its toll on the soil and daisies. The soil would have to be amended and leveled, but the greater puzzle was how to wrap the daisies around the plaque in a way that wouldn't obscure it during their bloom.

Pondering possibilities, I thought that the moor grass could be shifted to make room behind the plaque for the daisies. Then an appropriate ground-hugging species could move in along the bed's edge. Himalayan fleece flower (*Polygonum affine* 'Darjeeling Red') came to mind. The moor grass, however, was important to this bed's winter interest. This area would have to be redesigned in winter and changed in early spring.

A Return to the Edge

The last chore of the day was to put a new edge on the bed next to the reviving lawn. There was very little root to remove, as the lawn had been kept in check by my slicing along the edge several times during the summer. The object now was to reestablish an air trench that would prevent the passage of the rhizomes during the coming cool season. This took less than twenty minutes but would probably save at least thirty minutes of weeding and edging in the spring.

Don't Rush the Season

The results of all my efforts were pleasing. My attempt to keep fading foliage and seed pods to a minimum except where such appearance might contribute had paid off. Summer was passing gracefully and fall stepping in. Cardinal flower, still blooming, and blackberry lily, with seed pods just opened, were making a fine show in the center of the bed and keeping watch for the monkshood that might follow. Both ends of the bed were neat, if less full after the moves I'd made.

The combination of foliage colors at the east end was already attractive, and giving it one more look

made me realize that the 'Lambrook Silver' artemisia had recovered significantly from its summer stress. It would make a fine backdrop for the others.

There's something calm about a garden in fall, a feeling conducive to reflection, learning, and planning. It was now clear, for instance, that there would never be *Belamcanda flabellata* seedlings in this bed. I wouldn't leave any volunteers in future spring weeding in hope of having more of that species. All the information had been there since mid-summer, but now it was clear. The seed pods on 'Halo Yellow' were still quite green, very unlikely to ripen and open before fall clean-up took them away. The only blackberry lily volunteers in this bed would be children of the earlier-blooming *Belamcanda chinensis*.

A long fall shadow from the west-end oak made me think again about shade, root competition, and substitute species in that quarter. Shade was definitely going to increase there next year, and more redesign would be needed. Competition for nutrients and water was going to become greater, too. Just another inevitable change underway!

Digging to transplant sedum (A), I found 1 inch diameter oak roots 4 to 5 inches below the surface. A tree's roots spread at least as far as its branches. Perennials there face not only shade but also vigorous competition for water and nutrients.

Weeding to Last a Winter

NEW ENGLAND ASTER (*Aster novae-anglaie*) is in full bloom, fall crocus (*Colchicum autumnale*) is causing a stir in the beds where it's suddenly opened 4-inch lilac flares, and both red maple (*Acer rubrum*) and serviceberry (*Amelanchier canadensis*) are in full, glowing fall color.

There had been a hard frost since my last look at Bed Three. The top 2 feet of the cannas were black, and the crocosmia was a collapsing shock of yellow.

Now, in mid-autumn (October for me) cutting back and dividing were tops on my "to do" list, along with weeding, edging, and mulching.

Weeds: A Fine Harvest of None

There were no weeds of any substance in the bed, and the edge cut in early fall was still doing its job. There is nothing finer than seeing the season's work pay off in such a fine harvest each fall.

You know about the optimist, the pessimist, and the glass of water? Anyone who hadn't been in this garden all year might have seen my weed bucket as empty this month. They would wonder at calling it a harvest. My view was that it was a full bucket — full of time to spend as I wished.

Do Overhanging Woody Weeds Count?

Walking past the east oak, I ducked left to avoid that low limb. It had grown since spring. I'd forgotten the problem for much of the season, until noticing how badly worn the sod had become along that edge of the bed. All the traffic had been forced to dodge there just as I had. Hundreds or thousands of people had threaded this opening, and every left foot had touched down on the same tiny strip of lawn (photo on page 9).

I wrote a note for the arborist to let her know about the situation. There was no need to mark the tree or draw a diagram; the limb in question was betrayed by the shiny, bare spot in the lawn below.

Look for a Long-term Solution

A long-term solution might be required, though. If the oak was limbed up and the grass repaired, the lawn would still wear out quickly.

Perhaps the bed could be enlarged to include the east tree and a paved path laid to replace this narrow ribbon of grass. Then the pressure would be better distributed, since feet could land on wide flagstones rather than directly on the soil. The stones would have to be set in soil, however. Digging there to lay a footing for any other kind of paving would be death to the underlying tree roots. Changing the shape of the bed to include the tree would affect traffic flow and visual relationships among several beds. Resodding or adding paving would probably involve additional university departments. I saw these were suggestions for the horticulturist to ponder over winter. How sweet, sometimes, to be an independent gardener!

Withholding the Mulch

My normal procedure in the fall is to renew the mulch around each plant after I cut it down. With a slightly deeper mulch — 3 to 4 inches — the soil is protected over the winter, soil temperature changes are moderated, weed seedlings smothered, and soil microorganisms are fed. Even after five months of decomposition, the mulch may still be thick enough to carry the bed through the spring almost weed-free.

I couldn't use this approach here. Voles had to be discouraged, so all mulching would be put off until January or spring. This meant I would forfeit the weed-inhibiting benefits of mulch. Most of the current weed seedlings were destined to be killed by planting and dividing, but other seeds would germinate. Some children of the fall would still be there next spring, large enough then to defy smothering. I'd have to hoe or pull more weeds in early spring than normal.

It would all be for a good cause, though. My Ms. Hyde was there again, smiling at the idea of voles shivering in the cold and being pounced on by hawks.

Helping Nature Thin the Pests

Another pest-control tactic widely touted as a fall rule is to dispose of old foliage and other debris. It's said to harbor pests. Certainly some debris does this, but the same material also is likely to harbor eggs and overwintering adults of predatory insects and beneficial fungi and bacteria. When I remove foliage in fall clean-up, very little of it comes out as a pest-control measure; most of it is removed for aesthetic purposes or to make spring work easier.

The Bed Three phlox is a good example, where just one-sixth of the foliage was of concern from a pest-control standpoint. It was now clear that one of the six plants was having an inordinate amount of trouble with leaf spot. I not only removed that plant's foliage from the bed, but I took out the plant, roots and all. Something about that individual rendered it less resistant to disease, so it was undesirable in terms of looks and amount of care required.

It also was undesirable in terms of its fellows' health. The others might be more resistant to fungus, but resistance is not immunity. If you put a healthy person in a room with enough sick people, eventually he or she will fall prey to one bug or another. The same seems to hold true for plants. I sacrificed the sickly one to reduce the group's total exposure to contagion.

Don't Forget to Water

Watering is sometimes necessary in the fall, but it is often overlooked. Check new plants and transplants to make sure the soil around them is moist for optimal root growth. For instance, the horticulturist had noticed that Bed Three's transplanted potentillas had wanted water about a week after being moved, and she'd seen to it. Now they were making a fine show, and the soil around them was moist and cool.

The whole bed was moist, but this isn't always the case in October. During a dry fall, a few plants or a whole bed may need water. Evergreens that go into a winter dry are especially vulnerable to desiccation. Steady moisture throughout the fall is the answer, rather than heavy watering just before a freeze. Plant hardiness research indicates that heavy, late watering after plants have been stressed may cause woody stems to split and die. That's why I keep the hose handy until the ground freezes for the sake of evergreen perennials, shrubs, and trees.

Lifting Tender Bulbs

It was time to lift tender plants. The cannas no longer contributed to the monkshood area and were even detracting from it. It took five minutes to insert a garden fork under each canna and lift it out. I shook the soil off and dropped them at the botanical garden's greenhouse. They would be air-dried for a couple of days, have their tops cut back, then be stored until spring.

This left the oriental poppy on its own once again and set me to thinking about a companion for next spring. The cannas had not produced a healthy number of flowers per stem. I still favored the idea of planting variegated *Canna* 'Pretoria', since lack of bloom wouldn't be a problem in the presence of such a colorful leaf. Nevertheless, it seemed wise to consider alternatives. Castor bean was an option worth thinking about. The seeds could be tucked in around the poppy in spring. I put this on my slate for consideration in January.

Planting Hardy Bulbs

Finally I could add plants to give Bed Three some spring color — hardy bulbs! Daffodils and daylilies are a classic combination. The daffodils come up readily around daylily crowns, state their cases, and fade back before the daylilies need the stage. The similarity in foliage between the two makes it less likely that the fading daffodil leaves will stand out as an eyesore. Once I'd determined to split the daylilies, it was a natural move to add some spring color by doubling up this way.

I planted six all-yellow early daffodils (*Narcissus* 'Carlton'). In a perennial bed, spring bulbs look more at home if planted in clumps of one variety rather than singles. That's why I arranged them in two clumps of three. Planting in clumps is also simpler, usually requiring less disturbance around the crowns of perennials. I excavated one spot to a depth of 8 inches, inserted three bulbs, covered them, and then planted the other three.

Somehow I left the companions to these bulbs, six more yellows plus six with bicolor flowers, at home that day. I planted what I had with me, to avoid carting

them back and forth another time, even though this presented its own problem. I marked the diagram to show approximatly where the 'Carlton' bulbs were located, but by the time I returned with the balance of the bulbs, I wouldn't be able to tell exactly where the earlier bulbs were. That situation invariably leads to at least one sliced bulb.

To solve this problem, I placed four short pieces of bamboo into the bulb planting hole when it was half filled with soil. Laid horizontally, with ends crossed as

A Partnership of Bulbs

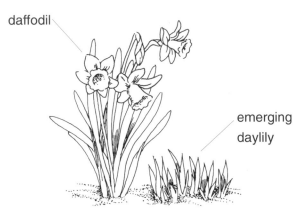

daffodil

emerging daylily

Bulbs and perennials can share space on a time-share basis. Daffodils are up and blooming before daylily foliage expands to fill its allotted space.

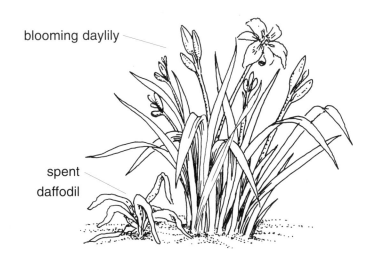

blooming daylily

spent daffodil

As the daffodil fades, the daylily gradually covers its space. This combination can continue for many years, until the daylily root mass becomes too thick to permit the daffodil to emerge.

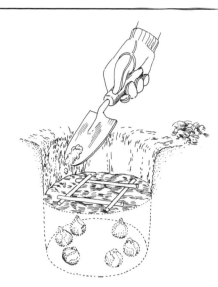

Before covering the hole where I planted the bulbs, I laid down crisscrossed pieces of bamboo to remind me of the location. These might also stop my spade from slicing through the bulbs in the future.

in a basket's weave, these pieces would stop my spade before it reached the bulbs. They would not impede the bulbs' growth and might last as a warning for several years.

The garden staff also was planning to add bulbs, but they had decided to wait until the ground was nearly frozen. Chipmunks and other rodents might be less likely to dig bulbs planted so late, a fate that even can apply to distasteful bulbs such as daffodils. This practice allows less time for roots to get established before the soil freezes around them, however, one of those trade-offs that are sometimes necessary in gardening.

The Final Word on Pest Control

The monkshood was finally in bloom. The flowers weren't impressive in quantity, and the plants were still losing leaves and stems to disease. Still, the flower was colorful enough to catch the eye of a photographer in search of fall-blooming plants.

Through the lens, with proper framing that excluded the foliage, that monkshood could still look beautiful. Its blue hooded flowers may well have graced the pages of a magazine, since that photographer was on

such an assignment. This is just a reminder that looking at plants and gardens only on the pages of a magazine, catalog, or coffee-table book is something like viewing this bed while wearing blinders.

Make an effort to see the whole picture, for the sake of your confidence as a gardener. Published photographs can be seductive. With no clues to the amount of manipulation practiced by the photographer, pictures can make you believe that a perfect garden exists ... which is true only for the second it takes to snap the shutter.

Once the camera in question was out of the way, I finished removing dead leaves and stems. I saw that the rot had infected even the monkshood's tuberous roots. The decayed stems were rotted well below ground level.

Perhaps there was still a chance for this plant, but it would have to be lifted in spring, every infected root destroyed, and all the surrounding soil dug out and replaced. Were these few blooms and all that handpicking of leaves worth that task? I began to dream of the ferny leaves and white autumn flowers of fall fairy candle (*Cimicifuga ramosa*). That would be something to look for come February. Maybe I could find the variety *Cimicifuga ramosa atropurpurea*, with purple foliage.

My uncertainty over the fate of the monkshood eliminated the second dividing chore for the day. The 'Early Sunrise' coreopsis could do with a rejuvenating split and redistribution throughout the area. That could wait for spring, though, when the identity and placement of other species in the area were decided.

Overall Review

Finished with all the work at hand, I was still mindful of my oversight with the daffodil bulbs and aware that there would be only one more chance to plant this year. I decided to review the notes I'd made about when and where the color in Bed Three needed a boost. The first to pop up was a mention of the Missouri primrose's sad appearance. I stepped over and dug out that plant. Let the husky clump in sunny, moist Bed Nine demonstrate what this species should look like.

I'd forgotten my dream of red hybrid lupine for early summer punch in the east end. It was too late for that, now, as there was no room left at that sunny end. The lupine was worth keeping in mind for spring, however, when I would be evaluating the daisy and moor grass area.

I'd also forgotten to record which of the rock rose plants were the right color, so that the off colors could be replaced. That would be another job for next year.

Even with additional daffodils, would the spring show be too skimpy? I made a list of other plants that would stretch and vary the color in mid-spring: little yellow allium (*Allium moly*) and bulbous Dutch iris (*Iris Xiphium*). Imagining the rest of the bed next spring, I was pleased about the leopard's-bane (*Doronicum caucasicum*) I was planning to add at the west end. Its yellow daisies would combine with the chartreuse of the myrtle euphorbia as a counterbalance to the east-end bulb show.

In that shady west side, astilbe seemed the perfect answer. A variety such as 'Glut' would bring a touch of bronze foliage in spring. More important, it would add

A good combination of foliage types and bloom times: hosta (background), astilbe (middle), and leopard's-bane (foreground), as they might be seen from the lawn northwest of Bed Three.

red flowers to the mid-summer scene, dominated previously by yellow and white, coreopsis and daisy. I tried not to get my hopes up, though. The competition from that oak might make it too dry for such a moisture-loving species as astilbe.

This summer's combination of maroon foliage backed by gray — purple-leaf sedum and silvermound artemisia — had been dramatic. If the silvermound eventually had to be taken out of the shade, white-edged *Hosta* 'Sugar and Cream' could stand in. It would make an equivalent light-colored backdrop for the maroon leaves of *Astilbe* 'Glut'. 'Sugar and Cream' also was recommended for having shown itself to be slug-resistant.

When to Chance Late Planting

Mid-fall — October — marks my normal "last new plant" date, but I had every intention of pushing it beyond the limit on the west side. A minor sense of urgency impels me when it comes to changing species in advancing shade. Nothing will stop the tree from growing. Every passing season means increased shade, more root competition, and slower establishment of new perennials. This applies even to shade-tolerant perennials.

Both *Astilbe* 'Glut' and *Hosta* 'Sugar and Cream' had proved hard to find but might still turn up before garden centers restocked in the spring. Late planting was better than no planting. If they failed over the winter, little would be lost. If they thrived, they would be a season ahead of the next best alternative.

I often plant late in my own garden, for different reasons. Clean-up there is usually the last chore on my schedule. Thus it's often very late in the fall when "orphaned" plants and divisions not used elsewhere are given a berth in my beds. More often than not, such late additions do take hold and so have a jump on anything I could plant in the spring.

Putting the Garden to Bed

AMERICAN WITCHHAZEL (*Hamamelis virginiana*) blooms now at the beginning of November in Zones 5 and 6. Its yellow flowers are often lost in the gold fall foliage. Callery pear trees (*Pyrus calleryana*), known for dropping their leaves well after the last raking, now show their first dollops of fall color.

There have been killing frosts, and most of the perennials have been affected. I've been putting gardens to bed for a month by November 1, but I'm happiest working on the last few, those that have been appreciated to the very end. I'm happy, but not always comfortable in the typical cold and dampness of early November. Often the best working days of fall are at mid-month, during a dry, blue-sky spate of Indian summer.

The essential agenda for this month is cutting back, weeding, edging, and mulching.

Go in Cutting

I started out, as in early spring, cutting down the unnecessary foliage. Working with sharp pruning snips, I completed the carnage in about thirty minutes. This made the bed temporarily look as if a bomb had exploded and flattened all but the sturdiest plants.

Pruning shears are my choice because they're sharp, precise, and easy on the hand. Hedge shears sometimes come in handy for serious production work, as when I'm cutting down that 80-square-foot bee balm area at home.

The bulk of the garden's plants went down. I'll discuss the exceptions following this primer on fall cutbacks.

Three Strikes against Laissez-Faire

First, I cut to make room for the gardener, the eye, and spring growth. This gardener needed access to weed, divide, and plant. Fall weeding is probably the biggest time-saving strategy in horticulture, and you've already heard my pitch for fall planting (see page 142). Both are simple to do if the ground-obscuring, eye-poking perennial remnants can be cleared out of the way first.

Second, I cut to improve the bed's off-season appearance. As one who enjoys the presence of perennials in the snow and works for or teaches others who want winter interest, I can attest to the tremendous differences in opinion in this arena. What looks good to one is an irritating mess to another. Well placed, a species can add interest to one scene. In another situation, the same plant may be wasted or distracting.

We train ourselves for months to look at a garden. Perhaps we turn toward it every morning after pouring a cup of coffee, or we glance at it every evening as we pull into the driveway. We rebel against the depressing prospect of looking at bare ground all winter.

Sparing some plants for winter interest is as much a design skill as a maintenance function. Sturdiness and a pleasant off-season aspect are not absolute qualifiers. What counts more is whether they are located well both within the bed and in relation to other elements. Harmony and contrast should remain along with the assorted leaves, stalks, and seed pods. Some of what I cut down could remain, but my design sense says it should not.

The third reason to cut is to clear the way for spring. It's faster and easier to cut and compost crisp fall remains than it is to do the same in a bed layered with tangled, half-rotted debris. Perennials can emerge through this layer, but they do so more quickly and gracefully if we help.

My records in this area indicate that the first maintenance visit in spring can be shortened by as much as 75 percent if fall work is done thoroughly. Cumulative savings run between 30 and 50 percent. Consider a bed given the clean-up described here. Sixty minutes might be required in the fall, followed by sixty to ninety minutes in the spring to bring it back up to snuff. If the fall work isn't done, initial spring clean-up may take four hours.

It's always encouraging to realize that the work I do in late fall might save time the next spring. It was clear last spring that Bed Three had not been edged in the late fall a year before. Clearing the perimeter then took ninety minutes; it might require only sixty minutes or less next spring.

Cut Those Who Wobble

The easiest place to start cutting in Bed Three was species that simply wouldn't make a splash over the winter. There are two categories of nonsplashers: those that turn into mush and those that you wish would turn into mush.

In the mush category, Bed Three had blackberry lily, foxglove, daylily, cardinal flower, lychnis, oxeye,

'Early Sunrise' coreopsis, phlox, and lamb's ear. Left on their own, these would largely disintegrate by spring. They fell more to facilitate weeding than to improve the bed's looks or to reduce spring work. I lopped off just the upright portions; the ground-hugging bases of cardinal flower and lamb's ear remained.

Established clumps of golden marguerite, daisy, oriental lily, 'Silver King' artemisia, Carolina lupine, oxeye, and monkshood won't go away entirely over the winter, but they will collapse in a heap if left uncut. By spring, they'll be a disgusting sprawl that will gum up clippers and soak through gloves.

It's a telling point that all twenty-seven stakes and several cages I recovered during fall clean-up came out in this first cutting pass. Most plants that can't hold up their heads over the summer can't withstand the winter either.

Consider the Seed Before It Falls

I handled several of these plants gently while cutting and pitching them out of the bed. The standard blackberry lilies (*Belamcanda chinensis*) and remaining stalks of golden marguerite were loaded with seed. Every seed that dropped off into the bed was a potential weed, so I avoided jiggling or jerking the stems. They came out with as smooth a motion as possible.

The foxglove was a different story. The species may be short-lived, so a few seedling replacements

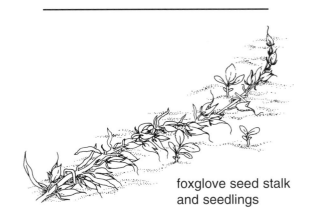

foxglove seed stalk
and seedlings

One way to remember to encourage and save seedlings of short-lived perennials is to peg down a complete seed stalk where you want the seedlings to sprout. During spring weeding, you will recognize this signal, know the species by its seed stalk, and allow those seedlings to grow.

would be welcome. After I cut the stems, I shook them sharply to dislodge seed over the space where volunteers would be welcome.

Many perennials might be treated this way. "Weakly perennial" is one flag you'll learn to recognize in plant encyclopedias. On first meeting one that may be short-lived, I shake the seed stalk in fall, as for foxglove. Then I peg down one of the cut stalks, using a bit of wire bent in a **U** or two short pieces of bamboo inserted at sharp angles so that the ends cross securely over the stalk.

In spring, I recognize seedlings of familiar species such as foxglove. An appropriate number can be saved from the hoe or smothering mulch. Without the sanction of a pegged-down stalk, strange seedlings might not be so lucky.

Evergreens Get Kid-Glove Treatment

Just as some species are in the "always cut" group, others get a "hands off" classification. These are the true evergreens, species that keep live leaves into the next spring. Some even qualify as woody subshrubs, as they set leaf buds on their stems rather than hiding them in their crowns at soil level or below.

Evergreens keep their leaves for the advantage it gives them over plants laid low by frost. They photosynthesize whenever conditions are right, even in early and late winter. Their foliage and forms also can be attractive additions to a snowy scene. For their health and our enjoyment, we leave their leaves intact during fall clean-up.

You met Bed Three's complement of untouchables in early spring: penstemon, 'Lambrook Silver' artemisia, blue fescue, rock rose, euphorbia, silvermound artemisia, poppy, dianthus, rue, and coralbells.

Flower stalks and excess growth can be snipped off any plant, even an evergreen. A few of the evergreens were shaggy, so I gave them a haircut. 'Lambrook Silver' artemisia, rue, and rock rose felt the clippers just enough to even up their ends. If the local wildlife had not already razed the dianthus, it would have been shorn a bit, too.

People often have trouble identifying evergreens. If a species is a stranger to you and is still green and lively after a hard frost, don't cut it at all or cut it back to 6 inches tall. Avoid cutting it all the way to the ground as

cutline

Evergreens, such as this silver mound artemesia, can be given a haircut in fall to keep them dense, but don't remove all the foliage.

for a known deciduous species. An evergreen can make it through the winter with at least 6 inches of leaf, partial leaf, or woody stem. The following spring, you can give it a critical look as described in Chapter 4. Then you'll know if it's an evergreen or just faking, and you can treat it accordingly thereafter.

Stalky Plants Get a Bye

Still standing at this point to accompany the evergreens were Bed Three's sturdy species: purple-leaf sedum, moor grass, 'Golden Showers' coreopsis, and blood grass. Their height and persistence can be the bones of a winter garden. Grasses also add movement and sound by swaying and rustling in the wind.

I raked out the debris and then stood back to view the bed from the angle it was most likely to be seen in winter. That was from the north, where a paved walkway runs through the botanical garden.

The tan moor grass, flanked by blue fescue and bright red blood grass and backed up by blue-green rue, was impressive and well-balanced. This group formed a steady triangle, corners flung wide to offset the moor grass's height. The cluster was full enough to have visual impact, but elements were separate enough to be distinctive. Those would all stay.

There were hints that one day the far left and right ends of the bed would have interest, too. Eventually, the purple-leaf sedum would be an equal partner with

Bed Three would be attractive over the winter, with moor grass flanked by blue fescue (left) and blood grass (right).

---

the 'Lambrook Silver' artemisia. As yet, it was too skimpy to be seen. On the west end, the rock rose and myrtle euphorbia held promise.

Only 'Golden Showers' coreopsis didn't fit into this picture. Neat and dense enough to be seen, it upset the balance that centered on the moor grass. It also partially hid the blood grass.

I cut 'Golden Showers' to the ground, along with the purple leaf sedum. That was it for cutting.

How Much Can We Cut?

What about that nagging question, raised in early spring, about whether winter stubble serves any purpose in a perennial garden? There can be good reasons to leave a uniform stubble, perhaps 6 inches high.

If you are unfamiliar with a garden and have little time to spend there, leaving 6 inches of stem is a quick, sure tactic. This cuts everything low enough to get the seed pods out but not so low as to kill any plants that may be evergreen. In the spring, visible remains will help you remember where desirable plants can be expected to emerge. The stubs can be cut out when and if they get in your way or block emerging foliage.

Another rationale for stubble is to hold a loose mulch against winter winds. For me, this was entirely theoretical, since Bed Three wouldn't be getting a winter mulch. If the bed did get a mulch, it would be compost, shredded leaves, finely ground bark, or a combination of these. Sometimes I shred the debris just removed from the bed and use it as mulch. None of

these materials blows away readily, but loose leaves and straw might. That's where a stubble can come in handy.

Are Power Cutters Desirable?

On the subject of theoretical questions, look at the issue of power cutters. Many gardeners like to use them or wonder whether they might gain by doing so.

Power tools don't appeal to me. In pursuit of speed and ease, some professionals use long-handled string trimmers or cutters with circular or reciprocating blades. My objections to these tools have to do with practicality and environmental considerations.

Practicality

From a practical standpoint, power tools can make more work than they save. Picture this typical episode of fall power cutting in a perennial bed.

You aim to cut stems of perennials at ground level or a few inches high. They topple in all directions, landing on areas already cut and still to be cut. To continue trimming without stopping every few feet to clear the debris, you must cut through fallen debris. Some of the stems and leaves are mushy and make the blade bog down or stall the engine.

Now you must rake — no, a blower won't budge the tangled mess! As you rake, you'll find stems that were not severed. Perhaps they were hidden under fallen plant parts, flattened as if cut by the weight of other stems falling, or just not sliced clean.

These attached stems will become tangled in the rake. Take care not to yank the rake free, though. If the plant in which it's tangled is a shallow-rooted perennial, a hearty tug might dislodge the crown. Instead, you need to disentangle the tines, then use a combing motion to carry loose materials over the incompletely cut area.

Now what do you have? A bed partially cleared of old plant parts. Some stems lie broken but still attached. Many small pieces of stalk and leaf are scattered about. You have to reach down to and cut the remaining stems by hand, then rake again so that the ground is clear enough for you to weed.

Weeding might be a problem, though. Here and there in any perennial bed are weeds that have snuggled into the crown of a perennial and escaped notice all season. Fall is the best time to remove them. The trouble is that in a power-cut bed, those weeds were sliced off with the perennials, still unnoticed. Unless there is some distinct difference between the weed's stalk base and the perennial's stalk base, you probably won't see the weed and won't go after it. You will definitely meet it again in the spring, in larger form.

I've done this and watched it done, and I still fail to see much reduction in time, if any. When I cut Bed Three, I grabbed a handful of stems in my left hand and made two or three cuts at the crown to release them. My left hand kept tension on the stalks, whether mushy or crisp, so they could be cut clean. As soon as the handful was loose, my left hand went up and back, tossing the debris out of the way. Raking was minimal and did not include additional bending to clean up stragglers.

There weren't many weeds in the crowns of the plants — few enough that I made a note of a single curious blade of grass in the 'Silver King' artemisia. Yet I was in a position to see those weeds that were hiding in the crowns and leave their greenery in place when I cut. It would be easy to find them when it was time to make the weeding pass.

It's my guess that a power cutter makes sense only in nursery rows or the largest beds, perhaps 1,000 square feet or more.

Environmental Considerations

My second objection to power tools revolves around noise and air pollution. We are exposed to a nerve-racking din and unfiltered exhaust from power tools every day from April to November. The noise is so great that safety and health regulations in most areas recommend or require ear protection for string trimmer and blower operators. Some communities have passed ordinances restricting the use of these machines to certain days and times. The pollution is real, shocking in amount, and beginning to come under regulatory scrutiny.

Perhaps you work in an office that blocks or muffles some of this racket. I live with its effects every day, as do children, retirees, vacationers, pets, and backyard wildlife. It's likely that few of us would begrudge power

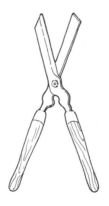

hand pruners

hedge shears

Most of the fall cutting can be done with hand pruners. Hedge shears may be useful for large stands of rigid stems.

tools to people who otherwise couldn't do the work they must do or want to do. Yet we could applaud those who don't need the extra strength and dexterity if they stop using those machines at every turn or out of habit.

What About Fertilizer?

One more theoretical question. Bed Three doesn't need fertilizer. If it did need elements other than nitrogen, such as sulfur to lower the pH or potash to correct a potassium deficiency, immediately after cutting down a garden would be a good time to apply them. The granules would then be mixed in during weeding and planting.

A 2-inch blanket of compost can serve as both winter mulch and fertilizer. It can be applied after weeding and planting so that it remains undisturbed on the surface. Don't assume the compost is supplying useful nutrients to the bed, however. I've seen analyses of some composts produced by large-scale operations and been surprised to see alkaline reaction, sometimes quite high. In some cases, soluble salt levels also were high for elements not necessarily helpful, such as sodium.

In reading technical reports and studies from other areas in the Midwest where compost technology is booming, I've noticed that my observations are not unusual. I continue to use compost as a good source of organic matter and to encourage microbial activity in the soil. However, you may want to follow my lead when it comes to compost as fertilizer: if you use it in bulk, ask whether an elemental and pH analysis is available. If not, don't rely on it to correct fertility problems.

On to the Weeds

Once again, there was only a handful of seedlings. These were sprouting wherever the mulch had gotten thin or been lost to early fall's soil renovation. Onstage, as expected, was a new batch of golden marguerite.

Most of these nuisances I would turn under or smother in planting new bulbs and the west-end perennials. I scuffed the soil with my hand hoe to wipe out two small clutches of oxalis. All the while, I knew it was hopeless. Every scrape that cut off one seedling's root exposed fresh seed. That seed would germinate later, before the spring weeding and mulching.

Indulging in the meditative state that can come from weeding, I recalled a report tucked within some no-till farming research. Fields tilled at night had yielded significantly fewer weeds than fields tilled by day. My fantasy of coming back at night to do one last, late-fall "hoe down" in Bed Three was interrupted by visions of security guards arriving to take me away — another experiment best left for my own garden.

Two legitimate weeds, in the "nice plants gone bad" category, were Carolina lupine and crocosmia. With a spade, I sliced down along the acceptable limit of their sprawl, popped up the soil, and removed the spreading roots. This was an exact repeat of early spring's work to reduce 'Golden Shower' coreopsis and 'Silver King' artemisia.

Loosening and Fluffing

A dearth of weeding all season did have one drawback: some parts of the bed were no longer loose and fluffy. My trampling through the bed to cut and rake hadn't helped. I loosened these areas with a spading fork. To perform this task, I walked into the center of the bed, inserted the fork and rocked it back once. Then I stepped backward toward the edge, loosened where I had just been standing, and continued this way until reaching the lawn.

While raking and loosening, it was important to avoid dragging too much loose soil to the outside edge of the bed. The trench was doing a very respectable job of deterring lawn creep, so I kept it cleared of this fill.

Root Out the Problem

At the west end of the bed, I came across a number of tree roots within a few inches of the surface. I exposed these by scraping loose soil out of the 3-inch trench that barred the lawn. Although these roots were closer to the surface than those I'd seen within the bed while moving the sedum, they weren't unexpected. They're one of the reasons that a solid, vertical root barrier around a tree is not a good idea.

It's common to find tree roots just beneath the sod. The soil beneath sod is often compacted from the start, or it becomes that way if traffic is heavy. So tree roots grow at the surface, where compaction is less. Years later, as the roots increase in diameter — a mirror of the branches' development — irritated gardeners claim that the roots are "surfacing." The irony is that those roots have been there all along; they've just grown thick enough to be visible.

If you combine compacted soil beneath a tree's outspread limbs, roots searching for loose soil, and a plastic or metal root barrier encircling the tree five inches into the soil, you have a recipe for a dead tree. Under these conditions, it's not unusual to see a shade tree go into decline fifteen or twenty years after it's planted. Tips die back and pest problems begin to mount, all because the tree has been stressed by limited root space. If you take the edging away from that tree, you'll

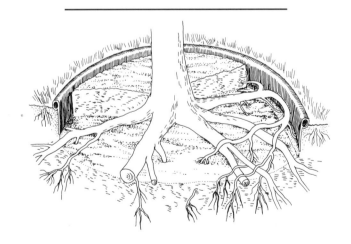

These tree roots were stopped in their lateral spread by edging and stopped from diving under the edge by compacted soil. To prevent this, loosen soil 6" to 9" deep, 12" to 24" beyond the tree's dripline each fall.

be amazed at the solid wall of thick root circling within the edging, starved and girdling itself.

As these "girdling" roots increase in diameter, they will press on and kill underlying roots. The tree will decline and eventually die from loss of root or secondary complications.

That's sad, because a fifteen-year investment in shade may have only just begun to pay off when the problems arise. To avoid this scenario, loosen the soil 12 to 18 inches deep all around the tree when it's planted. Keep loosening the soil in a widening ring, staying ahead of the spread of the branches. Lawn aeration can help, but deeper work with a fork is better. Finally, don't put in edging unless the soil beneath is loose and deep.

More Moves and Additions

All the existing plants were attended to now. I could turn my attention to the new perennials and bulbs: a clump of *Astilbe* 'Glut' and another of *Hosta* 'Sugar and Cream', each of which would produce three respectable divisions; three leopard's-banes; sixteen daffodils of two types; thirty alliums; and thirty *Iris xiphium*.

Happily, the additional daffodils went in without causing injury to the existing bulbs. I plugged in the alliums in groups of three, digging ten holes 4 inches deep around the sedum.

The irises required a bit more work. My vision was to have blue and blue-violet irises coming up through and around the 'Silver King' artemisia. In the spring, cool-color flowers often look best when given a light background such as the gray artemisia would provide. To achieve this look, I cut a square out of the center of the artemisia, excavated that area to 8 inches, and planted about half the irises. As I filled the hole, I included some young pieces of artemisia from the edge of the clump. This would ensure that the hole was plugged and address the dead-center syndrome that is a given with this artemisia. The remainder of the irises went into the ground in groups of three around the perimeter of the 'Silver King'.

Planting the astilbe, hosta, and leopard's-bane followed the pattern described in Chapters 4 and 9, with the only difference being that after planting I cut their foliage back for the winter. I also watered them in especially well, knowing the oak would take its share of water. The diagram indicates the locations of these newcomers.

Pros and Cons of Not Mulching

In any other year, I would have topped off this work with a layer of mulch. Three or 4 inches of shredded leaves tucked around the crowns would be perfect. The

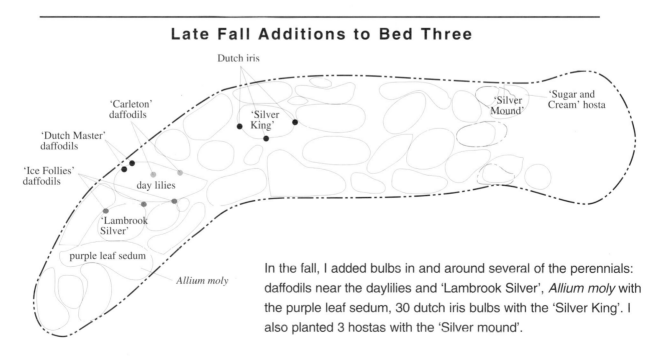

Late Fall Additions to Bed Three

Dutch iris

'Carleton' daffodils

'Dutch Master' daffodils

'Ice Follies' daffodils

'Silver King'

day lilies

'Lambrook Silver'

purple leaf sedum

Allium moly

'Silver Mound'

'Sugar and Cream' hosta

In the fall, I added bulbs in and around several of the perennials: daffodils near the daylilies and 'Lambrook Silver', *Allium moly* with the purple leaf sedum, 30 dutch iris bulbs with the 'Silver King'. I also planted 3 hostas with the 'Silver mound'.

layer is usually gone by spring, consumed by the soil animals, from microbes to worms.

In late fall in my own garden, sometimes I don't have time to shred the leaves, so I use them whole. Oak, sycamore, and other leaves tend to mat because they are slow to disintegrate. Usually the water-repellent, air-blocking features of a mat aren't desirable. To avoid this, I mix persistent leaves with other types that decay more quickly, such as apple, cherry, or elm. Whole-leaf mulch needs a cover of twigs or flattened wire cages to keep the leaves from flying back to the neighbors who donated them.

Mulch, leafy or other, wasn't an option here because of the voles, which might use the mulch as a home or for cover from predators. So an absence of mulch can be a pest-control measure. What could sound more benign? But remember that every pest-control strategy has drawbacks.

The drawback I most regretted was that the soil would be unprotected over winter. Without a mulch shield, Bed Three's surface soil particles would be pummeled by winter rains.

Have you ever noticed what happens to soil after a winter thaw, when water can't penetrate the frozen layer just below the defrosted mud? Where a foot falls or car tire rolls across, its particles are crushed by the downward pressure. This pulverized soil acquires the consistency of thick paste. By spring it has a disheartening floury texture that repels both water and the gardener's rehabilitative efforts.

This also happens to soil where there are no plant parts or mulch particles to disperse the force of falling rain or dripping meltwater. The downward pressure is not as great as from an automobile tire, but the blows are numerous and continue all winter. The upper particles' crumbly texture declines, and a fine skin of clay forms at the surface. One year without protection usually will not result in irreversible deterioration, but those who work hard for good tilth hate to see any backsliding.

Who Needs a Blanket?

The absence of mulch didn't make me worry about losing the plants themselves. All these species are hardy to USDA zone 5 and had proved themselves recently by returning after the coldest winter in fifty years. Also in their favor, they were well established and had adequate moisture and good drainage.

Even within a hardy species, individuals exhibit varying degrees of cold resistance. Older, healthier individuals like these fare best. The new additions might be at risk, but that wasn't going to bother me, because I knew that they were chancy latecomers.

Tender Care for New Plants

When plants have been added or moved late, water them well if the bed gets dry before the ground freezes. Avoid waterlogging, though. Put an airy, deep mulch over the crown and the whole root zone after the soil gets frosty. Use something you can remove easily in very early spring before it can smother the crown. When I have perennials to protect, I use discarded Christmas trees and partial bales of straw for cover.

New trees and shrubs are another matter. For example, deer, rabbits, and mice prey on young dogwood, fruit trees, viburnum, and burning bush in winter when other food is scarce. The soft twigs and buds are candy to rabbits and deer. Mice favor the cambium layer and so strip the bark to gnaw this sap lifeline.

Rabbit cages that protect perennials in summer move over to guard saplings and shrubs from rabbits and deer in winter. A temporary girdle of hardware cloth around the base of each vulnerable trunk or stem is protection against mice. Be sure the wire is pressed down into the soil around the trunk to close any gaps at its base.

Tasty When Cold

Some plants need protection over the winter from hungry animals. Squirrels and chipmunks may dig for bulbs in late fall or early spring. They seem to aim for new plantings, as if drawn by the freshly disturbed soil.

Some gardeners report that soaking new bulbs in a distasteful substance such as Tabasco sauce or rodent repellent, is an effective deterrent.

Irritants such as pepper or sneezing powder also may be sprinkled into the planting hole. I watched a squirrel digging for tulips in a botanical garden display area one fall. Bulbs must have been a known delicacy for this animal, which kept digging until only its rump and tail showed above ground. Suddenly, it erupted from the hole as if blown up and out. It stood for a minute, sneezing and wiping its face, and then ran off. I asked several of the gardeners about the bed. They didn't recall whether it had been treated with any animal repellent, but the image stayed with me. Clearly, the squirrel had met and been discouraged by some irritant, natural or applied.

Bulb-planting time isn't one of my peak organizational times, though. You know that I couldn't even remember to bring all the daffodil bulbs all at once, let alone buckets for soaking, repellents and annoying powders. That's why I rely on chicken wire or flattened rabbit caging where squirrel damage is likely. I lay it down on the ground over the new planting to make digging difficult if not impossible.

Underground sabotage is possible, such as oriental lily bulbs being devoured by mice or voles. The hardware cloth baskets I constructed in early summer are one defense against this damage. Filling directly around and over a new bulb with gravel before topping off the hole with soil is said to discourage tunnelers, too.

Even these pest-control tactics have side effects. Don't use any that aren't worth the trouble. A neighbor suggested one day that an animal might catch its head in my chicken wire. The thought of a squirrel adorned with a square yard of chicken wire collar amused more than upset me, but clearly my neighbor was concerned.

Evaluating Spring-Applied Mulch

It was high time to look at the differences between the various mulches applied in spring. I had not seen any significant differences in plant growth or health in any of these mulches, so I looked at other effects. The cocoa hulls had lasted well until early fall and then rapidly disintegrated. That's good timing for a perennial bed mulch. Fall tends to be a period of digging and moving. Mulch can get in the way at such times, unless you don't mind digging it into the soil.

Rotted and half-rotted mulch mixed into the soil is not a problem, but you should avoid raw wood mulch which can set up a chronic nitrogen deficiency.

The cocoa hulls had not developed the thick white mold that sometimes covers them and disturbs the gardener's aesthetic sense. Certainly it had been there, working to break down the hulls on the bottom layer next to the cool soil. I attributed its subdued presence to a bed that was just moist, not wet.

The leaves were completely gone and had been for some time. I supplement leaf mulches at midsummer or as needed. It's obvious when the mulch needs replenishment, because weed seeds sprout in thin spaces as green signal flares. That's where I add more shredded leaves, a thin layer of bark, or grass clippings, but no clippings from lawns treated with broad-leaved weed killers within the previous two weeks.

The rough bark chips were still evident, though thinning. The more finely ground bark also was still in place but had matted. Both were still attractive, but matted mulch can exclude air and water. This is a common problem with finely ground wood and bark, so be prepared. I've found that cultivating its surface two or three times a season prevents matting.

Cocoa hulls or shredded leaves get my vote for the best mulches. Unfortunately, the first is more expensive than any other material I use, and the other is seasonal in availability. Shredded bark in small bits will still be my backup when money is limited and there are no leaves at hand.

Weighing the Matter of Debris

Bed Three boiled down to three stacked wheelbarrows of debris, plus a plastic bag of sorry monkshood foliage, stems, and infected roots. I added the stems from the phlox to the monkshood bag because I did not know whether the compost in this botanical garden was produced by regular heating and turning or by slower, cool decomposition. The heat of an active, turned compost pile kills most disease organisms and seeds; this isn't true of a cool pile. I didn't want Bed Three's mildew to cause trouble for any other phlox next year.

Reducing Maintenance and Reflecting on the Season

ALL THE LEAVES HAVE FALLEN that will fall this year, and fruit left behind calls for attention even from nongardeners. Sargent crabapple *(Malus sargentii),* Washington hawthorns *(Crataegus phaenopyrum),* and American cranberry viburnum *(Viburnum trilobum)* suddenly get notice. Ice has formed and cleared several times on the pond. I don't mind December's cold coming, though my southern friends pity me as I descend into winter stillness three weeks or a month before they do.

This is my chance to tie up loose ends and reflect on the season past. I wouldn't miss it. Once a good friend urged me to move to some part of the country or world where outdoor gardening goes on all year. It wasn't something I'd ever considered, but when I opened my mouth to say so, something else came out: an answer so ready that it must have been churned and turned out long ago to be on hand when it was finally needed.

No, thank you. Winter is such a blessing after a busy season. It's for sitting back and looking over what's happened, making connections that didn't click earlier, and congratulating myself for accomplishments that were lost in the rush. There's no pressure to run out and get things done, but every good reason to savor and digest notes, thoughts, and photographs.

It's also time to account for hours and dollars spent throughout the season. At the beginning of the year, I estimated that the 504 square feet in this bed would require about thirty-five hours' work. I expected five hours' work each month on average. That's what it turned out to be. You'll notice on the chart on page 153 that April was a heavyweight in terms of total time spent; July and August were much lighter. This is common. It's also common to see that difference reduced during the second year of maintaining a bed by this schedule.

Applying These Times to Your Garden

My journal records 35.25 hours spent in the garden. It includes time spent purchasing materials, researching problems, actually working in the garden, and assembling and putting away tools. It also includes some allowance for fun, especially from June through August when the garden's needs were minor. For instance, one day I spent an unknown amount of time looking for my photographer who had wandered off to immortalize pansies and butterflies. Another day I walked the grounds and discussed species hardiness with a professor I admire. Every gardening schedule ought to have some time for this.

Divide by five the total time spent in this 500 square feet to find a base figure for estimating the time needed to care for 100 square feet of garden. For Bed Three, as for so many other gardens, this computation gives an answer of seven to eight hours per year, or just over an hour each month of a seven-month season.

You can use this figure to estimate how long it will take to maintain your garden. Over the past twelve years I've found that the time required is consistent. This base figure applies to spaces of 100 square feet as well as to large beds of more than 1,000 square feet.

To use the base figure, you need to know the size of your garden. If it's 20 feet long and 5 feet deep, it's 100 square feet in area. For that bed, you can use the base figure without modification. A bed 50 feet long and 6 feet deep has an area of 300 square feet. Simply multiply the base figure by three to forecast the hours you'll need to keep that garden up to the standards set in this book. For that bed, you could expect to spend about twenty-one hours during the year, an average of three hours per month — perhaps five or six hours in early spring and as little as one hour in the summer months.

The professional gardener should keep in mind that travel time is not included in these figures. It would not be possible to maintain eight different 100-square-foot beds in an eight-hour day unless those gardens were all on the same property.

Material Costs

Costs will vary widely, but it's often helpful to have a starting point. Maintenance necessities for Bed Three cost $515. Records I have kept on other gardens confirm that it's common to spend about one dollar per square foot of perennial garden each year on materials, replacements, and new plants.

Adjust Costs to Fit Your Needs and Dreams

It's easy to imagine spending less or more than I did. Look at plant costs. A gardener with a little patience and willingness to shop can buy fewer and smaller replacement plants to accomplish the same end. One who values change and variety over economy might make even more changes and more purchases.

Mulch cost could be eliminated if shredded leaves are available in quantity and one is willing to augment that material with midsummer grass clippings. Cocoa hulls were the most expensive mulch I used this year. Although using cocoa hulls would be much more costly than mulching with another material, cost might be unimportant to someone who prefers the appearance of cocoa mulch.

My Journal Records

Date	Materials	Hours
4/7	5 pounds 14-14-14 fertilizer	5.0
4/24	2 bags composted cow manure	6.25
	2 bags cocoa hull mulch	
	1.25 cubic yards hardwood and bark mulch	
	5 bags shredded leaves	
	14 perennials	
5/9	12 perennials	2.0
	Fencing for support cages	
	Bamboo stakes; twine	
5/23	3 perennials	2.5
	8 annuals; 3 cannas	
	Fencing for support cages	
	Lab diagnostic fee (monkshood)	
6/5	3 perennials	3.0
	Fencing; bamboo stakes; Hardware cloth;	
	Fungicide, fertilizer (21-7-7 soluble)	
	Soil test (Cooperative Extension)	
6/12	Fungicide	1.0
6/26	Bamboo stakes; insecticide	2.0
	Fertilizer (21-7-7 soluble)	
	3 perennials	
7/19	Fungicide, insecticide	1.0
8/10	Bamboo stakes	1.25
8/31	Beneficial nematodes	2.25
10/9	6 daffodils	1.5
11/1	9 perennials; 88 bulbs	2.25
Total seven months		35.25

Low-Maintenance Realities

The figure many gardeners want to negotiate is time. The concept of low-maintenance gardening probably sells more books, plants, and gadgets than any other. The catch is that it's all relative.

Low is a relative term. We can't discuss it productively until we work out a standard on which it can be based. This means describing the work that must be done, the standard of work expected, how much time that may require, and what the results should be.

Often the standard figure of one hour per month per 100 square feet turns out to be satisfactory. The gardener can afford or even enjoy that commitment. That's all it takes to make it "low" maintenance. For the person who can't or won't spend that much time, the discussion must continue, to look at what can be done differently to reduce that figure.

The conclusion of this chapter is a description of things that you can do to get gardening done more quickly or to reduce an area's overall need for maintenance. Several times in this book, I've warned you that every action has consequences. In keeping with that theme, each time-saver that follows also includes a brief explanation of what that tactic may "cost."

The how-to explanations and descriptions of consequences are very brief. The common ground we have after being through a gardening year together makes this possible.

All of these suggestions are strategies I use myself. My family's gardens cover about 8,000 square feet: our entire suburban lot excluding the space given to house, garage, driveway, patio, a tiny lawn, and two hedges. Although it's a family garden, the bulk of it is my responsibility, by choice. Once I could maintain all of it to the standards in this book, in increments of an hour or two every night and two full days every weekend. That ended when I began gardening professionally, and this list of shortcuts began to grow.

I've left some of my favorite tactics out of this chapter because I covered them thoroughly during the season. Two you should remember are **fertilizing before weeding** and **getting out early in spring**. Along with other methods already described, they're built into the standard of one hour per month.

This chapter includes more in-depth coverage on shortcuts I used while caring for Bed Three but mentioned only in passing. It also goes into techniques and devices that weren't applicable to Bed Three but that can help you in different circumstances.

It's impossible to say how much time any one of these materials, techniques, or design features will save. To figure that out, I would have to give up a timesaving technique on some occasions to do a controlled study. That has always been impossible for me. Every time I realized that working a particular way saved me time, I just couldn't give it up. Not even for science.

Timesaving Materials and Equipment

A **root barrier** can save edging time if it's well installed. Some people don't like the appearance of certain edging materials. Others are deterred by the initial cost or time required to put in a root barrier. Chapter 4 gives advice for installing edges. Don't forget that barriers should be used with care around young trees. See pages 148–149 for more on this.

Using **slow-release fertilizer** can mean telescoping three applications into one. The entire season's allotment may be applied in early spring before weeding and mulching a bed. One consideration is that some slow-release products are more expensive than conventional granular products, and others are bulkier. Another consideration is the effect a dry summer can have on water-soluble slow-release products. If the season is very dry or fertilizer granules are not in good contact with moist soil, spring-applied fertilizer may not dissolve and won't be available to plants. Fertilizer is discussed on pages 83–85.

Preformed kits and hoops for staking can be lifesavers in a busy spring. The initial cost per plant is often much higher than for bamboo stakes, wire cages, or twigs and string. However, preforms can be reused and often last many years. Some of my peony hoops have lasted for more than ten years, although they sometimes stay in the garage for years at a time. Kits and hoops have the disadvantage of taking up storage space

Watering Systems

A **sprinkler system** can be wonderful if it is well installed and you take the time to evaluate and adjust its effects. It can eliminate the time needed to drag hoses from storage and move hose-end sprinklers around at regular intervals. For best results, the system should put gardens and shrub areas in zones that are controlled separately from lawn zones. You should be able to operate sprinklers in garden zones manually even if those in lawn zones turn on and off automatically. Water should be applied to gardens only as needed, not on any calendar basis. Lawns respond best to frequent light watering.

It seems to be a well-kept secret in the irrigation industry that adjustments are always necessary immediately after a sprinkler system is installed and whenever the garden design changes. A plan that was adequate on paper may not deliver enough water to some areas or may deliver too much to others. Transplanting that results in tall plants where short species previously grew can block sprinklers. You must be willing to observe the system in action. It's often necessary to change spray heads, add flow reducers, redirect, and even move heads. Otherwise you can expect to see some plants fail "mysteriously" in what you would normally recognize as watering problem spots.

Soaker hoses are a specialized irrigation system that can save time and water. The hoses allow water to seep through countless pores and gradually soak into the garden soil. The layout of hoses and the frequency and duration of their use has to be evaluated as for any other system. One of this system's unique advantages is a potential reduction in fungal and bacterial diseases of the type that proliferate on wet foliage. A related drawback is that some insects and mites can flourish where overhead soaking doesn't occur to rinse these pests off the foliage.

Buy several **patching kits** when you buy your soakers. The kits are easy and quick to use, but buying one when the need arises often involves a time-consuming shopping trip. Whether you set the hose out above ground and hide it under mulch or you bury it, you will probably cut into it with a spade or pierce it with a fork at some time during the season. If the hose is sealed at its far end, use a hose repair kit to put a cap on that end so that you can open it and flush the hose annually. If your water is very hard, expect to replace soakers every four or five years, as the pores will become clogged. Check soaker hoses that are left in place over the winter; animals often chew them.

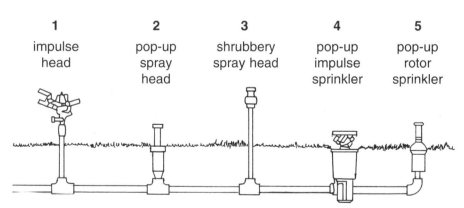

1	2	3	4	5
impulse head	pop-up spray head	shrubbery spray head	pop-up impulse sprinkler	pop-up rotor sprinkler

There are many different types of sprinkler heads and flow regulators to solve various irrigation problems. Most are easily obtained and installed. Beware of spray heads such as (1) and (4) that may spray water with such force that it flattens perennials.

in winter. The kit described on page 90 is attractive not only for its practicality in the garden but also because it collapses flat for storage.

Larger wheelbarrows save time, provided they are not so awkward and heavy that the gardener can't use them to capacity. My wheelbarrow holds a bit more than 5 cubic feet. This allows me to move a cubic yard of mulch or soil in just five or six trips. Fiberglass barrows of this size are very light and durable; I sometimes wish I had one. My husband prefers his construction-grade wheelbarrow, which carries more than 6 cubic feet of material. I avoid using it, having found that one 6-cubic-foot spill takes more time to clean up than I would have saved by using this bigger barrow.

Two-wheeled garden carts are handy for moving large amounts of material easily. They are shy on maneuverability, though. Also, I haven't yet met a standard garden gate that is wide enough to allow passage of the cart we use on a friend's herb farm.

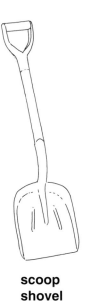

scoop shovel

Scoop shovels save a surprising amount of time. Six or seven scoops can fill a wheelbarrow or cart when you're loading a lightweight material such as bark, mulch, soil, or compost. The one disadvantage is the initial cost.

Five-gallon buckets may be the greatest laborsaving devices ever given to gardeners. With one at your side, you eliminate the need to carry either a bucket to soak transplants or a bag to hold small tools or debris. You'll also find that you have a portable stool and a sturdy aid for rising after being too long on your knees.

Cameras don't often make it onto lists of garden tools, but they are a boon. Coupled with a **journal or garden diary,** photos form the basis for solid, time-saving plans made during the winter. Show them sparingly to friends to avoid driving off those who don't find the details of your garden as exciting as you do. If you were not going to be with me throughout the season, I would have shown you only the first eight pictures in Chapter 1.

Dress for Success

I've been accused of looking as if an animal chewed on me when I'm out in my garden. I'll admit that my favorite garden clothes tend to be tattered from use. Sometimes they miss their turn in the wash, too, but that's because I can't get along without them.

Some people carry a kneeling pad around with them. My kneeler is built-in. The **knee pads** in my Greenknees (see Appendix, "References and Tools") are so thick, light, and long-wearing that I forget they are there. I can fall on my knees without discomfort, and it takes a sizable stone to make its presence felt through that foam. One day when I was out in my yard, I dropped down to the lawn to join a neighbor child in examining a new insect. I'd forgotten that I was wearing civilian clothes. The shock nearly brought tears to my eyes.

How do knee pads save time? Savings come in tiny bits, the difference between springing up to move to a new place and creaking to a stand. They might come from eliminating constant searches for the kneeling pad. There's also a good chance that I'd avoid early-spring work if not for the waterproof lining in the knee pockets. Losing the jump on spring would cost a lot.

Garden pants should be sturdy and comfortable and have a pocket suitable for carrying pruning shears. Mine win good grades on the first two counts. The tear in the back pocket speaks volumes for their failure on the third. I'll stick with this style because after five years I haven't found anything to beat them, but it's probably time to buy a pruner holster.

Frequently at outdoor gardening workshops or community gardening events I'm told, "You must have strong legs. I can't cut that sod at all, but you can."

It's not the legs. It's the **boots.** Not only do they save time, but they protect the only two feet you have. I recall preboot times with pain, when I often walked tenderly for several days after preparing a new bed.

Buy a pair with a **steel arch.** You'll be able to get the spade into the soil with one or two pushes, versus three, four, or not at all. Boots are expensive, but they last. Even with daily wear almost year-round and shamefully few oilings, mine last two or three years.

Shaving Time in Spring

• Whether you buy materials in bags or have it delivered in bulk, **get enough material to do the whole job.** This saves both the time and the aggravation of leaving your garden to buy or call for

Take Care of Tools

• **Keep spades, shovels, and saws sharp.** One cut is always quicker than three. A disadvantage is that a sharp spade is more of a threat to a soaker hose or sprinkler line. Sharpening spades is a good chore for bored teenage children. A sharp edge can last half the season, and getting it sharp cures the kids for as long.

• **Organize your tools** and equipment so that your standard kit is easy to find and put away. The only drawback this has is that other people can find your tools easily, too.

• Put your **hand tools in a bucket** and hang that from the handle of your wheelbarrow. Don't believe that advice about painting handles a bright color so you won't lose tools. Even the brightest fluorescent paint will disappear until winter if it slips under the garden canopy. Once you get used to plunking your shears back into a bucket when it's time to switch activities, you'll eliminate those searches for the world's most lost tool. One drawback to putting hand tools in a bucket is that you might be tempted to carry more than you need.

• **Spread a tarp** on the lawn before you begin stripping sod. Park a wheelbarrow on the tarp. Pitch the unwanted sod into the barrow, and you can eliminate raking the debris that misses its mark. This sometimes saves wear and tear on underlying sod, too.

• If you have wood chips or soil dumped on your lawn, spread a tarp there to make clean-up quicker and less traumatic for the sod. Don't spread a tarp if the truck will dump its load on your driveway. It's easy to clean every scrap off of a paved driveway. Scooping the last bits off a tarp is tougher.

more. This is most often the case when making raised beds. Such efforts require more soil than most people think. One cubic yard of material can raise a 5-by-10-foot area just 6 inches. The drawback to having six or seven yards of anything delivered is that the family may have to live with the pile for a few weeks while the gardener whittles away at it. Don't be concerned that they'll complain. They know that doing so will result in an invitation to join the chain gang.

• **Have mulch delivered as close as possible to the garden.** If this means dumping it on the street and hustling to get it moved before evening traffic begins, do it. Often the neighbor's driveway is closer, and you might be able to get permission to have material dumped there. Think carefully about the pros and cons of each delivery location. Most delivery companies require a signed waiver before backing into private drives. The weight that can crack pavement also can mire a truck in your septic field.

• **Do more pruning during the off-season** and in late summer, less during the late spring season of peak growth. One hard cut on a deciduous shrub in very early spring can eliminate one or two shearings later. Shear evergreens before growth begins or in late summer after the next year's buds are set. Remember to go over the shrub first with your hand pruners to thin the tips before you shear, as described on page 39.

• **Put a ball of string in your back pocket when pruning.** Unroll a yard of string and spread it out on the ground near the shrub you're pruning. Toss your clippings to fall across the string. Periodically tie up the bundle and start a new one. If you compost twigs and branches, you'll have to snip or untie the bundle when you arrive at the compost or shredder.

• **Restrain the urge toward constant change.** I moved, divided, and added plants in early spring for more than three hours. Little of this work was essential in terms of plant survival. Most of it was "should" work that can be done every three or four years rather than every two. Postponing the dividing has a drawback: a plant here and there will disappoint you each summer as it reaches its limit. It

One Cubic Yard of Soil

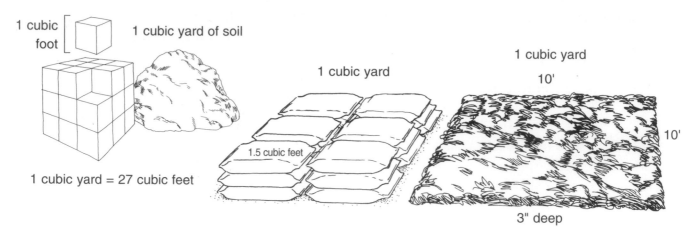

1 cubic foot

1 cubic yard of soil

1 cubic yard = 27 cubic feet

1.5 cubic feet

1 cubic yard

1 cubic yard

10'

10'

3" deep

Make sure you have as much material as you need. Remember there are 27 cubic feet in 1 cubic yard. One cubic yard will cover 100 square feet (a 10' X 10' area) just 3" deep.

might "lodge" (stems falling in all directions) as it gets too crowded. It may fall prey to a leaf disease, again from crowding. The flowers may be less than glorious in size and quantity. Learn to recognize these signs and put the signaling plants on your list for fall division.

• **Water new additions with the leaky buckets** or bottles described in Chapter 6. Unless you have a ready collection of matching containers, this can be visually distracting. If it saves the time and trouble of fighting with a hose, it's worth it. Was there ever such a double-edged sword as a garden hose?

• **Install hose reels in several places** where they are most often needed. I dream of the day when I will get connecting lines and hose bibs installed in all the proper places in my garden.

Buy several hoses and hose reels and leave them where they are most often used.

• **Use weeds and trimmed bits of perennials as mulch.** Lay them down where they came out. This eliminates some of the raking and carting of weeds. It also returns to the soil everything that went into the unwanted plant. Be sure to leave any roots high and dry so the plants die. This can look shabby while weeds are fading to brown. Get around that by scattering a thin layer of more attractive mulch on top. Don't mulch with weeds if they have ripe seed pods.

• **Make minicomposts in several places** around the garden. It's called sheet composting if you spread the materials thin and far. Perhaps a low mound of organic debris behind that huge peony, next to the woodpile, or along the base of the hedge. These small piles will decompose more slowly than large, so your supply of finished compost may fall off.

I rarely make the time to turn my compost pile. There are so many other things that are more fun to do with my gardening time. Left on its own, that pile of weeds, sod, and clippings will break down in a year. I've established a second compost site and move back and forth between the sites every other spring so that the previous year's accumulation can rot.

• **Reduce staking time by giving in.** Let the floppers flop. When they do, cut them back and bring the flowers in the house for vases and gifts. The disadvantage of this advice is obvious, but I derive great satisfaction from skipping this chore.

High-Summer Shortcuts and Fall Sprints

Once you get a taste of the rewards of lower maintenance and a chance to weigh the disadvantages, it's simple to do things you never dared. When you can use the next tactic, you've arrived.

Removing Problem Plants

If the plant is sickly or a bother, pull it out and send it to the compost. Ornamental gardening embraces thousands of species and tens of thousands of varieties. It only makes sense that a few won't be suited to your site, style, or handling. Loyalty to our purchases and protégés can blind us to how much time a struggling plant requires. As for bothersome plants, it's probably good that we aren't wired to blood pressure monitors while we're in the garden. I bet my blood pressure goes up every time I walk past that aggravating honeysuckle.

This lightening of the load can reduce our choices in species, but survivors will be healthier and easier to tend. It's the route to abundant green. A desire to preside over a lush garden comes up often on gardeners' wish lists. More people might throw away struggling plants if they understood this move as the key to that dream garden.

If, after removing a plant, you find that two or three different replacement species fail as well, take a step back and reevaluate the site and your expectations. You will probably find that the soil conditions, the light, or your own vision are not aligned with horticultural reality. Then you should apologize to the departed spirits of the plants you discarded and come back down to earth in your next choices.

Deadheading

Deadheading can be an enjoyable way to relieve stress, but it also accounts for the majority of summer maintenance time. To save time, **deadhead each species only once.** Use hedge shears or a weed whip as the plant passes its prime and begins the descent into shabbiness. You'll benefit from the economies of scale, although the plant will necessarily be browner than otherwise for the last part of its reign.

As a variation on all-at-once deadheading, **use conventional culling methods only where plants are close to the viewing public.** Let distance hide the gradual browning of other flowers until you dispatch them with your hedge shears. The disadvantage of leaving flowers to go brown is an increased chance of seed production and weed problems. I make mass cuts earlier than some. I'd rather see a shorter bloom period and an armload of cut flowers than be forced to weed out a mob of volunteers.

Drastic Measures in Fall

How desperate are you to reduce maintenance time? You can **cut down the whole garden in fall, leaving only the evergreens.** It's a drastic reduction in winter interest but considerably less work in spring. By the time I level our ornamental grasses in early spring, they've started to disintegrate, so raking is required. For a large species like maiden grass (*Miscanthus sinensis*), the fallout can spread 10 feet or more in every direction.

Defining Your Limits

Cure yourself of wandering. One fall, I did this by linking three bamboo stakes with 10-foot lengths of clothesline. By jabbing them in the ground and stretching the cords taut, I could define the back and side of a square area 10 feet on a side. I vowed to complete everything that needed to be done within this square before doing anything else. In an hour, that space was put to bed. It was clear what I had accomplished, and it felt good in contrast to days when a little work here and there added up to a visual zero.

You can do this without the physical demarcation that helped me stay in bounds. Choose an area of 100 to 200 square feet and stick with it until it's done. Ignore the things that lure you just a bit farther away. They'll wait. By doing so, you'll omit the time waste inherent in starting, dropping, and restarting a task. The disadvantage is that adjacent areas within a large garden may look distinctly different. Use this tactic in fall and spring, when you need the time savings most and inconsistent appearances are easier to tolerate.

Mulching

Apply a heavy mulch in fall. Do all the dividing you can before tucking this blanket between the plants' crowns. Use 5 to 6 inches of shredded leaves or 3 to 4 inches of shredded bark. This material will decompose over the winter and will be nearly perfect in depth for the next growing season. This means paying for or making both fall and spring mulches at the same time. In addition, in spring mulch will have to be raked away from areas that still need dividing.

Designing for Low Maintenance

Design and maintenance are not separated by any clear line. A good garden or landscape design anticipates and facilitates normal maintenance. The designer of Bed Three and the surrounding perennial display area used many strategies to keep maintenance within reason. Here are just a few tips to reduce maintenance before it starts or to redesign for lower care.

• **Avoid invasive plants, or use them to advantage as groundcovers.** If you must have an invasive plant within a more refined bed, install a root barri-

Root barriers of an appropriate depth can save time. There may be less need to untangle an invasive plant from its neighbors every spring.

Plan for a maintenance path between a wall and the garden, or between a hedge and border garden. This allows you to circulate and reach all parts of the bed easily. It also allows better circulation of air. This reduces the incidence of fungal diseases such as leaf spot and powdery mildew.

---

er deep enough to prevent its spread. Keep in mind that running plants such as 'Silver King' artemisia, bee balm, aster, and mint tend to put their energy into their perimeter growth and wear out at the center. It will be necessary every year or two to cut out the center, renew the soil there, and move outside pieces into that space.

• For island beds deeper than 6 feet and one-sided beds deeper than 3 feet, **build in maintenance paths.** Few people can reach more than 3 feet without falling into the garden they're tending. Working in deep beds without maintenance paths can cause back strain, compacted soil, and plants flattened by you losing your balance.

Large, flat paving stones can make a path that passes behind or between tall plants along the garden's left-right viewing axis. Such a path is easily seen in spring but lost under foliage in summer. The gardener never loses it, however, reaching it by stepping over an edging plant or walking into the far left or right side of the bed.

• **Use long-lived plants** that don't require frequent division. In Bed Three, 'Lambrook Silver' artemisia, daylily, blue fescue, moor grass, rue, blood grass, monkshood, and oxeye all fit this description. The astilbe and hosta added in fall qualify, too. Check the perennial chart in Chapter 14 for species that rate the April note "Divide every 2nd or 3rd year." These are species to avoid or to limit in number where low maintenance is important.

• **Plant species that don't require deadheading.** These include late-blooming species plus plants with short, sturdy flower stalks and attractive seed pods. To achieve the minimum of care, pick species that don't set a great deal of seed. In our trial garden, 'Halo Yellow' blackberry lily, potentilla, purple-leaf sedum, moor grass, rue, 'Golden Showers' coreopsis, 'Silver Carpet' lamb's ear, blood grass, cardinal flower, monkshood, and rock rose all fit the ticket.

• **Choose plants that will thrive on the site.** Avoid plants said to "tolerate" the prevailing conditions. Aim for those that will be so healthy that their natural enemies will be unable to get the upper hand. These also will give you the best bloom and foliage effects.

• **Use fewer gravel and stepping-stone walking paths.** These are attractive and can lend a romantic air, but they also can become weeding nightmares. Sod paths edged with root barriers are practical and comfortable even in bare feet. Just ask my kids, who have never forgiven me for taking out our sod paths. Make paths wide enough to allow the mower to

Reshape bed to eliminate un-mowable areas. This saves time that might have been spent arguing with a mower or hand-trimming where a mower couldn't reach. Dotted lines indicate an easier-to-maintain edge.

───────────────────

pass without dropping a wheel off the edge. Wood-chip paths can be practical if the mulch is thick and renewed at least once a year. Wood chips are perfect for these paths, as any nitrogen deficiency that results will work primarily against unwanted plants trying to establish in the path.

• **Check that a garden's edge will be mowable.** Wheel the mower along the proposed line, or walk it heel to toe. If you can do either comfortably, it's a mowable line.

To All Things a Season . . .

It's been an enjoyable and productive season. Enjoy the winter and all the plans you're making for next year.

Care of Particular Perennial Species

IN THIS CHAPTER, you can look for a particular perennial species to plan for its unique needs. This is where you can find *what* needs to be done *when*. On the facing page is a chart of general care and timing for activities in a perennial bed. A list of tasks is included for each month, with priorities indicated in bold type. These priority items are the "must-do" jobs. The distinctions between "must-do," "should-do," and "might-do" tasks are described in the Introduction. Below the chart is space for you to enter the perennials in your own garden.

Beginning on page 164 you will find a seasonal account of what should and might be done specifically for 90 perennial species. For instance, "deadhead" is a priority for the whole perennial garden in July, but it may be done in May for lungwort (*Pulmonaria saccharata*). Observing for pests and disease is a general priority in early summer, but you can begin looking for insect damage on bee balm (*Monarda* species) in late spring.

It is assumed that all the whole-garden activities, such as weeding, watering, and mulching, are done for individual species as part of treating the whole area per the general schedule. Those broad items are not repeated for each species.

Species are listed in alphabetical order by the plant's scientific name. This is the only way to avoid confusion, since one plant may have several different common names. If you do not know where to look on the chart because you are unfamiliar with plant scientific names, use the Index, which contains both the common and scientific names.

Customize the Chart for Your Use

The general chart is ready for you to copy and customize. Remember to adapt the column headline "Your Dates" to fit your hardiness zone and microclimate. (See page 6 for guidance.) Make a list of the plants in your garden. Check the species chart and write in the name of each plant that requires individual attention. Write the care it needs under the appropriate months in that row of your chart.

For instance, adding columbine to the chart will add a May-June note to watch for two insects, the columbine skipper and columbine leaf miner. You also might decide to add the note "cut back hard" in late June. That's one way to deal with both the insects and the plant's own tendency to go dormant. It will deny the pests a meal ticket, starving many. It also will encourage a second flush of leafy growth that will make the summer garden more attractive. For more information on pests and diseases, see page 178.

General Care and Timing

ZONES 5-6 ► YOUR DATES ►	APRIL	MAY	JUNE	JULY	AUGUST	SEPTEMBER	OCTOBER/ NOVEMBER	NOTES
THE WHOLE PERENNIAL GARDEN NEEDS:	Weed/edge Mulch Plant bare-root plants	Weed Mulch Water Fertilize Plant potted plants	Weed Water Check pests	Weed Water Fertilize Check pests	Weed Water	Edge Water Move/add	Weed Edge Mulch Water Move/add Winterize	
SOME PLANTS MAY NEED:	Protection off Cut down Check pests Thin/divide	Pinch Stake Thin	Pinch Deadhead Cut back Shear Stake	Pinch Deadhead Stake	Deadhead Stake	Cut back Divide	Fertilize Divide Protect if tender	

Customized Chart for Individual Species

YOUR DATES ► YOUR PLANTS ▼								NOTES

Care of Particular Perennial Species:
A Customized Chart

ZONE 5/6 ▶ YOUR DATES ▶	APRIL	MAY	JUNE	JULY
Achillea filipendulina **Fernleaf Yarrow** (Yellow)	Divide annually or every 2 years; discard center; relocate 4th–5th year	Stake (hoop) if any shade		Deadhead
Achillea millefolium **Milfoil** (Red, Pink, White)	Divide annually or every 2 years; discard center; relocate 4th–5th year	Stake (hoop) if any shade	Deadhead	Cut back hard
Aconitum species **Monkshood**		Observe for fungal, bacterial leaf diseases and remove/burn any affected foliage	May need staking if light strong from only one side	
Ajuga repens and varieties **Ajuga**	Cut out portions if it has outgrown its area	Shear/mow to remove flower stalks	Foliage declines temporarily esp. if in sun and not sheared	Rogue out any reversions
Alchemilla mollis **Lady's Mantle**		Observe for four-lined plant bug	Deadhead (optional; seed heads can be decorative)	
Anemone x *hybrida* (syn. *A. japonica*, *A. hupehensis*)	**Japanese Anemone**	Observe for four-lined plant bug		
Anthemis tinctoria **Golden Marguerite**	Divide every year or two	Stake and/or pinch		Deadhead
Aquilegia species **Columbine**		Observe for insect damage; columbine leaf miner, and skipper; (both overwinter in/on soil nearby as pupae)	Deadhead; can be cut back hard to starve pests, and renew foliage	May go through 4–6 week dormancy
Artemisia ludoviciana **Silver King/Silver Queen**	May need root barrier; divide every other year			
Artemisia schmidtiana **Silvermound**	Shear; divide every few years			Deadhead (shear) if heavy bloom

AUGUST	SEPTEMBER	OCT/NOV	NOTES
Cut back hard (unless winter effect desired)		Can be attractive over winter	Excess nitrogen or moisture contributes to lodging and fungi **Problems occasionally seen:** Fungi — rust; powdery mildew; stem rot. Bacteria — crown gall.
			Can suppress or inhibit the growth of adjacent plants **Problems occasionally seen:** Fungi — rust; powdery mildew; stem rot. Bacteria — crown gall.
		Remove/burn stalks	All parts dangerous if eaten **Problems occasionally seen:** Virus — leaf pale, stunted.
		Evergreen	May develop crown rot, root rot, or blights (fungi); most often associated with poor aeration, poor drainage, and heat **Problems occasionally seen:** Root nematodes.
			Low care: no serious problems.
	Deadhead		Good cover over spring bulbs **Problems occasionally seen:** Cultural — spotted, distorted, or dwarf flower (usually caused by heat/drought). Fungi rust (may account for abnormal spring development as well as leaf spot); downy mildew; smut; leaf spot; rhizome rot; collar rot. Insects — aphids; black blister beetle. Nematodes — fern nema (brown/black blotch on leaf as on mum and various other ornamentals); stem nema (as in phlox).
		Cultivate soil at base, leave bare until freeze to expose pests to birds and frost	**Problems occasionally seen:** Fungi — crown rot; leaf spot; root rot; rust (native grasses are alternate hosts; other host genera Anemone, Clematis, Delphinium). Virus — mosaic. Insects — aphids, stalk borer.
			Most artemisias irritating to hayfever sufferers when in bloom **Problems occasionally seen:** Fungi — rust (on leaf); stem rot. Insects — aphids.
		Don't cut hard before winter - Woody Evergreen	**Problems occasionally seen:** Fungi — rust (on leaf); rot (occurs most often in heavy, poorly drained soils). Nematodes.

| ZONE 5 ▶ | APRIL | MAY | JUNE | JULY | |
YOUR DATES ▶	_____	_____	_____	_____	
Aruncus dioicus **Goatsbeard**				Deadhead (optional: attractive in seed)	
Aster novae-belgii and hybrids **Aster**	Divide every other year	Stake (hoop); pinch tall varieties	Pinch tall varieties; check for rust or mildew fungi	Pinch tall varieties	
Astilbe arendsii, A. simplicifolia **False Goatsbeard, Astilbe**			Observe for mites	Deadhead; observe for Japanese beetle	
Astilbe chinensis varieties; _A. chinensis taquetii_ **Dwarf & Late Astilbe**	Observe for root weevil damage		Observe for leaf damage — weevil	Observe for Japanese beetle	
Athyrium japonicum 'Pictum' **Japanese Painted Fern**			Leaves may scorch in dry heat		
Brunnera macrophylla **Bigleaf Forget-me-not**		Seed stalks usually disappear under foliage	Leaf scorch usually cultural problem from heat and sun		
Calamagrostis acutiflora stricta **Feather Reed Grass**				Usually not deadheaded	
Campanula carpatica (Blue Clips, White Clips) **Carpathian Harebell**	Divide every other year		Deadhead; observe for crown rot fungus (correct drainage)	Shear	
Campanula persicifolia **Peach-Leaf Bellflower**	Divide every 3–4 years	Stake (optional); observe for slug damage	Deadhead; observe for leaf spot fungus	Deadhead	
Campanula poscharskyana **Serbian Bellflower**				Deadhead or shear	
Centaurea montana **Mountain Bluet, Perennial Bachelor's Button**	Weed out seedlings		Cut to ground after strong bloom is past		
Coreopsis hybrids ('Sunray,' etc.) **Lanceleaf Coreopsis**	Divide every 3 years	Monitor for four-lined plant bug	Deadhead	May be cut back hard	

| --- | --- | --- | --- |
			Long-lived, low care ***Problems occasionally seen:*** Fungi — leaf spot; rust. Insects — whitefly (reintroduced annually from greenhouse plants.) Mites.
Deadhead early varieties			Rabbits esp. fond of aster ***Problems occasionally seen:*** Fungi — leaf spot; fusarium blight; rusts (alternate hosts include Austrian pine, sedges, grasses). Virus — aster yellows. Insects — Japanese beetle; aphids; stalk borer (as in Lilium); root aphids; chrysanthemum lace bug; six-spotted leaf hopper. Foliar nematode (as in mum).
		A dense stand with heavy seed heads can be attractive in winter	Long-lived ***Problems likely to happen:*** Spider mite. Insects — black vine weevil. ***Problems occasionally seen:*** Cultural (from drought, heat) — leaf tip burn and scorch.
Deadhead			A. chinensis can spread aggressively ***Problems occasionally seen:*** Cultural (from drought, heat) — leaf tip burn and scorch. Spider mite (also often related to heat).
			Long-lived, low care, clump-forming.
			Can spread aggressively.
		Don't cut back: attractive in winter	Long-lived, low care, clump-forming ***Problems occasionally seen:*** Rot over winter (if in container or poorly drained area).
			Problems occasionally seen: Fungi — rust; leaf spot; crown rot; rot (poor drainage and air circulation usually to blame). Insects — foxglove aphid; onion thrips. Mites.
			Problems occasionally seen: Fungi — root rot; crown rot; rust. Insects — aphids.
			Problems occasionally seen: Fungi — crown rot, leaf spot.
			Spreads rapidly by seed ***Problems occasionally seen:*** fungi — downy mildew; stem rot; rust. Insects — stalk borer; aphids.
			Problems occasionally seen: Fungus — leaf spot. Insects — potato aphid; spotted cucumber beetle.

ZONE 5 ▶ YOUR DATES ▶	APRIL	MAY	JUNE	JULY	
Coreopsis verticillata: **Threadleaf Coreopsis**	Variety 'Golden Showers' needs restraint: divide regularly			Monitor variety 'Moonbeam' for gold-flowered sports and rogue out	
Delphinium elatum **Delphinium**	Divide every 3 years; replant only healthy side shoots in new site	Stake; monitor for fungi and bacteria: leaf spots, discoloration	Stake (tie in); monitor for occasional insects	Deadhead	
Dendranthemum x *morifolium* *(Chrysanthemum)* **Hardy Mum**	Divide every other year	Pinch; monitor for four-lined plant bug and aphids	Pinch; monitor for rust or mildew fungi	Pinch; monitor for rust or mildew fungi	
Dianthus gratianopolitanus **Cheddar Pinks**			Shear		
Dianthus plumarius **Pinks**	Restart from cuttings every other season		Deadhead	Cut back	
Dianthus x *alwoodii* **Cottage Pinks**			Deadhead	Deadhead	
Dicentra eximia hybrids and varieties **Fringed Bleeding Heart**			Deadhead for better repeat bloom		
Dicentra spectabilis **Bleeding Heart**	No special care needed				
Digitalis purpurea and other biennial spp. **Foxglove**		Stake (each stem)	Deadhead; monitor for mildew fungus	Stake (tie in); deadhead	
Echinacea purpurea **Purple Coneflower**				Deadhead	
Echinops ritro (E. exaltatus) **Blue Globe Thistle**		Can be pinched for shorter plant, later bloom; monitor for four-lined plant bug	Observe for caterpillars (new leaves sewn together): Painted Lady butterfly	Deadhead	
Epimedium species **Bishop's Hat**					

August	September	Oct/Nov	Notes
Deadhead (unless winter effect desired)		Can be attractive in winter	***Problems occasionally seen:*** Fungi — stem/root rot (in heavy, poorly drained soil).
Cut back all old growth when new basal growth seen		Remove/burn stalks	***Problems occasionally seen:*** Fungi — leaf spot; powdery mildew; crown rot (may also be bacterial). Virus — cucumber mosaic; curly top; aster yellows; regrowth after cutting back is very yellow, may be nutritional problem or aster yellows. Mites. Insects — stalk borer; aphid; Japanese beetle.
		Need extra protection if planted new in fall	***Problems occasionally seen:*** Fungi — wilt; powdery mildew; leaf spot (foliar nema is also confused with mum leaf spot). Bacteria — blight. Virus — mosaic. Insects — various leaf beetles; corn earworm; leafhopper (a disease vector); chrysanthemum lace bug. Mites (especially where air circulation is poor). Nematodes.
		Do not cut back hard for winter—woody evergreen	Eaten by rabbits, voles, deer ***Problems occasionally seen:*** Fungi — stem rot; botrytis blight (especially where moisture abundant at surface in winter); rust. Bacteria — leaf spot. Insects — onion thrips; aphids. Mites.
		Do not cut back hard for winter—woody evergreen	Eaten by rabbits, voles, deer ***Problems occasionally seen:*** Fungi — stem rot; leaf spot; botrytis blight; rust. Insects — onion thrips; aphids. Mites.
			Eaten by rabbits, voles, deer ***Problems occasionally seen:*** Fungi — stem rot; rust. Bacteria — leaf spot. Insects — onion thrips; aphids. Mites.
			Problems occasionally seen: Fungi — stem rot (check drainage). Insects — aphids.
Goes dormant: cut back hard as soon as foliage yellows			Long-lived, low care ***Problems occasionally seen:*** Fungi — stem or crown rot (spring growth suddenly wilts and dies; poor drainage to blame). Insects — aphids.
Allow some seed to set		Do not cut down basal foliage of 1st-year plants	***Problems occasionally seen:*** Fungi — leaf spot; root rot; stem rot. Virus — curly top virus; tobacco mosaic. Insects — Japanese beetle, foxglove aphid.
		Birds appreciate winter seed	Eaten by groundhogs and rabbits ***Problems occasionally seen:*** Fungi — leaf spot. Insects — Japanese beetle. Unknown virus (sudden black, shriveled lower leaves, progresses up stem — remove and destroy).
Cut back			***Problems occasionally seen:*** Fungi — crown rot. Insects — peach tree aphid.
		Don't cut hard: semi-evergreen	Long-lived, low care ***Problems occasionally seen:*** Insects — vine weevil. Fungi — leaf spot.

Care of Particular Perennial Species | 169

ZONE 5 ▶ YOUR DATES ▶	APRIL	MAY	JUNE	JULY	
Eupatorium coelestinum **Blue Mist Flower**		Slow to emerge in spring; cut out unwanted portions now	Monitor for mildew fungus	Monitor for mildew fungus	
Eupatorium purpureum, E. fistulosum **Joe Pye**		Can be pinched for shorter plant			
Euphorbia polychroma **Cushion Spurge**		Do not deadhead; bracts attractive through summer	If lodges, consider dividing in fall		
Festuca ovina glauca **Blue (Sheep's) Fescue**	Cut back hand; divide every 3–4 years		Deadhead; can cut back to renew foliage		
Gaillardia grandiflora **Blanket Flower**	Divide every 2–3 years			Deadhead	
Geranium, tall spp. such as *Geranium himalayense, G. platypetalum* **Cranesbill**		Monitor for leaf spot fungus	Deadhead		
Geranium, groundcover types such as *Geranium macrorrhizum* **Perennial Geranium**	Cut out unwanted portions				
Geranium, repeat-blooming short spp. such as *Geranium endressi, G. sanguineum* **Perennial Geranium**		Monitor for leaf spot fungus	Shear		
Grasses: See *Calamagrostis, Festuca, Helictotrichon, Imperata, Miscanthus, Molinia, Pennisetum, Phalaris*					
Gypsophila paniculata **Baby's Breath**		Stake (hoop) if in anything less than full sun	Deadhead	Deadhead	
Helictotrichon sempervirens **Blue Oat Grass**	Cut down		Deadhead or cut back		
Heliopsis helianthoides (*H. scabra*) **False Sunflower**		Monitor for four-lined plant bug		Cut back	
Hemerocallis hybrids **Daylily**			Deadhead	Deadhead	

AUGUST	SEPTEMBER	OCT/NOV	NOTES
			Can spread aggressively; good cover for spring bulbs ***Problems likely to happen:*** Fungi — mildew. Insects — chrysanthemum leaf miner. ***Problems occasionally seen:*** Fungi — leaf spot. Insects — scale; aphids.
Deadhead			Spreads rapidly by seed in moist soil ***Problems occasionally seen:*** Fungi — mildew; leaf spot.
			Long-lived, low care ***Problems occasionally seen:*** Fungi — root rot (in pots and in poorly drained soil).
		Do not cut hard: ever-green	Seedling may be inferior in leaf color. ***Problems occasionally seen:*** Fungi — crown rot (in poorly drained soil).
Cut back			***Problems occasionally seen:*** Fungi — leaf spot; powdery mildew; rust. Insects — leafhopper; aphids; stalk borer.
			Long-lived, low care ***Problems occasionally seen:*** Insects — four-lined plant bug.
			Long-lived ***Problems occasionally seen:*** Fungi — leaf spot.
			Long-lived; some spread rapidly by seed ***Problems occasionally seen:*** Fungi — rust.
			Rodents may damage crowns over winter ***Problems occasionally seen:*** Fungi — crown or root rot over winter, especially if grown in pots.
Deadhead			***Problems occasionally seen:*** Fungi — stem or crown rot (spring growth suddenly wilts and dies; poor drainage to blame). Bacteria — crown gall (especially on grafted forms — a soil-dwelling pest). Virus — aster yellows. Insects — aphids.
		Do not cut: attractive in winter	Long-lived, low care, clump-forming
Deadhead			Spreads rapidly by seed ***Problems occasionally seen:*** Insects — aphids. Fungi — leaf spot. Unexplained problem, perhaps a virus — chlorosis (pale yellow growth) in early spring.
Cut back deteriorating foliage			Long-lived, low care ***Problems occasionally seen:*** Fungi — leaf spot. Insects — flower thrips. Mites. Daylily "spring sickness" — yellow early foliage, may be crumpled (nutrient deficiency).

ZONE 5 ▶ YOUR DATES ▶	APRIL	MAY	JUNE	JULY	
Heuchera x *brizoides* 'Palace Purple' etc. **Purple-Leaf Coralbells**	Divide every 3 years; observe for root weevil		Observe for leaf damage by weevil	Deadhead	
Heuchera sanguinea **Coralbells**	Divide every 3 years; observe for root weevil		Deadhead; observe for leaf damage by weevil	Deadhead	
Hibiscus moscheutos **Hardy Hibiscus**		Late to emerge		$\frac{1}{3}$ of stems can be cut back $\frac{1}{3}$ now for later bloom on regrowth	
Hosta species **Hosta**	Monitor slugs: pinholes in leaves become huge by late summer; control in April-May				
Iberis sempervirens **Candytuft**			Shear		
Imperata cylindrica 'Red Baron' **Blood Grass**	Cut down	Watch for and remove tall blades without red — reverting to type			
Iris germanica **Dwarf & Standard Bearded Iris**	Clean all debris early — borer eggs on old leaves	Deadhead	Monitor for borer		
Iris pallida (I.p. variegata) **Zebra Iris**	Deadhead	Observe for borer			
Iris sibirica hybrids **Siberian Iris**				Deadhead (unless winter effect desired)	
Kirengeshoma palmata **Japanese Wax Bell**					
Lamium maculatum varieties, etc. **White-leaf Lamium, Spotted Dead Nettle**	Cut out portions to reduce spread as needed	Observe for fungi: leaf spot	Cut back to renew		
Lavandula angustifolia **Lavender**	Shear			Shear	
Leucanthemum x *superbum (Chrysanthemum)* **Daisy**	Divide every 2–3 years	Monitor for four-lined plant bug Deadhead	Cut back hard after bloom		

AUGUST	SEPTEMBER	OCT/NOV	NOTES
Deadhead		Do not cut hard: ever-green	Eaten by deer **Problems occasionally seen:** Insects — mealybug. Fungi — leaf spot; powdery mildew; stem rot.
		Do not cut hard: ever-green	Eaten by deer **Problems likely to happen:** Fungi — stem rot. Insects — root weevil. **Problems occasionally seen:** Insects — mealybug. Fungi — leaf spot; powdery mildew.
			Long-lived, low care **Problems occasionally seen:** Fungi — leaf spot. Insects — Japanese beetle; leaf skeletonizer (perhaps abutilon moth).
Deadhead			Eaten by deer; long-lived, low care **Problems occasionally seen:** Fungi — leaf spot; crown rot (in heavy mulch or when set too deep in pot). Foliar nematodes.
		Do not cut hard: ever-green	**Problems occasionally seen:** Club root disease (remove and destroy, replant with species not in mustard family). Insects — oystershell scale.
		Do not cut: attractive in winter	Species can be invasive in areas without cold winter.
Lift and divide every 2–3 years; check/discard borer damage			**Problems occasionally seen:** Fungi — soft rot (associated with borer damage; control it by controlling borers); leaf spot; rust; blossom blight. Cultural — flower buds dry, shrivel unopened (excessive heat or drought early in spring). Insects — aphids.
			Problems occasionally seen: Insects — iris borer.
		Seed heads can be attractive through winter	Long-lived, low care **Problems occasionally seen:** Insects — iris thrips; Japanese beetle (eat roots as well as foliage); borer.
		Flowers late; buds may be killed by frost	Long-lived, low care. Locate in protected area if frost likely by early October in your area.
		Do not cut hard: semi-evergreen	**Problems occasionally seen:** Fungi — stem rot (especially in heat, poor drainage; some varieties resistant). Insects — four-lined plant bug.
		Do not cut hard: woody evergreen	**Problems occasionally seen:** Fungi — leaf spot; crown/root rot (heavy soils, wet areas). Insects — four-lined plant bug.
			Problems occasionally seen: Fungi — wilt; powdery mildew; leaf spot. Virus — distorted growth/foliage. Insects — aphids; stalk borer; thrips.

ZONE 5 ▶ YOUR DATES ▶	APRIL _____	MAY _____	JUNE _____	JULY _____	
Liatris spicata **Blazing Star/Gayfeather**				Deadhead	
Linum perenne **Blue Flax**	Short-lived; replace every 3rd year		Shear	Shear (allow some seed set for renewal)	
Matteucia pensylvanica **Ostrich Plume Fern**		Cut out portions to reduce spread as needed			
Miscanthus species and varieties **Maiden Grass**	Cut down				
Molinia species **(Purple) Moor Grass**	Cut down				
Monarda didyma, M. fistulosa **Bee Balm**	Divide every 2 years	Monitor for four-lined plant bug	Monitor for powdery mildew fungi	Deadhead	
Pachysandra terminalis **Pachysandra**	Can be cut to ground now and bed renewed if needed		Chlorosis if in too much sun or alkaline soil		
Paeonia hybrid **Peony**		Stake (hoop); fertilize when new stalks are just emerging	Deadhead; monitor for leaf & flower blight fungi and remove affected stems	Monitor for Japanese beetle	
Papaver orientale **Oriental Poppy**			Deadhead	Dormancy	
Pennisetum alopecuroides **Perennial Fountain Grass**	Cut down; divide every 4–5 years	Slow to begin growth in spring			
Penstemon species **Penstemon/Beardtongue**	Divide every 3 years			Deadhead as desired	
Perovskia atriplicifolia **Russian Sage**	Cut woody stems down to live in basal buds				
Phalaris arundinacea picta **Variegated Ribbon Grass**	Requires root barrier		Cut back now to deadhead and renew foliage		
Phlox divaricata **Woodland Phlox**			Shear; observe for powdery mildew fungus		
Phlox maculata, P. paniculata **Tall Phlox**	Divide every 2-3 years		Monitor for: mildew and leaf spot fungi (*P. maculata* has some resistance)	Monitor for fungi: mildew and leaf spot fungi	

August	September	Oct/Nov	Notes
Cut back before foliage dies back			***Problems occasionally seen:*** Fungi — leaf spot; crown rot.
			Problems occasionally seen: Fungi — infects and "pinches" frond mid-rib while young; causes summer death of tip. Insects — distorted summer foliage may be from minor spring insect damage when fronds unfurling.
		Don't cut: attractive in winter	Long-lived, low care.
Don't deadhead- seed stalks attractive in fall		Don't cut: attractive in winter	Long-lived, low care.
Cut back hard			***Problems occasionally seen:*** Fungi — rust.
		Do not cut hard: ever-green	***Problems occasionally seen:*** Fungi — leaf blight. Insects — scale. Mites.
		Cut and destroy all debris if any leaf disease noted	***Problems occasionally seen:*** Fungi — leaf spot; downy mildew; stem wilt. Insects — lily scale, flower thrips; rose chafer.
Best time to transplant mid-July while dormant		Do not cut new basal foliage: evergreen and essential	***Problems occasionally seen:*** Insects — four lined plant bugs; rose chafer; tarnished plant bug. Bacteria — blight. Fungi — downy mildew.
		Do not cut: can be attractive in early winter	Can spread rapidly by seed.
			Problems occasionally seen: Fungi — crown rot (usually attributable to poor drainage).
		Do not cut to ground: semi-evergreen	***Problems occasionally seen:*** Fungi — leaf spot. Insects — four-lined plant bug.
		Do not cut hard: ever-green	Eaten by groundhog and rabbit.
Deadhead			Eaten by groundhog and rabbit ***Problems occasionally seen:*** Stem nema (distorted new growth). Insects — spittlebug; phlox plant bug. Cultural — leaf blight (from poor growing conditions). Two-spotted mite.

ZONE 5 ▶ YOUR DATES ▶ _____	APRIL _____	MAY _____	JUNE _____	JULY _____	
Phlox subulata **Creeping Phlox**			Shear		
Platycodon grandiflorus **Balloon Flower**		Late to emerge	Stake tall varieties	Deadhead; stems cut back by ⅓ before mid-July often bloom in fall	
Polystichum acrostichoides **Christmas Fern**	Groom foliage (year-old leaves may be tattered)				
Potentilla species **Herbaceous Potentilla**	Divide every 3–4 years		Deadhead		
Pulmonaria species **Bethlehem Sage**		Deadhead (optional — seed stalks usually fall below foliage)	Monitor slugs		
Rudbeckia fulgida 'Goldsturm' **Black-Eyed Susan**	Cut out unwanted portions now	Monitor for four-lined plant bug			
Ruta graveolens **Rue**	Prune to shorten and remove any winter-killed stems	Deadhead	If caterpillars, consider welcome (Eastern black swallowtail butterfly)		
Salvia, ornamental species (*S. azurea*, *S. superba*, *S. verticillata*)	**Perennial Sage**	Monitor for four-lined plant bug	Deadhead	Cut back	
Sedum acre, *S. kamschaticum*, *S. spurium* **Groundcover Sedum**				Deadhead (mow)	
Sedum sieboldii 'Vera Jameson' **Sedum Vera Jameson**	No special care needed				
Sedum spectabile; *S. maximum* 'Atropurpureum' **Cabbage Rose**	Cut down; divide every 4–5 years				
Stachys lanata **Lamb's Ear**	Divide every 3 years			Deadhead; observe for fungus crown rot	
Tradescantia species **Spiderwort**			Cut back hard	Normal for foliage to deteriorate	
Veronica species **Veronica/Speedwell**		Monitor for four-lined plant bug		Deadhead	

August	September	Oct/Nov	Notes
		Do not cut to ground: evergreen	**Problems occasionally seen:** Fungi — rust. Stem and bulb nematodes (in spring, center dies out).
			Eaten by rabbits and slugs **Problems occasionally seen:** Fungi — crown rot (improve drainage). Insects — aphids (reduce nitrogen levels).
		Do not cut down: evergreen	Long-lived, low care.
			Problems occasionally seen: Fungi — leaf spot.
			Eaten by deer **Problems occasionally seen:** Fungi — powdery mildew (especially in dry shade; some varieties resistant).
		Attractive in winter	**Problems occasionally seen:** Fungi — leaf spot; powdery mildew; downy mildew. Insects — stalk borer; (red) aphid.
		Do not cut to ground: evergreen	Oil in leaf can cause dermatitis **Problems occasionally seen:** Insects — black swallowtail butterfly caterpillars (plant tolerates this damage easily).
			Spreads rapidly by seed **Problems occasionally seen:** Fungi — leaf spot. Insects — stalk borer; scale.
			Problems occasionally seen: Fungi — leaf spot; crown rot.
			Problems occasionally seen: Fungi — leaf blotch; leaf spot; stem rot; crown rot. Insects — aphid.
		Do not cut: attractive through winter	Eaten by deer **Problems occasionally seen:** Fungi — leaf blotch; leaf spot; stem rot; crown rot. Insects — aphid.
			Can be invasive **Problems occasionally seen:** Fungi — leaf spot.
Cut back			**Problems occasionally seen:** Fungi — leaf spot; downy mildew. Spring leaf distortion, summer flower deformity, and overall weakness — cause unknown, possible virus.

Pests and Diseases in General

Each plant species is accompanied by a list of problems that may occur. If this listing of problems causes you to shy away from gardening, please remember my advice to take time to smell the flowers. Most of the problems shown in the charts are possibilities, not probabilities.

I compiled the list over several years. Recently, I expanded it to include observations made by Department of Agriculture plant inspectors. So you're looking at a record of everything found on thousands of plants over decades, on plants in containers — with all the attendant stresses of that artificial environment — as well as those growing in open ground. You'll see that most were found only occasionally. You may not see any of these problems, or you may have two or three minor skirmishes a season, just as I did in Bed Three.

It's also worth noting that some species' problems have been under more critical review than others, here and in pest-management reference books. Species cultivated for cut flowers and pot crops often have the longest list of problems. This may not be a reflection of the plant's susceptibility to problems but a result of long, close observation under greenhouse conditions.

Problems that are most likely to occur are listed by month for the plant they affect. Those that are more unusual are listed as "Problems occasionally seen." If you want to fuss most productively over a plant, concentrate on learning to recognize those problems listed by month. Diseases and other pests that are occasionally seen are listed primarily for your easy cross-reference if you are also using more technical pest-control manuals.

When Dealing with Symptoms, Think About Culture

It has been estimated that more than 80 percent of the troubles we see in a garden are caused not by insects or diseases but by cultural mismanagement. Plants become susceptible to pests when they are underwatered, overwatered, given too little or too much sun, overfertilized, or denied the depth or spread of root to which their species is accustomed. Don't use the chart in this part of the book to treat diseases and kill bugs that are actually symptoms of environmental trouble.

If you find an "occasionally seen" problem, take a good look at the site and your maintenance practices. Unusual problems are more likely to crop up among stressed plants than among healthy ones. Fix any underlying problem before focusing on a symptom. Check a plant encyclopedia (see Appendix, "References and Tools," for my recommendations) and verify that you have planted that species in an appropriate site and are giving it proper care.

Categories of Pest and Disease Problems

Many diseases are caused by fungi. Three examples are powdery mildew on phlox, black spot on roses, and leaf spot on perennial geranium. Although three different fungi are involved, some general antifungal steps are effective against all.

Other diseases are bacterial, such as crown gall on baby's breath or bacterial leaf spot in monkshood. These two bacteria are distinct species, but both can be kept at bay by a gardener who understands the basic cycle of bacterial infection and spread.

Thus the general nature of a problem forms the basis for your first response. What you need to start any pest-management program is the knowledge that a condition is caused by insects, fungi, bacteria, and so on.

From that starting point, you can apply the general care that is appropriate in horticulture. Those basic steps are described below. If standard care procedures for that category don't seem to apply or fail to correct a problem, take the specific disease or insect name and consult one of the references listed in the Appendix, "References and Tools," for a more refined approach.

Cosmetic vs. Life-Threatening Problems

As you use the chart to manage pest problems, be clear as to the degree of harm that the plant actually faces. Your plan of action should be based on whether a situation is cosmetic or life threatening.

The majority of pest concerns we face are cosmetic. Most leaf damage is cosmetic, while extensive damage to woody parts or roots is more serious. Problems that recur year after year without killing or stunting a plant are also usually cosmetic in nature. You can check your estimate of the seriousness of almost any situation by looking it up in a disease or pest reference book. There, descriptions of specific cosmetic problems often contain the phrase "not serious."

Some things are obviously minor. You know that I accepted some slug damage in Bed Three without concern. I also made no effort to track down the culprit when a few daisy petals were eaten in June. If all the petals had been eaten off every daisy and every plant in the bed had been riddled with slug holes, the problems could have been described as more widespread. Yet it's unlikely that either situation would have escalated to life threatening. Those established plants in Bed Three could afford to lose 10 or 20 percent of their leaf surface to a leaf eater, just as they could spare that amount of foliage when I pruned and deadheaded them.

Take a good look at the most slug-damaged or insect-ravaged leaf you can find on an established plant. To figure the degree of stress the plant has experienced, estimate the ratio of green leaf to holes. You'll be surprised at how ugly a leaf can be and still have only minor damage — less than 20 percent of the tissue destroyed. Cosmetic problems become life threatening only when damage to the whole plant is greater than 20 percent or weak plants are involved — seedlings, transplants, or individuals recovering from earlier trouble.

Managing Legitimate Problems

So you've decided to try to manage a problem, either because it threatens to kill the plant or because it has wounded your sense of aesthetics so deeply that the trouble will be worth the effort. The following information will help you plan an effective campaign.

Fungi

Fungi grow over time. They don't suddenly appear to coat a leaf with white powder or rusty red spores. By the time you notice the infection, it's probably been growing for weeks within the leaf. Whatever you do to control the disease this season, make sure you mark your calendar to do it next year, earlier.

Many fungi require water to develop from an airborne spore into an organism capable of penetrating or attaching to a leaf. Moisture may be required for an hour or a day — it depends on the species of fungus. It always pays to keep foliage dry rather than wet. Check and change your watering routine if fungi become a problem.

Air is an ally in fighting fungi. Thin plants to let air flow freely between the stems. Leave space between solid walls or hedges and border plantings so that a breeze can find its way through.

Clean up infected foliage as soon as you see it, and get rid of the sickest plants. This reduces the sources of contagion. Swab your hands and tools with rubbing alcohol before moving on to other plants that also may be susceptible.

If you decide a fungicide is necessary, be aware that some chemicals kill some fungi but not others. Use one of known effectiveness, and time the application wisely. Do this by looking for the problem in the books listed in the Appendix, "References and Tools," and follow those recommendations for choosing a fungicide and timing the application.

When you spray fungicides, coat the bottom of each leaf as well as the top. Be sure to aim low on the plant, too, since lower leaves are more at risk of infection than higher foliage that's bathed in air and light. If the fungicide is water-soluble, reapply it after any heavy rain. This applies to commercial products as well as homemade fungicides such as baking soda and water.

Learn to let go. If a plant is so susceptible to fungal problems that your best efforts can't keep it clean, throw it out and start over with a variety that is resistant to the disease.

Bacterial Problems

Treat bacterial problems as if they were fungi, up to the point of applying fungicides. Some bacteria can be killed or suppressed with fungicides such as Bordeaux mixture, which contains copper. This is not always the case, however. If increased ventilation, reduced water, and cleanliness don't help, hit the books before you mix up a fungicide.

Bacterial growth is encouraged by nitrogen. Avoid using a fertilizer with a high nitrogen content where bacterial problems exist.

Viruses

Virus-infected plants may have distorted leaves, stems, or flowers. There also may be a pattern of discoloration on the leaves that is well described by the term *mosaic*.

Many viral infections are so minor that they can exist for years in a plant without attracting attention. The virus weakens its host, but while growing conditions are good, the plant continues to grow. It may be similar to a person who continues to function while nursing a head cold. You may see significant symptoms only when the plant is undergoing some other stress.

The summer described in this book was exceptionally hot. Plants were stressed, and I noticed unusual symptoms. I saw purple coneflower (*Echinacea purpurea*) with "double yoke" flowers, purple loosestrife (*Lythrum salicaria*) with flattened flower spikes that resembled cockscomb celosia, and blue veronica (*Veronica longifolia*) with curled and flattened spikes. All of these distortions were probably the result of latent viruses. None of them warranted immediate attention, but now I had my cue to watch for further developments.

If I see that those plants are weak even in normal conditions, I'll act. We don't have cures for viruses, so I will have only one option — destroy the plant. That will reduce the chances that others of its species will become infected. Commonly, viruses move around via insects that feed on both infected and healthy plants, spreading the trouble between plants of the same susceptible species.

Insects

The best advice I can give you about insects is to read my accounts of Bed Three's black vine weevil problem and my family's four-lined plant bug crusade in Chapters 5 and 7. After you trace a problem to an insect, you still need to know something about its life cycle so that you can interfere at a critical juncture.

Many insects are easiest to identify but hardest to kill when they reach maturity. They may simply be more mobile as adults — harder targets. Also, they may have developed a waxy shell that sheds insecticidal solutions. When you first identify an insect problem, your best course may be to wait, research it, and act when the next "hatch" is due — often that's the following season.

The majority of insects do the most damage when they are young, hungry, and growing rapidly. Coincidentally, young insects are quite vulnerable to physical controls such as squashing or knock-down sprays of water. They also may be easily controlled by the introduction of beneficial insects and biological weapons such as bacteria that infect only that insect. You may have a wider selection of control tactics to choose from, and their effectiveness may be greater, if you wait to attack the young insects. Check one of the reference books listed in the Appendix, "References and Tools," to pinpoint the critter's location when it's young and soft. Focus your time and energy there.

Useful Books

Following is a list of the references that I used at one time or another in compiling this book. It's lengthy yet incomplete. It would be impossible to list all the Cooperative Extension Service publications used or all the periodicals from which I regularly cut and file useful articles. I encourage you to make use of your Extension office and your library's *Reader's Guide to Periodical Literature* for guidance in this area.

General Gardening, Locating Plants, and Identifying Useful Organizations

Brickell, Christopher, editor-in-chief. *The American Horticultural Society Encyclopedia of Gardening.* New York: Dorling Kindersley, 1993.

Bubel, Nancy. *The New Seed Starter's Handbook.* Emmaus, Pennsylvania: Rodale Press, 1988.

Heriteau, Jacqueline, and H. Marc Cathey. *The National Arboretum Book of Outstanding Garden Plants.* New York: Simon and Schuster, 1990.

Huxley, Anthony, editor-in-chief. *The New Royal Horticultural Society Dictionary of Gardening.* New York: Stockton Press, 1992.

Isaacson, Richard T. *The Andersen Horticultural Library's Source List of Plants and Seeds.* Chanhassen, Minnesota: Andersen Horticultural Library, 1993.

McGourty, Fred. *The Perennial Gardener.* Boston: Houghton-Mifflin, 1989.

Reilly, Ann. *Park's Success with Seeds.* Greenwood, South Carolina: Geo. W. Park Seed Company, 1978.

Wright, Michael. *The Complete Book of Gardening.* New York: Warner Books, 1979.

Wyman, Donald. *Wyman's Gardening Encyclopedia.* New York: MacMillan Publishing Company, 1986.

The Encyclopedia of Associations. Gale Research, Inc., Detroit, 1995.

Perennial Plant Association, "Standards: Landscape Specifications" for bed preparation and maintenance of perennials. Available for a fee and to members. For information, contact Steven Still, Executive Secretary, 3383 Schirtzinger Road, Hilliard, OH 43026.

Soil Preparation, Fertilizers, and Component Interactions

Baird, Jack V., and Charles D. Sopher. *Soils and Soil Management.* Reston, Virginia: Reston Publishing Company, 1982.

Carleton, R. Milton. *Your Garden Soil: How to Make the Most of It.,* New Jersey: D. Van Nostrand Company, 1961.

Foster, Catherine Osgood. *Building Healthy Gardens.* Pownal, Vermont: Storey Communications, 1989.

Foth, H. D., and L. M. Turk. *Fundamentals of Soil Science.* New York: John Wiley & Sons, 1972.

Watson, Gary W., and Dan Neely. *The Landscape Below Ground.* Savoy, Illinois: International Society of Arboriculture, 1994.

Botany, Nomenclature, and Poisonous and Toxic Plants

Capon, Brian. *Botany for Gardeners.* Portland, Oregon: Timber Press 1990.

Erichsen-Brown, Charlotte. *Medicinal and Other Uses of North American Plants.* New York: Dover Publications, 1979.

Hortus Third. New York: MacMillan Publishing Company, 1976.

Kindscher, Kelly. *Medicinal Wild Plants of the Prairie.* Lawrence, Kansas: University Press of Kansas, 1992.

Lampe, Kenneth F., and Mary Ann McCann. AMA *Handbook of Poisonous and Injurious Plants.* Chicago: American Medical Association, 1985.

Preacher, James W., and Randy G. Westbrooks. *Poisonous Plants of Eastern North America.* Columbia: University of South Carolina Press, 1986.

Stern, Kingsley R. *Introductory Plant Biology.* Dubuque, Iowa: Wm. C. Brown Publishers, 1985.

Young, Paul. *The Botany Coloring Book.* New York: Barnes & Noble Books, 1982.

Lawn Care

Decker, Henry F., and Jane M. Decker. *Lawn Care.* Englewood Cliffs, New Jersey: Prentice-Hall, 1988.

Gilmer, Maureen. *Easy Lawn and Garden Care.* Yonkers, New York: Consumer Reports Books, 1994.

Trees and Shrubs

Austin, David. *David Austin's English Roses.* Boston: Little Brown & Company, 1993.

Cox, Peter. *The Cultivation of Rhododendrons.* London: B. T. Batsford Books, 1993.

Dirr, Michael A. *Manual of Woody Landscape Plants.* Champaign, Illinois: Stipes Publishing Company, 1990.

Giles, F. A. *Pruning and Care of Trees and Shrubs.* Bulletin U5040, Cooperative Extension Service, University of Illinois at Urbana-Champaign.

Harris, Richard W. Arboriculture: *Care of Trees, Shrubs and Vines in the Landscape.* Englewood Cliffs, New Jersey: Prentice-Hall, 1983.

Hightshoe, Gary. *Native Trees, Shrubs and Vines for Urban and Rural America.* New York: Van Nostrand Reinhold, 1988.

Hill, Lewis. *Pruning Simplified.* Pownal, Vermont: Storey Communications, 1979.

Martin, Alexander C., Arnold Nelson, and Herbert S. Zim. *American Wildlife & Plants: A Guide to Wildlife Food Habitats.* New York: Dover Publications, 1993.

Ray, Richard, and Michael MacCaskey. *Roses: How to Select, Grow and Enjoy.* Tucson, Arizona: HP Books, 1985.

Reddell, Rayford Clayton. *The Rose Bible.* New York: Harmony Books, 1994.

Shigo, Alex. *A New Tree Biology.* Durham, New Hampshire: Shigo and Trees Associates, 1989.

Taylor's Guide to Shrubs. Boston: Houghton Mifflin Company, 1987.

Taylor's Guide to Trees. Boston: Houghton Mifflin Company, 1988.

Vertrees, J.D. *Japanese Maples.* Portland, Oregon: Timber Press, 1987.

Zucker, Isabel. Revised and expanded by Derek Fell. *Flowering Shrubs and Small Trees.* New York: Grove Weidenfeld, 1990.

Perennials, Annuals, and Wildflowers

Aden, Paul. *The Hosta Book.* Portland, Oregon: Timber Press, 1993.

Clausen, Ruth Rogers, and Nicolas H. Ekstrom. *Perennials for American Gardens.* New York: Random House, 1989.

Crockett, James Underwood. *Crockett's Flower Garden.* Boston: Little Brown & Company, 1981.

De Hertogh, A. A., L. B. Gallitano, G. H. Pemberton, and M. E. Traer. *Guidelines for the Utilization of Flowering Bulbs as Perennial (Naturalized) Plants in North American Landscapes and Gardens.* Bulletin 37, Netherlands Flower Bulb Institute, 1993.

Harper, Pamela, and Fred McGourty. *Perennials: How to Select, Grow and Enjoy.* Tucson, Arizona: HP Books, 1985.

Hill, Lewis and Nancy. *Successful Perennial Gardening.* Pownal, Vermont: Storey Communications, 1988.

Hudak, Joseph. *Gardening with Perennials Month by Month.* Portland, Oregon: Timber Press, 1993.

Lewis, Peter, and Margaret Lynch. *Campanulas.* Portland, Oregon: Timber Press, 1989.

Lloyd, Christopher. *Clematis.* Deer Park, Wisconsin: Capability's Books, 1989.

Lund, Harry. *Michigan Wildflowers.* Traverse City, Michigan: Village Press, 1985.

Scott, George Harmon. *Bulbs: How to Select, Grow and Enjoy.* Tucson, Arizona: HP Books, 1982.

Still, Steven. *Manual of Herbaceous Ornamental Plants.* Champaign, Illinois: Stipes Publishing Company, 1988.

Taylor's Guide to Bulbs. Boston: Houghton Mifflin

Company, 1986.

Taylor's Guide to Groundcovers, Vines and Grasses. Boston: Houghton Mifflin Company, 1986.

Taylor's Guide to Perennials. Boston: Houghton Mifflin Company, 1986.

Thomas, Graham Stuart. *Plants for Ground-Cover.* Portland, Oregon: Timber Press, 1990.

Toogood, Alan. *Container Gardening.* New York: Gallery Books, 1991.

Voigt, T. B., Betty R. Hamilton, and F. A. Giles. *Ground Covers for the Midwest.* Urbana-Champaign: University of Illinois, 1983.

White, John W. *Geraniums IV.* Geneva, Illinois: Ball Publishing, 1993.

Wilson, Jim. *Landscaping with Container Plants.* Boston: Houghton Mifflin Company, 1990.

Problem Diagnosis and Pest Control

Buczicki, Stefan, and Keith Harris. *Pests, Diseases and Disorders of Garden Plants.* Toronto: HarperCollins, 1993.

Carr, Anna, and Miranda Smith. *Rodale's Garden Insect, Disease and Weed Identification Guide.* Emmaus, Pennsylvania: Rodale Press, 1988.

Daughtrey, Margery. *Ball Field Guide to Diseases of Greenhouse Ornamentals.* Geneva, Illinois: Ball Publishing, 1992.

Dietz, Marjorie, editor. *10,000 Garden Questions.* Garden City, New York: Doubleday & Company, 1982.

Garner, R. J. *The Grafter's Handbook.* London: Cassell Publishers, 1988.

Insect and Mite Management on Landscape Plants. Bulletin E-2088, Michigan State University Extension, 1988.

Insects of Eastern Forests. Publication 1426, United States Department of Agriculture Forest Service, 1985.

Johnson, Warren T., and Howard H. Lyon. *Insects That Feed on Trees and Shrubs.* Ithaca, New York: Cornell University Press, 1988.

Johnson, Warren T., Howard H. Lyon, and Wayne A. Sinclair. *Diseases of Trees and Shrubs.* Ithaca, New York: Cornell University Press, 1987.

Lindquist, Richard K., and Charles C. Powell. *Ball Pest & Disease Manual.* Geneva, Illinois: Ball Publishing, 1992.

Managing Insects and Mites with Spray Oils. Publication 3347, University of California Division of Agriculture and Natural Resources, 1991.

Muenscher, Walter Conrad. *Weeds.* Ithaca, New York: Cornell University Press, 1980.

Orton, Donald A. *Coincide: The Orton System of Pest Management.* Flossmoor, Illinois: Plantsmen's Publications, 1989.

Pirone, P. P. *Tree Maintenance.* New York: Oxford University Press, 1988.

Pirone, Pascal P. *Diseases and Pests of Ornamental Plants.* New York: John Wiley & Sons, 1985.

Putnam, Cynthia, ed. *Controlling Vegetable Pests.* San Ramon, California: Ortho Books, 1991.

Pyle, Michael. *The Audubon Society Field Guide to North American Butterflies.* New York: Chanticleer Press, 1981. Includes useful Host Plant Index.

Shurtleff, Malcolm. *How to Control Plant Diseases.* Dubuque: Iowa State University Press, 1966.

Smith, Cheryl, ed. *The Ortho Home Gardener's Problem Solver.* San Ramon, California: Ortho Books, 1993.

Spencer, Edwin Rollin. *All About Weeds.* New York: Dover Publications, 1968.

Thomson, W. T. *Tree, Turf and Ornamental Pesticide Guide.* Fresno, California: Thomson Publications, 1992.

Ware, George W. *The Complete Guide to Pest Control, With and Without Chemicals.* Fresno, California: Thomson Publications, 1988.

Yepsen, Roger B., ed. *Natural Insect and Disease Control.* Emmaus, Pennsylvania: Rodale Press, 1984.

Your Gardening Questions Answered. London: Reader's Digest Associated, 1988.

Tools and Other Materials

These are the tools I find indispensable. The numbers in parentheses following each tool refer to the company where I purchased mine. Those suppliers are listed in the next section.

- Spade with sharp, squared blade. Mine is made by Ames Co. (10)
- Spading fork (7)
- Metal-tine leaf rake, adjustable to rake a wide or narrow path (8)
- Five-gallon bucket (10)
- Short-handled weeder (7)
- Hand pruners with bypass cutting blades. Mine are made by Felco. (5, 10)
- Sturdy knife (6)
- Garden diagram and mechanical pencil, both inside a clear plastic page protector (10)
- Pruning saw with fixed, curved blade (4)
- Pruning saw that folds. Mine is made by Felco. (5)

Following are some other helpful tools and materials.
- Beneficial nematodes, also called predatory nematodes (11, 13, 14, 15, 16)
- Carpet runner for deep edging (10)
- Composts and organic fertilizers (12, 10)
- Garden pants with padded knees (2)
- Scoop shovel (1, 10)
- Shower-type watering attachment for a garden hose (3, 6)
- Slow-release granular fertilizer (Osmocote or Once) (6, 10)
- Staking kits, peony hoops, and single-stem stakes (5, 9)
- Soaker hose (1, 8)
- Two-wheeled garden cart (1, 7)

Suppliers of Tools

My tools were originally purchased from the following companies. I continue to buy replacement tools and materials from these suppliers. The list is not meant to be all-inclusive. By including a company here, I do not mean to imply that the prices or quality are necessarily better than those from any other source.

There may be other sources for some of the tools and materials listed in the previous section. Some of the suppliers listed below even carry the same items that I purchased from a different company on the list.

(1) A.M. Leonard, Inc., P.O. Box 816, 241 Fox Drive, Piqua, OH 45356; (800) 543-8955

(2) Denman Co., 187 West Orangethorpe Avenue, Suite L, Placentia, CA 92670; (714) 524-0668 (Greenknees garden pants; available in men's sizes only. Author is 5'4", weighs 135 pounds, wears a men's small; suspenders are necessary.)

(3) The Dramm Company, P.O. Box 1960, Manitowoc, WI 54221; (414) 684-0227

(4) Karl Kuemmerling, Inc., 129 Edgewater Avenue NW, Massillon, OH 44646; (216) 477-3457

(5) Kinsman Company, Inc., River Road, Point Pleasant, PA 18950; (800) 733-4146

(6) MacKenzie Nursery Supply, P.O. Box 322, 3891 Shepard Road, Perry, OH 44081; (800) 777-5030

(7) Smith and Hawken, 25 Corte Madera, Mill Valley, CA 94941; (415) 383-2000

(8) Stanley Forge Company, Inc., 1415 Guinotte, Kansas City, MO 64120; (816) 421-4265

(9) Walter Nicke Company, P.O. Box 433, 36 McLeod Lane, Topsfield, MA 01983; (508) 887-3388

(10) Readily available at local hardware and department stores

Suppliers of Beneficial Organisms and Organic Products

The beneficial nematodes I used in Bed Three were packaged under the brand name Biosafe. This product is available in garden centers in many cities. Equivalent products and other beneficial organisms may be obtained by contacting the following companies for a catalog.

(11) Biologic, P.O. Box 177, Springtown Road, Willow Hill, PA 17271; (717) 349-2789

(12) Bricker's Organic Farm, 842 Sandbar Ferry Road, Augusta, GA 30901; (404) 722-0661

(13) Natural Gardening Research Center, Gardens Alive, 5100 Schenley Place, Lawrenceburg, IN 47025; (812) 537-8650

(14) Necessary Trading Company, Natural Solutions, One Nature's Way, New Castle, VA 24127-0305; (703) 864-5103

(15) "Nature Guard for Gardens" beneficial nematodes can be purchased directly from the producer, Farnham Company, Security Products Division. Call (602) 267-5211. Ask for "Nature Guard for Gardens," item #1585. One bottle will cover 3,200 square feet.

(16) Nematec Biological Control Agents, P.O. Box 93, Lafayette, CA 94549-0093; (415) 866-2800

INDEX

Page references in *italic* indicate illustrations; **bold** page references indicate charts/tables.

Other Storey Titles You Will Enjoy

The Big Book of Gardening Skills, by the Editors of Garden Way Publishing. A comprehensive guide to growing flowers, fruits, herbs, vegetables, shrubs, and lawns. 352 pages.
Paperback. $18.95 US/$26.50 CAN. Order #795-5.
Hardcover. $29.95 US/$41.95 CAN. Order #796-3.

Bulbs: Four Seasons of Beautiful Blooms, by Lewis and Nancy Hill. A season-by-season approach to adding the beauty and color of bulbs to home and garden. 224 pages.
Paperback. $18.95 US/$26.50 CAN. Order #877-3.
Hardcover. $28.95 US/$40.95 CAN. Order #878-1.

Daylilies: The Perfect Perennial, by Lewis and Nancy Hill. In a warm, readable style, the authors discuss how to create dramatic, colorful, and long-lasting displays with minimal care. 208 pages. Paperback. $14.95 US/$20.95 CAN. Order #651-7. Hardcover. $24.95 US/$34.95 CAN. Order #652-5.

Easy Garden Design: 12 Simple Steps to Creating Successful Gardens and Landscapes, by Janet Macunovich. Includes site-assessment and combinations of plantings to create a workable and attractive garden and landscape. 176 pages.
Paperback. $14.95 US/$20.95 CAN. Order #791-2.

The Gardener's Bug Book: Earth-Safe Insect Control, by Barbara Pleasant. How to identify and control more than 70 common garden insects using the best homemade and commercial control strategies. 160 pages. Paperback. $9.95 US/NCR. Order #609-6.

The Gardener's Complete Q & A, by the Editors of Garden Way Publishing. Provides answers to thousands of often-asked questions on lawns, landscaping, perennials, annuals, herbs, fruits and vegetables. 736 pages.
Hardcover. $39.95 US/$55.95 CAN. Order #904-4.

The Gardener's Guide to Plant Diseases: Earth-Safe Remedies, by Barbara Pleasant. The antidote for the 50 most common plant diseases. The only organic plant disease reference guidebook available. 192 pages.
Paperback. $12.95 US/$17.95 CAN. Order #274-0.

The Gardener's Weed Book: Earth-Safe Controls, by Barbara Pleasant. This comprehensive guide for beginners and experts explains how to understand, identify, and control weeds using earth-safe methods. 144 pages.
Paperback. $12.95 US/$17.95 CAN. Order #921-4.

Pruning Simplified (Updated Edition), by Lewis Hill. This timeless guide to pruning is based on the premise that pruning, if done right, strengthens and rejuvenates plants. 208 pages.
Paperback. $14.95 US/$20.95 CAN. Order #417-4.

Secrets of Plant Propagation: Starting Your Own Flowers, Vegetables, Fruits, Berries, Shrubs, Trees, and Houseplants, by Lewis Hill. Step-by-step techniques including starting plants from seeds and cuttings, dividing, layering, and grafting. 168 pages.
Paperback. $14.95 US/$20.95 CAN. Order #370-4.

Step-By-Step Gardening Techniques Illustrated, illustrated by Elayne Sears. Written in a clear, concise style by 7 different gardening experts and illustrated in beautiful and detailed line drawings. 224 pages.
Hardcover. $22.95 US/$32.50 CAN. Order #912-5.

Successful Perennial Gardening: A Practical Guide, by Lewis and Nancy Hill. Covers how to divide and propagate perennials, keep them pest and disease free, cut and dry them, and much more. 240 pages.
Paperback. $18.95 US/$26.50 CAN. Order #472-7.

These books and other Storey books are available at your bookstore, farm store, garden center, or directly from Storey Publishing, Schoolhouse Road, Pownal, Vermont 05261, or by calling 1-800-441-5700.